ALL THE —

SH*T

YOU SHOULD

HAVE LEARNED

A Digestible
Re-Education in
SCIENCE, MATH,
LANGUAGE,
HISTORY...and
All the Other
Important Crap

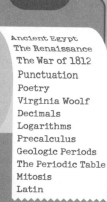

Ancient Egypt
The Renaissance
The War of 1812
Punctuation
Poetry
Virginia Woolf
Decimals
Logarithms
Precalculus
Geologic Periods
The Periodic Table
Mitosis
Latin

PAUL KLEINMAN

ADAMS MEDIA

NEW YORK   LONDON   TORONTO   SYDNEY   NEW DELHI

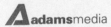

Adams Media
An Imprint of Simon & Schuster, Inc.
57 Littlefield Street
Avon, Massachusetts 02322

First Adams Media trade paperback edition December 2019

ADAMS MEDIA and colophon are trademarks of Simon & Schuster.

For information about special discounts for bulk purchases, please contact Simon & Schuster Special Sales at 1-866-506-1949 or business@simonandschuster.com.

The Simon & Schuster Speakers Bureau can bring authors to your live event. For more information or to book an event, contact the Simon & Schuster Speakers Bureau at 1-866-248-3049 or visit our website at www.simonspeakers.com.

Interior design by Colleen Cunningham
Interior images by Ivan Ryabokon; © 123RF/abscent

Manufactured in the United States of America

10 9 8 7 6 5 4 3 2 1

Library of Congress Cataloging-in-Publication Data
Names: Kleinman, Paul, author.
Title: All the sh*t you should have learned / Paul Kleinman.
Description: Avon, Massachusetts: Adams Media, 2019.
Identifiers: LCCN 2019037995 | ISBN 9781507212400 (pb) | ISBN 9781507212417 (ebook)
Subjects: LCSH: Curiosities and wonders. | History--Miscellanea. | Literature--Miscellanea. | Mathematics--Miscellanea. | Science--Miscellanea.
Classification: LCC AG244 .K54 2019 | DDC 031.02--dc23
LC record available at https://lccn.loc.gov/2019037995

ISBN 978-1-5072-1240-0
ISBN 978-1-5072-1241-7 (ebook)

Contains material adapted from the following title published by Adams Media, an Imprint of Simon & Schuster, Inc.: *A Ton of Crap* by Paul Kleinman, copyright © 2011, ISBN 978-1-4405-2935-1.

CONTENTS

PART 2: LANGUAGE ... 87

PART 3: MATH ...

PART 4: SCIENCE ... 207

PART 5: FOREIGN LANGUAGE ... 267

INTRODUCTION

When did the Ming Dynasty rule?
What is the Pythagorean Theorem used to calculate?
How many layers does the Earth have?

At some point, you probably knew the answer to at least one of these questions. Sure, you may have no idea what the answer is right now, but that's not your fault. You've got a lot going on, and *All the Sh*t You Should Have Learned* understands that. What follows is a digestible re-education in everything you *probably* learned at one time or another, but forgot because your head is filled with so much other crap; crap like the dates of every family member's birthday (your second cousin included), the roads you should avoid during rush hour, and the ingredients for your favorite meat sauce recipe.

In the following pages, you'll be schooled in five academic subjects: History, Language, Math, Science, and Foreign Language. All the major players from your school days. But instead of getting one long lecture that makes your head pound, each subject is broken down into smaller topics, like Ancient Egypt, Logarithms, the Solar System, French, and Poetry. These nuggets of information avoid a brain dump of information, and help you retain all the wisdom you've accumulated instead of flushing it down the toilet.

So get comfortable, relax, and get ready to learn (or relearn) all the sh*t you should *really* already know.

PART 1

History

MESOPOTAMIA AND THE FIRST CIVILIZATIONS

THE SUMERIANS Six thousand years ago, the first civilizations developed between the Tigris and Euphrates Rivers in what is now Iraq. The first civilization was known as Sumer, and the different villages developed self-governing city-states with a pyramidal temple, or ziggurat, at the center of each city-state. As a result of the location, there was seasonal flooding and a hot, dry environment. This led to very fertile ground, which farmers took advantage of, producing crops such as wheat, barley, sesame, and flax.

ZIGGURATS The ziggurats at the heart of each city-state served many purposes. Not only were they there for religious reasons, but they were also the center of daily life for the Sumerian people. The Sumerians believed there were many powerful gods in the sky, and they dedicated these large temples to them with steps leading to the top. The ziggurats were built of mud brick. At the very top of each, religious ceremonies were held.

THE AKKADIANS The Akkadians were a Semitic people from the Arabian Peninsula who increasingly came into conflict with the Sumerians as they migrated north. In 2340 B.C., Sargon, the Akkadian military leader, conquered Sumerian city-states and established an Akkadian empire over the land. Sargon established his rule in the city of Akkad, and created the largest empire known to humankind at that time. The empire was short lived, and in 2150 B.C., the Akkadian Empire fell.

BABYLONIA As the last Sumerian dynasty fell, the Amorites came to power, basing their capital in Babylon. One of the most notable legal texts in history comes from this time period, when the king, Hammurabi, created one of the first sets of written laws. This is called the Code of Hammurabi. These laws were written out so that all would know the punishments if they disobeyed them. One of the most famous paraphrases of this code is "An eye for an eye, and a tooth for a tooth."

THE HITTITES No one knows the origins of the Hittites, and until recently, their language was undecipherable (it was in the Indo-European family). Their invasion brought the end of the Old Babylonian Empire; however, as they conquered Mesopotamia, they adopted the laws, literature, and religion of Old Babylon. The Hittites are most notable for their work involved in trade and commerce, which spread Mesopotamian literature and thought all over the Mediterranean.

INVENTIONS Many important inventions came out of Mesopotamia. The seed plow was revolutionary in agriculture, and allowed seeding and plowing to occur simultaneously. The people of Mesopotamia also created a writing system based on images called cuneiform, developed irrigation and sanitation methods, created glass, and around 3500 B.C., invented the wheel. They were also the first to harness wind energy by creating sails.

XIA DYNASTY

REAL OR LEGEND? The Xia Dynasty, said to be the first imperial dynasty of China, is supposed to have lasted from the twenty-first to the seventeenth century B.C. with seventeen emperors. It is still up for debate whether the Xia Dynasty actually existed or whether it is merely a legend told in the ancient texts.

YU THE GREAT
Da Yu, meaning "Yu the Great," was the founder of the Xia Dynasty. He is famous for his involvement in stopping the great flooding of the Yangtze River, a process that lasted thirteen years. Yu the Great united the various ethnic groups, divided the land into nine provinces, and most notably, taught the people methods on how to control floodwater through the building of canals.

THE POLITICAL SYSTEMS
Yu the Great chose to set up the Xia Dynasty under an abdication system, which meant choosing a leader based on ability. Following his death, his son, Qi, made himself emperor, officially ending the abdication system and creating a hereditary system. Fifteen offspring of Qi succeeded him, forming the first imperial dynasty in China.

DECLINE OF THE XIA DYNASTY
The Shang Dynasty followed the Xia Dynasty. The last leader of the Xia Dynasty, Jie, was an oppressive and tyrannical emperor who killed many of his people. Eventually, the people of the Xia Dynasty began to revolt and followed the leadership of Tang, chief of the Shang tribe. The successful uprising led to the demise of the Xia Dynasty and the beginning of the Shang Dynasty, which would hold power from 1766 B.C. to 1122 B.C.

CONTROVERSIES TODAY
In the 1920s, Gu Jiegang created a school of scholars in China called the Doubting Antiquity School. It was the first group of people to question whether the Xia Dynasty actually existed or whether it was just a legend; they cited the lack of archaeological findings corresponding to the historical texts. Today, scholar Sarah Allan argues that the Zhou

Dynasty created Xia to justify their conquest of the dynasty that followed Xia, the Shang Dynasty.

ARCHAEOLOGICAL FINDINGS In 1959, a site was excavated in the city of Yanshi. The site included large palaces, and archaeologists at the time believed that this could be the capital of the Xia Dynasty. Over the next twenty years, many sites were uncovered, revealing tombs, urban sites, and bronze implements. These were discovered in areas where the ancient texts claimed the Xia Dynasty to be, and radiocarbon dating places the site to be from around 2100 to 1800 B.C. Recent research from 2016 employing stratigraphic data and radiocarbon dating confirms that the flood did occur at the beginning of the Xia Dynasty, around 1900 B.C. The debate as to whether this is the Xia Dynasty, or whether the Xia Dynasty even existed at all, continues to this day.

ANCIENT EGYPT

PREDYNASTIC EGYPT Egypt's history began similarly to that of Mesopotamia. Civilizations congregated around the Nile River around 5500 B.C. The largest civilization, the Badari, inhabited the northern part of Egypt, and was most known for high-quality stone tools, ceramics, and pottery and their use of copper. In the southern part of Egypt, the Naqada civilization arose. Over the course of 1,000 years, the Naqada controlled the tribes along the Nile, and created a full system of hieroglyphics for writing.

EARLY DYNASTIC EGYPT Around 3100 B.C., Upper and Lower Egypt united under the pharaoh Menes. Memphis, a part of

Lower Egypt, was established as the capital of the land and became critical in trade and agriculture. It also provided a workforce. Notable from this time period were the mastaba tombs, which were large rectangular, flat-roofed structures made of stone and mud bricks that were built to celebrate pharaohs who had died.

THE OLD KINGDOM The Old Kingdom refers to the rule of the Third Dynasty to the Sixth Dynasty from 2686 to 2181 B.C. This is a time defined by a flourishing economy, a well-defined justice system, and a strong government. It was during this time that the famous pyramids of Giza were built, marking great artistic and technological advancements. A new class of educated scribes also arose.

THE MIDDLE KINGDOM The central government of the Old Kingdom collapsed in 2160 B.C., and around 2055 B.C., the prosperity and stability of Egypt was restored when Mentuhotep II came to power, beginning what is known as the Middle Kingdom. Once again, art, literature, and great monuments defined this period. One stark contrast between the art of this time and that of the Old Kingdom is that this work focused more on the individual and a democratization of the afterlife in which every person possessed a soul and was greeted by the gods and goddesses when they died.

THE NEW KINGDOM The New Kingdom lasted from the sixteenth to the eleventh century B.C. and was defined by military campaigns that made the Egyptian empire the largest it had ever been. Amenhotep IV, who changed his name to Akhenaten, instituted new and radical worship of a new sun god, Aten. Attacking the priestly establishment, Akhenaten eventually made Aten the only god. When Tutankhamun came to power after Akhenaten's death, he returned Egypt to a polytheistic religion.

THE LATE PERIOD The Late Period lasted from 664 to 323 B.C. It is considered the end of the once-great Egyptian Empire. From 525 to 404 B.C., Egypt was part of the Persian Empire. The Twenty-Eighth Dynasty, led by Amyrtaeus, saw a revolt against the Persians; however, by the Thirtieth Dynasty in 343 B.C., the Persians had once again reoccupied the land.

THE HUNS

WHO WERE THEY? In the fourth and fifth centuries A.D., a nomadic group of people from Central Asia spread to the Caspian Sea, coming into contact with the Roman Empire toward the end of its reign. These people were fierce warriors (with a specialty in archery), animal herders, and expert horsemen. The tribes were called the Hsiung-nu; however, in the West, they were referred to as the Huns.

CONQUERORS The Huns first overcame another nomadic group that lived between the Don and Volga Rivers, the Alani. From there, they attacked the Ostrogothic kingdom, and in 376, the Huns attacked the Visigoths. During the fifty years following their conquest of the Visigoths, the Huns firmly established their status with both the Western and Eastern Roman Empires through constant raids and attacks.

WEAPONRY The Huns relied on two powerful weapons: composite bows and horses. The Huns were excellent horseback riders and fought as cavalry. The groups they attacked could not escape their hit-and-run tactics, and using their bows and arrows allowed the Huns to attack their enemies and inflict injury from long ranges. Warriors of the Huns also carried swords, lassos, and lances.

ATTILA THE HUN In 432, the Huns became centralized under the leadership of one ruler, Rugila. Two years later, Rua died and his throne was passed on to his two nephews: Bleda and Attila. In 445, Attila killed his brother, taking complete control of the government and the Huns. Under Attila's reign, the Huns defeated and conquered several rivals and made several attacks on the Roman Empire. Attila was one of the most-feared rulers of the time.

AFTER ATTILA Upon Attila's death, Ellac, one of his sons, overcame his two brothers and became ruler of the Huns. However, former subjects of Attila began to revolt and united under Ardaric, the ruler of the Gepids. The Huns would fight Ardaric's men in the Battle of Nedao in 454, and lose, ending their supremacy over Europe.

LEGENDS The stories of the Huns' conquests played an important part in the folklore of the Germanic people. In particular, the Old Norse *Volsunga Saga*, an epic poem from thirteenth-century Iceland, and the *Hervarar Saga ok Heiðreks* make considerable mention of the Huns and the battles they fought. In the *Hervarar Saga*, a battle is depicted between the Huns and the Goths, and in the *Nibelungenlied*, another epic poem, a woman marries Attila the Hun.

THE OTTOMAN EMPIRE

WHAT THE OTTOMAN EMPIRE WAS The Ottoman Empire was based in Turkey and lasted from 1299 to 1923. In the sixteenth and seventeenth centuries, the Ottoman Empire was at its peak, with territory ranging from North Africa to southwestern Asia and southeastern Europe, across twenty-nine provinces. For six centuries, the empire's capital city, Constantinople, was the center of interaction between the East and the West.

RISE OF THE OTTOMAN EMPIRE The Ottoman Empire arose in the early fourteenth century, just as the Roman Empire began to fall. It was originally created when the empire of the Seljuk Turks broke down. As the Ottomans began absorbing other states, by the reign of Muhammad II (or Mehmed II) in 1451, all local Turkish dynasties had ended. Under Osman I and subsequent rulers, many attacks were aimed at the Byzantine Empire.

THE OTTOMAN EMPIRE EXPANDS From the reign of Muhammad II onward, the Ottoman Empire expanded widely over the land. In 1453, the Ottomans took over Constantinople, the capital of the Byzantine Empire. Expansion of the Ottoman Empire reached its peak in the sixteenth century under Sultan Selim I and Süleyman I. The empire expanded to include Hungary, Transylvania, Persia, Egypt, Syria, and Greece.

SOCIETY OF THE OTTOMAN EMPIRE One of the reasons the Ottoman Empire was so successful was its ability to unify a variety of people through its tolerance of other religions. This was done by establishing millets, which were religious groups of people that were able to practice and retain their own laws, language, and traditions of their religions. The many different ethnicities, however, led to a weakness in nationalism, one of the contributing factors of the empire's decline.

DECLINE OF THE OTTOMAN EMPIRE From the sixteenth to the eighteenth century, the Ottoman Empire faced many wars, rebellions, and treaties. This took a great toll on the empire economically. The Ottoman Empire would come to lose control of

Serbia, Montenegro, Bosnia, Romania, Herzegovina, Greece, and Egypt. By 1914, the once-flourishing Turkey was being referred to as "The sick man of Europe."

COLLAPSE OF THE OTTOMAN EMPIRE In 1908, a nationalist and reformist group called the Young Turks forced the restoration of the 1876 constitution. In 1909, the sultan was deposed by Parliament and replaced by Muhammad V. In the two Balkan Wars, Turkey lost nearly all of its European territory. During World War I, Turkey aligned with the Central Powers, and in 1918, the resistance collapsed, thus ending the Ottoman Empire.

THE MAGNA CARTA

KING JOHN OF ENGLAND TAXES HIS PEOPLE King John came to power in 1199 and became one of the most controversial monarchs in the history of England. Though never liked as a ruler, King John, after a failed attack on France, set in motion the events leading to the creation of the Magna Carta in 1215. The mission against the French proved costly, and King John raised taxes on his people, causing outrage.

KING JOHN AND THE POPE In 1207, King John fought with Pope Innocent III over who should become Archbishop of Canterbury. As a result, the pope excommunicated the king, leading to increased tensions between the king and his people. Though the king would come to apologize, the pope was wary, and in 1214, he proclaimed that anyone who tried to overthrow King John would be legally allowed to do so. That year, King John lost another battle against the French, resulting in England losing its possessions to France.

THE CREATION OF THE MAGNA CARTA Following the loss against the French, the English revolted against King John. In 1215, the Magna Carta was created. To this day, it is still one of the most celebrated documents ever written. Literally meaning "the Great Charter," the Magna Carta consisted of thirty-seven laws that greatly reduced the power of the king and allowed for the formation of a parliament. King John of England was forced to sign the document.

CLAUSE 61 A large section of the Magna Carta is referred to today as Clause 61. This established the creation of a committee composed of twenty-five barons or representatives who would have the power to overcome the rule of the king at any time should he defy what was written in the Charter. If necessary, these barons could seize the king's possessions and castles. Both King John and the pope refused to allow this, and England entered into a civil war, known as the First Barons' War. The Magna Carta was only valid for three months, and was considered to be a failure.

THE MAGNA CARTA TODAY Today, only three of the original sixty-three clauses are still valid in England. The first clause guaranteed the liberties of the English Church. The second clause declared that London and all of the other cities, towns, ports, and boroughs would be allowed to enjoy their ancient customs and liberties. The last clause, and the most well-known of the three, states that no free man shall be imprisoned, seized, or stripped of his rights except by a lawful judgment by his equals, and that no one will be denied justice.

LASTING EFFECTS OF THE MAGNA CARTA The Magna Carta greatly influenced the United States Constitution, the Declaration of Independence, and the Bill of Rights during the writing of these documents. The third clause from the Magna Carta, which stated accused persons shall not be imprisoned until found guilty by their peers, is perhaps the most obvious influence, as it appears in the Fifth Amendment of the Bill of Rights. Also, the first clause included the principle of the separation of church and state.

THE REFORMATION

POWER OF THE CHURCH By the beginning of the sixteenth century, Roman Catholicism was the only religion in Western Europe. The Church believed that it alone had the power to interpret the Bible. However, with the Renaissance and the invention of the printing press, people started believing the Church had too much control. In the fourteenth century, a man named John Wycliffe became the first to translate the Bible from Latin into English. This idea was soon picked up by Jan Hus of Bohemia, who began preaching his own sermons.

MARTIN LUTHER'S 95 THESES In 1517, Martin Luther, an Augustinian monk, became fed up with the Church's policies of selling indulgences and misleading people. Luther wrote a series of theses against the practices of the Church (such as indulgences), as well as new ideas for a better religion (such as rejecting the authority of the pope). Luther nailed his 95 Theses on the door of the church at Wittenberg.

THE REFORMATION SPREADS THROUGHOUT THE LAND At the same time that Luther's ideas began to spread, Ulrich Zwingli led a similar revolt in Switzerland. The printing press enabled the ideas of Luther and Zwingli to reach the general public; however, there were differences in some of their ideologies. The teachings of Luther would become established as Lutheranism. Soon, another voice would rise and become a prominent figure in the Protestant Reformation: John Calvin.

JOHN CALVIN In 1536, John Calvin, a lawyer, published *Institutes of the Christian Religion,* which is a statement of his theology. Calvin's teachings gained in popularity, and soon Calvin would reform the Catholic Church in Geneva and force its citizens to follow his practices. Although Calvin and Luther were contemporaries and shared many similar beliefs, there were considerable differences. In particular, Calvinism espoused the idea of predestination, that a person was destined at birth to either be saved or doomed to damnation.

THE AFFAIR OF THE PLACARDS On October 18, 1534, citizens of Paris awoke to find the city covered with placards denouncing the Catholic Mass and condemning the Eucharist, among other things. These placards were also posted all around northern France and even on the king's door. A group of Huguenots, French adherents of Calvinism, were deemed the culprits, and were burned at the stake. Suppression of Protestantism soon followed.

THE COUNTER-REFORMATION Initially, the Catholic Church thought nothing of the Reformation, but as it spread from country to country, the Church established the Council of Trent to repair the schism that was occurring. A Spanish nobleman named Ignatius of Loyola, who had renounced his military life, founded the Jesuits, a group that made reforms from within the Church. By the end of the sixteenth century, half of the lands lost to Protestant Reform returned to the Catholic Church, a divide that still exists today.

ROME

THE FOUNDING MYTH
According to legend, Romulus and Remus were the children of the god Mars. Mars feared they would one day kill him, and decided to drown them. They were rescued by a she-wolf and raised by her until ultimately being found by a shepherd and his wife. When the boys grew older, they decided to build a city. In a fight over who would rule the city, Romulus killed Remus with a rock. Romulus then named the city after himself, calling it Rome.

THE ROMAN KINGDOM
The Roman Kingdom lasted from 753 to 509 B.C. Rome was established as a village on the Tiber River and was ruled by seven kings (with Romulus as the first) who were elected by the village to serve for life. According to legend, Romulus's followers were mostly men from all classes, including slaves, and the shortage of women brought about the abduction of women from the neighboring tribe, the Sabines. The Roman Kingdom expanded to 350 square miles at this time. Most notably, a Senate of 100 men was created to act as an advisory council to the king.

THE ROMAN REPUBLIC
After the last king, Tarquin Superbus (meaning Targuin "the Proud") was overthrown, a republican system based on elected magistrates was put into effect, and along with the Senate, there was a new focus on separation of powers, and a system of checks and balances. The Roman Republic lasted from 500 to 30 B.C. During this time, Rome expanded throughout the Mediterranean and into North Africa, Greece, and the Iberian Peninsula. Toward the end of this time period, one of the most famous rulers, Julius Caesar, came to power and attempted to become a dictator of Rome.

THE ROMAN EMPIRE

The Roman Empire, which lasted from 27 B.C. to A.D. 1453, began when Octavian took control of the empire after his great-uncle Julius Caesar was assassinated by a group of senators. The republic was never re-established, as the emperor held most of the power, but the Senate continued. Rome continued to expand, and by the time Trajan ruled (A.D. 98–117), the Roman Empire had expanded 2.5 million square miles. To better control the vast empire, authority was divided between four co-emperors. These divisions would ultimately divide the Roman Empire into a Western Empire and an Eastern Empire.

THE FALL OF ROME

The Western Empire of Rome collapsed in 476 with an attack from the Visigoths. In 1453, the Eastern Empire collapsed, thus ending the great Roman Empire. There were several contributing factors that led to the fall of Rome, including its grand size, which made it hard to control its people; the influence and spread of the newly formed religion, Christianity; the spread of Islam; attacks from barbarians; inflation; and even lead poisoning.

THE COLOSSEUM

Construction of the Colosseum, one of the best-known monumental structures associated with Rome, began in A.D. 72 and was completed eight years later. The amphitheater could seat 55,000 spectators and was 159 feet tall. Free games were held in the Colosseum for the public, representing power and prestige, and the events included comedy acts and gladiatorial fights to the death with animals and with other gladiators.

THE MIDDLE AGES

THE EARLY MIDDLE AGES The Early Middle Ages, also known as the Dark Ages, followed the collapse of the Western Roman Empire, and lasted from the fifth century to the tenth century. From 400 to 700, Europe was greatly divided, and there was a great migration of Germanic and Slavic people. Besides the increase in migration, this time period was marked by an economic decline. Many empires rose and fell during this time, never being able to achieve the status or success of the Roman Empire. It was also during this time that feudalism started to appear.

THE HIGH MIDDLE AGES The High Middle Ages, which lasted from the eleventh to the thirteenth century, was defined by urbanization, a unifying religion in Christianity, and a rise in population and military expansion. It was during this time that the Crusades, a series of wars fought between Christians and Muslims over the Holy Land occurred. From the Crusades came contact with Arab science, math, and philosophy, which had been developed from the classical works of Ancient Greek philosophers. The contributions made by the Muslim world were passed on to Europe.

THE LATE MIDDLE AGES The Late Middle Ages, which lasted from 1300 to 1500, was defined by climate change, famine, disease, war, and social upheaval. The Great Famine of 1315 to 1317 and the Black Death led to an incredibly large loss of life. It was during this time that the Hundred Years' War was fought between England and France, and it was in the Late Middle Ages that the schism in the Catholic Church occurred.

THE BLACK DEATH In 1347, Europe was struck by the Black Death (now known to have been the bubonic plague). It is believed that one-third to one-half of the entire population of Europe was killed by this plague. The common belief is that rats in ships arriving from Asia were infected with the disease. The disease would then move from rats to fleas, and then the fleas would bite humans, infecting them. From there, the disease would spread from human to human.

SCIENCE OF THE MIDDLE AGES Science during the Middle Ages focused on the natural world. Much of the scientific advancements were from the Islamic world, learned by Europeans as they traveled during the Crusades. One of the major fields of science Europeans learned from the Arab world was the study of astronomy. Another important field of science studied during this time was known as alchemy (or what we refer to as chemistry today).

INVENTIONS OF THE MIDDLE AGES There were many major technological advancements made during the Middle Ages. Among the most important inventions were the use of gunpowder, vertical windmills, the mechanical clock, the printing press, eyeglasses, and improvements on water mills. Advancements were made in agriculture as well, with the introduction of the heavy plow and three-field crop rotation.

THE CRUSADES

THE FIRST CRUSADE The First Crusade lasted from 1096 to 1099. It was an attempt by Western Christians to recapture Jerusalem, the Holy Land, from the Muslims. Fearing that his country would fall to the Muslims, Alexius I of Constantinople called on Pope Urban II for help. The pope urged people to volunteer and repel the invading Turks, and the armies consisted of knights and, largely, of peasants. Eventually, Jerusalem was captured and the Kingdom of Jerusalem was created.

THE SECOND CRUSADE The Second Crusade took place from 1145 to 1149, and occurred after the city of Edessa, a crusader state established in the First Crusade, fell. This Crusade was announced by Pope Eugene III, and it was led by European kings from France and Germany. The armies of the two kings marched separately and were each defeated by the Seljuk Turks and the Crusade was considered a failure.

THE THIRD CRUSADE Also known as the King's Crusade, the Third Crusade lasted from 1189 to 1192. The Third Crusade was an attempt to reconquer the Holy Land after it was retaken by Saladin. The king of France and the king of England ended their conflict and united to fight Saladin; however, they achieved little beyond capturing the city of Acre. As the king of France left, the king of England and Saladin eventually came to a truce in which Jerusalem would remain under Saladin's control but unarmed Christian pilgrims were allowed to visit the city.

THE FOURTH AND FIFTH CRUSADES The Fourth Crusade lasted from 1202 to 1204 and was an attempt to once again conquer Jerusalem by going through Egypt. Instead of Jerusalem, however, the crusaders sacked Constantinople and established the Latin Empire. The Fifth Crusade, from 1217 to 1221, was an attempt to conquer Jerusalem by defeating the Ayyubid Sultanate in Egypt. The Ayyubid Sultan launched an attack that would lead to the surrender of the crusaders, and an eight-year peace agreement was made.

THE SIXTH AND SEVENTH CRUSADES

THE SIXTH AND SEVENTH CRUSADES The Sixth Crusade was from 1228 to 1229, and though there was very little fighting, control of Jerusalem was regained temporarily by the crusaders. The Seventh Crusade lasted from 1248 to 1254, and was led by King Louis IX of France. The Christians were defeated by the Egyptian army led by the Ayyubid Sultan, with support from the Mamluks, and the king and thousands of European soldiers were captured.

THE EIGHTH AND NINTH CRUSADES The Eighth Crusade of 1270 lasted only one year and was led by King Louis IX once again. It was originally meant to aid crusader states but was diverted to Tunis, where two months later, King Louis IX died. The Ninth Crusade was the final Crusade, and it lasted from 1271 to 1272. Prince Edward of England led the Crusade following the death of Louis IX. It failed due to the rising power of the Mamluks in Egypt and low morale among the crusaders.

THE RENAISSANCE

WHAT LED TO THE RENAISSANCE The Renaissance was a return to the classicism and humanism of Ancient Greece in Europe after the Middle Ages. Following the Black Death pandemic, there was a great change in the European economy. That, along with the invention of the printing press, the fall of the Byzantine Empire, and the Crusades, led to the birth of the Renaissance, where Classic Greek and Roman art, literature, and philosophy were reintroduced into European culture.

THE MEDICI FAMILY The Renaissance began in Florence, Italy. Much of the great artwork in the Early Renaissance can be traced back to a family of the noble class, the Medici family. In the thirteenth century, the Medici acquired great wealth as bankers and became the wealthiest family in all of Italy. With their wealth, they sponsored many artistic endeavors, such as the great paintings and architecture of this time.

EARLY RENAISSANCE The Early Renaissance was from 1330 to 1450, and took place in Florence, Italy. Artwork sponsored by the Medici family placed great focus on the art of Ancient Greece and Rome. The artwork once again focused on humanism, naturalism, and realism, and introduced new ideas about art, such as depth of field, linear perspective, and types of shading that indicated volume and texture. The most well-known artists to come out of the Early Renaissance are Sandro Botticelli (*Primavera*), Domenico Ghirlandaio (*Portrait of an Old Man and a Boy*), and Piero della Francesca (*The Baptism of Christ*).

HIGH RENAISSANCE The artwork of the High Renaissance, which was from 1490 to 1530, made advances on the techniques of artists of the Early Renaissance. The center of the High Renaissance was Rome, and artwork was now being commissioned by the popes. It was during the High Renaissance that the best-known works of Renaissance painters appeared. The most well-known artists to come out of the High Renaissance are Leonardo da Vinci (*Last Supper*), Michelangelo Buonarroti (*The Creation of Adam*), and Raphael (*Sistine Madonna*).

NORTHERN RENAISSANCE The Northern Renaissance was from 1500 to 1600, and it took place outside of Italy. The ideas of the Renaissance quickly spread throughout Europe, and some of the most notable artwork of the time came from the Netherlands and Germany. This artwork is distinctively different from the work produced in Italy, due to the increasing disenchantment with the Church. The figures appeared less classical, and more realistic. The most well-known artists to come out of the Northern Renaissance are the Flemish painter Jan van Eyck (*The Arnolfini Portrait*), the German painter and printmaker Albrecht Dürer (*The Knight, Death,* and the *Devil*), and the Dutch painter Hieronymus Bosch (*The Garden of Earthly Delights*).

ADVANCEMENTS IN TECHNOLOGY AND SCIENCE Not only was the Renaissance a time of great achievements in art, but there were also great advancements made in technology. It was during this time period that the first portable clock, eyeglasses, printing press, microscope, telescope, and even the first flush toilet were created. With the rise of technology and science, concepts such as gravity and the ability to study the universe led to the notion that the universe was not simply centered around humankind.

THE MING DYNASTY

FOUNDING OF THE MING DYNASTY The Yuan Dynasty, led by Mongols, left the economy and state of agriculture in shambles. A group of peasants, the Han Chinese, who were discriminated against during the Yuan Dynasty, rose up and revolted. Zhu Yuanzhang came to lead the group of rebels, and as the last Yuan leader fled north, Zhu Yuanzhang founded the Ming Dynasty in 1368. Zhu took control of the Yuan capital city, Dadu, officially ending the Yuan Dynasty.

THE EARLY REIGN When he came to power, Zhu Yuanzhang instituted a series of policies aimed at reducing the burden on the peasants, and placed great attention on punishing court officials involved in corruption and ending corruption. When Zhu Yuanzhang died, his son came to power; however, his son was soon overthrown in a coup led by Zhu Di, who would come to be known as Emperor Chengzu. The reign of Emperor Chengzu would be considered the most prosperous time in the Ming Dynasty.

THE GOLDEN AGE OF THE MING DYNASTY Emperor Chengzu's reign was known as the Yongle Period, and is considered the Golden Age of the Ming Dynasty. Emperor Chengzu launched a series of five wars against Mongolia, and most notably, it was during this time that the Forbidden City was constructed. Relations with minorities and different nationalities were strengthened, and Chengzu was the first to make Beijing the capital, a title it would hold for 500 years.

THE DECLINE AND FALL OF THE MING DYNASTY The Ming Dynasty began to decline under the reign of Emperor Shenzong, known as the Wanli Emperor. When Shenzong's chancellor, Zhang Juzheng, died, state affairs began to be neglected, and later, his army was defeated by the "Later Jin" regime. The last ruler of the Ming Dynasty was Emperor Congzhen, whose reign was defined by corruption and extreme hardship due to natural disasters. In 1628, rebel forces began attacking. In 1644, Beijing fell to a rebel army. Emperor Congzhen hanged himself, thus ending the Ming Dynasty.

THE ECONOMY OF THE MING DYNASTY The economy of the Ming Dynasty showed an end of feudalism and the beginnings of capitalism. From the reign of Zhu Yuanzhang and onward, porcelain making was the major source of finance, and there was a wide interest in foreign commodities from both Europe and America. Urbanization and commercial metropolises also arose during this time in cities such as Beijing, Nanjing, and Yangzhou.

THE GREAT WALL OF CHINA The majority of the Great Wall of China that exists today is from the Ming Dynasty, which lasted from 1368 to 1644. The project took more than 100 years to complete, and the wall was made in an effort to protect the citizens of the Ming Dynasty from outside Yuan tribes such as the Wala and the Dada.

COLUMBUS AND THE NEW WORLD

COLUMBUS DECIDES TO TRAVEL TO THE EAST Christopher Columbus spent much of his life sailing the Atlantic Ocean. He became very interested in traveling to the Far East, which he believed was just across the Atlantic Ocean. His idea was to create a sea route to India and obtain the gold and spices of the East Indies. Columbus met with King John II of Portugal to support his journey, but was soon rejected. He then met with the monarchs of Spain, King Ferdinand and Queen Isabella, who, although they initially had rejected him, would eventually agree to support his journey.

THE FIRST VOYAGE Columbus prepared three ships, the *Niña*, the *Pinta*, and the *Santa María*, for their journey. Columbus was the captain of the *Santa María*, and his brothers were the captains of the other ships. On August 3, 1492, they set sail. On October 12, they landed on what is now the island of San Salvador in the Bahamas and took possession of the island. Columbus soon found Cuba (which he believed to be China), and in December, he reached Hispaniola (which Columbus believed to be Japan), and established a colony of thirty-nine men. In March of 1493, Columbus returned to Spain with riches, spices, and human captives.

THE SECOND VOYAGE In October of 1493, Columbus set sail with a fleet of seventeen ships and 1,500 colonists. In November, they landed in the Lesser Antilles and discovered Puerto Rico and the Leeward Islands. Upon returning to Hispaniola, Columbus found that the original colony had been killed by the natives. Columbus established another colony and then set sail once again, exploring Cuba and finding Jamaica. As Columbus left for Spain, his brother stayed in Hispaniola and founded Santo Domingo, which was the first permanent European settlement of the Americas.

THE THIRD VOYAGE In 1498, Columbus set sail on his third voyage, and due to bad reports from Hispaniola, was forced to bring convicts to the New World. Columbus sailed farther south, finding Trinidad, and continued sailing until he realized that he had found a land mass. Columbus had to return to Hispaniola before exploring it any further, however. In 1500, due to the bad reports from Hispaniola, the monarchy sent a royal commissioner to survey the situation, which resulted in Columbus being sent back to Spain in chains.

THE FOURTH VOYAGE Columbus managed to get four ships together in 1502 for his fourth journey, which he hoped would restore his reputation. Columbus hit the coast of Honduras and was later marooned on Jamaica in an attempt to return to Hispaniola. Upon being rescued in 1504, Columbus was forced to return to Spain. Columbus died two years later, still believing he had reached Asia.

THE IMPACT ON THE NATIVE AMERICANS Over the course of a century, the population of natives on the island of Hispaniola was completely destroyed in a genocide brought on by the Spanish. In 1493, policies regarding slavery and mass extermination were implemented, and within a three-year time span, 5 million Native Americans were killed. Mass numbers of Native Americans were hanged, stabbed, shot, or worked to death as slaves.

THE SALEM WITCH TRIALS

ABOUT SALEM In Salem, Massachusetts, from 1692 to 1693, a series of witchcraft trials occurred, and nineteen people were executed. In Europe, from the 1300s to the 1600s, there was a strong belief in witchcraft and that the Devil could give people the power to harm others. At the time of the Salem witch trials, these feelings had pretty much subsided in Europe. During this time, however, a war between England and France brought conflict between the countries' respective colonies and Native American allies. The fighting displaced many people to Salem, leading to tensions and strain in the town. The villagers believed this strain and tension came from the Devil.

STRANGE OCCURRENCES WITH THE CHILDREN In January of 1692, Elizabeth (Betty) Parris, the daughter of Reverend Samuel Parris, the Puritan minister of Salem, and the minister's niece, Abigail Williams, began having bizarre fits in which their bodies contorted, and they screamed, threw things, and uttered strange noises. Another girl, Ann Putnam, was also having these fits. The local doctor blamed it on supernatural causes. When pressured to give names, the children accused Tituba, the Parris's slave; Sarah Good, a homeless woman; and Sarah Osburn, a poor elderly woman.

THE WITCH HUNT BEGINS Osburn and Good declared their innocence, but Tituba confessed that the Devil had come to her and made her serve him. She described images of a black man making her sign a book, and she told them there were other witches seeking to destroy the Puritans. The three women were put in jail, and paranoia spread throughout Salem. Dozens of villagers were brought in for questioning. While in prison, Tituba's bail was paid by an unknown person, and Tituba disappeared, never heard from again.

BRIDGET BISHOP On May 27, 1692, a special court was established. The first trial was that of Bridget Bishop. When she was asked if she had committed witchcraft, Bishop said, "I am as innocent as the child unborn." She was found guilty, and on June 10, she was hanged; the first of the Salem executions for witchcraft.

THE TRIALS Five days after the hanging of Bridget Bishop, a respected minister requested that the court not allow testimony about dreams and visions. His request was ignored, and in July, five more people were hanged. Another eleven more were hanged, and some, like Giles Cory, were tortured to death. A total of nineteen people were killed.

AN END TO THE WITCH TRIALS In response to the Massachusetts governor's own wife being questioned for witchcraft, the governor halted further arrests, released many of the accused, and dissolved the court. In May of 1693, the governor pardoned all who were accused of witchcraft. All in all, nineteen people were hanged, one man was tortured to death, and others died in prison. Nearly 200 people had been accused of witchcraft. Many involved with the trials and accusations issued public apologies, and in 1702 the trials were declared unlawful. In 1957, the state of Massachusetts apologized for the events that had happened more than 250 years before.

THE AMERICAN REVOLUTION

THE BATTLES OF LEXINGTON AND CONCORD
It is unknown which side the "Shot Heard Round the World" came from, but on April 19, 1775, the British troops and the American colonists fought the first battle of the Revolutionary War. A rumor was circulating that the Massachusetts Militia had been storing weapons in Concord, and 700 British soldiers were sent to quell their mission. The colonists quickly learned of the oncoming British troops, leading to Paul Revere's famous horseback ride. Though both sides faced casualties, more British soldiers were left dead or wounded.

THE BATTLE OF BUNKER HILL
Following the Battles of Lexington and Concord, the colonists besieged Boston from the surrounding hills. When they heard news of the British planning to attack Bunker Hill and Breed's Hill, the colonists sent 1,600 militiamen to set up fortifications. On June 17, 1775, 2,600 British soldiers attacked. Most of the fighting took place on Breed's Hill. By the third charge from the British, the colonists had to retreat, and though the British gained control of Breed's Hill, they suffered great losses and casualties.

THE EVACUATION OF BOSTON
The evacuation of the British from Boston was a very important victory for the colonists, and also the first victory for General George Washington. As a result of the Battle of Bunker Hill, even though the British won, they desperately needed reinforcements. To support Washington, Henry Knox, the chief artillery officer, brought fifty cannons from Fort Ticonderoga and positioned them to aim at the British fleet in Boston Harbor. On March 5, 1776, the British general saw the cannons aimed at them and took his men to Halifax, Canada.

THE BATTLE OF TRENTON Following a defeat, General George Washington planned a surprise attack on the British and Hessian soldiers on Christmas day of 1776. Washington led 2,500 soldiers across the Delaware River in a great snowstorm under treacherous conditions to reach Trenton, New Jersey. While the British soldiers slept, Washington and his men attacked, taking 1,000 prisoners and killing over 100 men without a single American killed.

THE BATTLE OF SARATOGA The Battle of Saratoga is considered to be one of the major American victories in the Revolutionary War and a turning point for the Americans. The British army wished to control the Hudson River and cut New England off from the other colonies. British troops had planned to join with other troops along the way to quell the colonists; however, intervention from the Americans prevented this. On September 19, 1777, the first battle of Saratoga occurred, followed by the second battle on October 7, resulting in the surrender of the British troops.

THE BATTLE OF YORKTOWN Though the battle of Yorktown did not end the American Revolution, it was the last major battle fought. On September 5, 1781, the French fleet arrived and defeated the British Navy. The British general, Lord Cornwallis, found his men trapped between the American colonists and the French, and on October 19, 1781, he and his 8,000 troops surrendered. The surrender had a huge impact on the British government, who concluded that the war was being lost.

THE US CONSTITUTION

THE DECLARATION OF INDEPENDENCE Before the Constitution was ever written, the Declaration of Independence needed to be drafted, declaring the colonies' freedom from the British. The Continental Congress met in the summer of 1776 to discuss the writing of the important document, and on June 11, Thomas Jefferson began the first draft. The final draft was submitted to the Continental Congress on June 28, and by July 2, the Continental Congress took a vote regarding their independence. On July 4, the document was released to the public.

THE ARTICLES OF CONFEDERATION

Upon winning their freedom, the thirteen states began to operate under their own rules, and a centralized government was strongly opposed, fearing another monarchy could arise. As a compromise, the Articles of Confederation were drafted in 1776 and ratified in 1781. Essentially, this was the country's first constitution. Each state would retain its freedom, and a committee of representatives—a Congress—would be responsible for declaring war, dealing with foreign affairs, and maintaining an army and navy. Though the document had a lot of good ideas, it had many shortcomings, and these led to the creation of the Constitution.

THE CONSTITUTIONAL CONVENTION OF 1787

In 1787, delegates from all of the states except Rhode Island met in Philadelphia to create a more centralized government. Two plans, the Virginia Plan and the New Jersey Plan, were presented. The Virginia Plan consisted of a powerful centralized government that had executive, legislative, and judicial branches. The New Jersey Plan would make changes to the Articles of Confederation and allow Congress to control taxes and trade to some degree. A compromise was reached, combining parts of both plans.

ARTICLES OF THE CONSTITUTION

The Constitution has a preamble, seven original articles, a list of twenty-seven amendments, and a certification from the Constitutional Convention. The first article establishes the legislative branch, defining Congress as a bicameral body with a House of Representatives and a Senate. Article II establishes the role of the presidency. Article III describes how the court system will work and includes the Supreme Court.

THE BILL OF RIGHTS The Bill of Rights are the first ten amendments made to the Constitution. These amendments establish the specific rights every American citizen has. The Bill of Rights was created due to the fears of Anti-Federalists who were wary of the Constitution and feared the presidency could turn into a monarchy. These rights include the freedom of speech and religion, the right to bear arms, and the right to have a fair trial by a jury.

AMENDMENTS TO THE CONSTITUTION During the writing of the Constitution, the framers were aware that over time, certain changes would be necessary, and included the ability to amend the Constitution. There have only been twenty-seven amendments to the US Constitution. Some of the most well-known are the Thirteenth Amendment, which abolished slavery; the Nineteenth Amendment, which established women's suffrage; and the Eighteenth Amendment, which prohibited the sale of alcohol. The Eighteenth Amendment was then repealed by the Twenty-First Amendment.

THE US INDUSTRIAL REVOLUTION

WHAT WAS THE INDUSTRIAL REVOLUTION? The Industrial Revolution can be broken into two parts: the first Industrial Revolution, which started in England and lasted from 1750 to 1850; and the second Industrial Revolution, which took place in America and lasted from 1850 to 1940. The Industrial Revolution was a great burst of technological advancement that changed the world from a rural, agricultural economy to that of an urban and industrial one.

TEXTILES

In 1750 England, the modern factory system developed in textiles as a result of power-driven machinery. Prior to these machines, textile work was done completely by hand. With the spinning machine, however, a person would just have to operate a foot pedal and let the machine do the rest. The most famous model of the spinning machine was the spinning jenny. In the 1740s, the first textile mills began appearing in England, and by the 1780s, there were over 120 textile mills.

STEAM POWER

The steam engine provided an efficient and cheap source of power. The first practical steam engine was created in 1712, and it was later perfected by Scottish inventor James Watt in the 1770s. The steam engine was an integral part of the Industrial Revolution. It provided power for machinery and soon moved from the factories to being used in locomotives and ships.

TRANSPORTATION

Prior to the Industrial Revolution, transportation was limited to horse-drawn carriages and boats. In the 1800s, the first steamboat was created by an American inventor, Robert Fulton. Within just a few years, steamboats appeared both in the United States and in England and traveled the Atlantic with goods and raw materials. Technological advancements soon led to better roads and the first steam-powered rail systems.

IRON AND COAL

Without iron and coal, there would not have been an Industrial Revolution. Coal provided the power for the steam engines as well as energy to fuel the smelting of iron. The iron was then used to build and improve machinery, ships, and bridges. The reason Great Britain became a leader in the Industrial Revolution, and in fact, the first industrialized nation, was due to their large coal and iron ore deposits.

THE COTTON GIN In America, the cotton gin, created by Eli Whitney, was revolutionary in the American cotton industry. Prior to Whitney's invention, farming cotton required hundreds of hours separating the raw fibers from the cottonseed by hand. With this new invention, however, up to 50 pounds of cotton could be cleaned in one day. Though its technological advancement was great, the cotton gin would ultimately revitalize slavery in the South.

THE FRENCH REVOLUTION

THE TENNIS COURT OATH Pre-Revolutionary France practiced a class system. The higher classes were given special privileges, such as not paying taxes. At a time when France had great debt, King Louis XVI refused to change the system. The Third Estate, which represented the underprivileged class, formed a National Assembly. On June 20, 1789, when the Third Estate was locked out of their meeting hall, they moved to a nearby tennis court. There, they took an oath to never separate until there was a constitution in France.

STORMING OF THE BASTILLE The Bastille was a royal prison that became a symbol of oppression. It was also an armory where the arms and gunpowder were held. On July 14, 1789, hundreds of angry citizens demanded the weapons. When they were refused, they stormed the prison. After gunfire from the prison guards left 100 men dead, some prison guards defected, shooting open the prison doors. The governor of the Bastille surrendered and was beheaded. His head was put on a stake.

WOMEN'S MARCH ON VERSAILLES
The women's march on Versailles was one of the most significant events of the French Revolution. On October 5 and 6, 1789, some 7,000 women of the marketplaces in Paris marched to the king's palace demanding the price of bread and food be brought down. The crowd forced the king and the French Assembly to return to Paris. The authority of the king had effectively been ended, and the balance of power began to shift toward the common folk.

OVERTHROW OF THE MONARCHY
On August 10, 1792, French citizens numbering as many as 30,000 marched to the Tuileries Palace in an effort to capture King Louis XVI. The king had heard the approaching mob and moved himself and his family to the Legislative Assembly building. The Swiss Guard protecting the castle was never made aware of these plans, and when the mob approached, they attempted to defend the palace, but ultimately surrendered. As the mob stormed the castle, they killed anyone inside. Leaving the castle, they advanced toward the Legislative Assembly building, where King Louis XVI was found and arrested, signaling the end of the monarchy.

THE SEPTEMBER MASSACRES
Starting on September 2, 1792, a mass killing of political prisoners took place. Following the overthrow of King Louis XVI, there was an imminent threat of invasion by Austrian and Prussian forces to restore the monarchy. The French feared the political prisoners were going to join together and create a counterrevolution. The killings lasted for five days, and 1,200 prisoners were killed.

A NEW REPUBLIC On September 22, 1792, the French First Republic was founded by the National Convention, an elected assembly comprised of professional men, businessmen, and tradesmen that ruled France from 1792 to 1795. The National Convention abolished the monarchy, created a new constitution, and a day later, declared France to be a Republic. The Republic would only last fourteen years, however, before Napoleon Bonaparte rose to power and established the First French Empire.

THE WAR OF 1812

WHAT WAS THE WAR OF 1812? The War of 1812 began in 1812 and lasted until 1815. The British, who were in a war with France, wanted to restrict trade between the newly formed United States of America and France, an act that the Americans considered illegal. Following years of Britain's restrictions and attacks on American ships, as well as their funding Native American attacks on American settlements, the US declared war on Britain and their Canadian colonies. This new war with Britain reaffirmed the stance that the United States had to be independent from Britain.

INVASION OF CANADA When war was declared against the British, the War Hawks (members of Congress who wanted to go to war with Britain and the Native Americans) set their sights on an attack of the British in Canada. The American forces divided into segments at Niagara, Lake Champlain, and Detroit, and invaded on July 12, 1812. The divided American troops were no match for the British, and fighting was pushed into American territory.

SURRENDER OF DETROIT On August 15, 1812, the British forces captured Detroit. In fact, no actual fighting took place. The British general Isaac Brock, along with the Native American British allies, tricked the American general William Hull. Though his men outnumbered the British and Native Americans, Hull thought otherwise and surrendered the fort and town of Detroit.

HARTFORD CONVENTION On December 14, 1814, Federalist delegates from Massachusetts, Connecticut, Vermont, New Hampshire, and Rhode Island met to discuss opposition to the war, and even the possibility of New England seceding. As a result of the Hartford Convention, constitutional amendments were proposed stating that war and laws that restricted Congress needed a two-thirds majority in Congress; that successive presidents could not be from the same state; that presidents were limited to a single term; and that the three-fifths clause would be eliminated.

TREATY OF GHENT The War of 1812 ended on December 24, 1814, with the signing in Belgium of the Treaty of Ghent between the United States and Britain. The treaty called for amnesty for all Native American participants, the return of prisoners of war and territory, the return of slaves, and a commitment to end the international slave trade.

THE BATTLE OF NEW ORLEANS Two weeks after the Treaty of Ghent, news of the treaty had not yet spread to the United States, and the United States fought in the Battle of New Orleans, its greatest military victory of the war. The British were 7,500 strong, while the Americans were only 5,000. A total of 2,036 British soldiers were killed, with only twenty-one American casualties, turning Andrew Jackson, the general of the battle, into a national hero.

THE CIVIL WAR

SECESSION FROM THE UNION Before Abraham Lincoln even took office as president of the United States, the state of South Carolina, perceiving his election as a threat, called all state delegates to a meeting. The delegates voted to remove South Carolina from the United States in December of 1860. Mississippi, Alabama, Florida, Louisiana, Georgia, and Texas followed South Carolina's move, forming the Confederate States of America on February 4, 1861. Four more states, Virginia, Tennessee, Arkansas, and North Carolina, would join the Confederate States of America on April 12, 1861.

FIRST BATTLE AT BULL RUN Though the events at Fort Sumter started the Civil War, the first major battle was at Bull Run on July 21, 1861. As pressure to crush the rebellion in the South grew, the Union army started to march toward Richmond, Virginia, the capital of the Confederacy. The Union army and the Confederate army met at Manassas, Virginia. Though initially losing, the Confederates had reinforcements, and Union soldiers began withdrawing. It was thought at the time that this would be the only battle of the war; however, as the battle came to a close, many came to the realization that this war was going to last much longer.

THE BATTLE OF SHILOH The Battle of Shiloh is known as one the deadliest battles of the Civil War. Approximately 23,750 soldiers were killed or wounded, 13,000 of whom were from the Union side. The Confederate army attacked General Ulysses S. Grant's soldiers by surprise at Pittsburg Landing in Shiloh, Tennessee, on April 6, 1862. Though not prepared, the Union army was able to fight until reinforcements could come. The next day, Grant led a counterattack, forcing the Confederates to retreat and securing a victory for the Union.

THE EMANCIPATION PROCLAMATION

In September of 1862, a preliminary form of the Emancipation Proclamation was ordered declaring that any slaves in the Confederate states would be freed unless the states rejoined the Union by January 1. The Confederate states did not take the offer, and on January 1, 1863, President Lincoln issued the Emancipation Proclamation, stating that slaves in all of the states would be granted freedom. The Emancipation Proclamation did not actually free all slaves, however. Rather, it freed the slaves who were living in the Confederate states and allowed blacks to fight for the Union. Though ending slavery was never a major goal of the Civil War, the Emancipation Proclamation turned it into one.

THE GETTYSBURG ADDRESS

On November 19, 1863, President Lincoln issued one of the most famous speeches in American history: the Gettysburg Address. The speech was delivered in Gettysburg, Pennsylvania, four and a half months after the Union had defeated the Confederates at the Battle of Gettysburg. The speech paid tribute to all lost soldiers, and featured no hatred or ill will but emphasized the principles of democracy.

THE SURRENDER OF ROBERT E. LEE

In the spring of 1865, Confederate general Robert E. Lee fled with his army to Appomattox County with Grant's army in pursuit. Seven days after the capture of Richmond, on April 9, 1865, Lee knew that Grant would win another battle, and decided to meet with Grant at Appomattox Court House. The two men showed great respect for one another, and Robert E. Lee surrendered. Though this did not end the war immediately, the loss of Robert E. Lee's army would lead to the surrender of the other Confederate armies.

THE SPANISH-AMERICAN WAR

CUBA'S STRUGGLE FOR INDEPENDENCE Cuba had been a colony of Spain since 1492. By the mid-nineteenth century, Cuba had become dissatisfied with Spain's corruption and sought independence. The Spanish denied the Cubans any freedom, and Cuban nationalists fought the Spaniards in the Ten Years' War, from 1868 to 1878. In 1896, the Spanish sent over General Weyler, a.k.a. "The Butcher," who established concentration camps where thousands of Cubans died. As news spread to the United States, President Cleveland vowed that even if Congress declared war, he would not send the military to Cuba.

YELLOW JOURNALISM Yellow journalism was the name given to sensational news stories being reported in the United States about the Spanish treatment of Cubans. Though based on truth, the articles were written to elicit strong responses. The two men most responsible for yellow journalism were William Randolph Hearst of the *New York Journal* and Joseph Pulitzer of the *New York World*. Yellow journalism would galvanize public opinion to go to war.

SINKING OF THE USS *MAINE* In 1897, the United States sent a warship, the USS *Maine*, to Cuba to investigate what was going on and to provide rescue to any Americans. On February 15, 1898, an explosion on the USS *Maine* left 266 Americans dead. Though the explosion was an internal problem with the ship and not an attack by Spain, the newspapers quickly placed blame on the Spanish, creating great anti-Spanish fervor among Americans.

DECLARATION OF WAR Though President McKinley did not want war, the pressure from the public, including that of the assistant secretary of the navy, Theodore Roosevelt, grew. On April 11, 1898, McKinley told Congress he supported going to war with Spain. On April 24, Spain declared war on the United States, and the next day, the United States declared war on Spain. To justify going to war, Congress passed the Teller Amendment, in which the United States promised to liberate Cuba.

THE PHILIPPINES Without permission, Theodore Roosevelt, the assistant secretary of the navy, ordered the officer in control of the US Asiatic Squadron to attack the Spanish fleet in the capital of the Philippines should the United States declare war. The fleet was quickly defeated. At the same time, Filipino rebel forces continued fighting the Spanish.

THE TREATY OF PARIS In 1898, the war officially ended with the Treaty of Paris. The Spanish-American War lasted a total of six months. Under the treaty, Guam and Puerto Rico fell under American control, Cuba was granted its independence, and for $20 million, America gained control of the Philippines. Due to the Platt Amendment, the United States was granted a military base at Cuba's Guantánamo Bay.

THE WRIGHT BROTHERS

ATTEMPTS AT FLIGHT PRIOR TO THE WRIGHT BROTHERS Humans have always had the desire to fly. In the 1480s, Leonardo da Vinci designed a concept for a machine that had bird-like wings called the ornithopter. In 1783, French brothers Joseph-Michel and Jacques-Étienne Montgolfier created the first hot-air balloon, and in the 1800s, Sir George Cayley created the first gliders capable of carrying humans. In 1891, German engineer

Otto Lilienthal created the first glider that could fly long distances. That same year, Samuel Pierpont Langley realized that in order to fly, power was needed. He built a model plane that ran on a steam-powered engine and flew for three-fourths of a mile. However, when he created a full-sized version called the Langley aerodrome, it was too heavy and crashed. In 1894, Octave Chanute created the biplane, which would become the basis for the Wright brothers' design.

THE STUDY OF BIRDS From 1897 to 1899, the Wright brothers, Wilbur and Orville, rode their bicycles to the Pinnacles, a picnic spot near Dayton, Ohio. Many birds flew around the area, and the unique geography of the Pinnacles created an updraft, perfect for large soaring birds. There they observed the birds and came to the realization that in order to fly, their model needed to be based on large birds that soar. In 1899, after observing buzzards, the Wrights came up with their wing warping theory. The Wright brothers realized that as birds soared into the wind, lift was created as a result of the air going over the surfaces that were curved. To turn, birds change the shape of their wings.

THE WRIGHT BROTHERS' GLIDERS The Wright brothers created a series of gliders over the next three years, and even corresponded with Octave Chanute. After a successful test, they created a full-sized glider, choosing Kitty Hawk, North Carolina, as the test site due to its hilly landscape, isolated location, and wind. The 50-pound, 17-foot-wingspan glider was tested at Kitty Hawk in 1900, both piloted and unmanned. A year later, the largest glider ever (weighing almost 100 pounds and with a 22-foot wingspan) was flown at Kill Devil Hills, North Carolina. Their glider faced some problems, and the Wright brothers realized that their calculations were not reliable. They built a wind tunnel to test various wing shapes, and soon planned on making a new glider with a 32-foot wingspan.

THE WRIGHT FLYER

In 1902, the Wright brothers tested their new 32-foot-wingspan glider. Their research showed that if the glider had a moveable tail, it would actually balance the glider. The Wright brothers connected a tail to the wires responsible for warping the wings. After successful tests were performed in the wind tunnel, the brothers decided they would try to make a powered aircraft. They studied how propellers worked, and created a motor and an aircraft that would be sturdy enough for the motor, as well as able to withstand the motor's vibrations. This new craft was known as the Flyer, and it weighed 700 pounds.

THE FIRST MANNED FLIGHT

In order for the Flyer to gain enough speed to launch, the Wright brothers created a movable downhill track. On December 13, 1903, after only two tries (one of which resulted in the Flyer crashing), Orville Wright flew for twelve seconds. This was the first piloted and powered flight in history to ever be a success. On November 9, 1904, the Flyer II, this time flown by Wilbur, flew for over five minutes.

THE *VIN FIZ*

On July 30, 1909, the US government bought its first airplane. It was a Wright brothers biplane, and it sold for $25,000 with an additional $5,000 because it had exceeded 40 miles per hour. In 1911, the Wright brothers' *Vin Fiz* became the first airplane to travel coast to coast. Calbraith Perry Rodgers purchased the plane from the Wright brothers and had only ninety minutes of training. The flight took a total of eighty-four days, stopped seventy times, and crash-landed so frequently that little of the original plane existed by the end of the journey.

THE PANAMA CANAL

ABOUT PANAMA Panama is at the southeastern end of the isthmus that bridges North America and South America. It is also between the Pacific Ocean and the Atlantic Ocean (when standing on the highest point, the summit of Volcán Barú, you can actually see both oceans). In its entirety, Panama is slightly smaller than the state of South Carolina. From 1538 to 1821, Panama was part of the Spanish Empire.

THE EARLIEST PROPOSAL FOR A CANAL The proposal to build a canal in Panama dates all the way back to 1534, when King Charles V of Spain, the Holy Roman Emperor, sought a route that would ease traveling between Spain and Peru and give the Spanish military an edge on the Portuguese. From 1788 to 1793, Spanish naval officer Alessandro Malaspina demonstrated that a canal would in fact be feasible, and he began making outlines for its construction. Other attempts to make use of the location were made in 1698 by Scotland, and in 1855 a railway was built across the isthmus. That same year, an employee of the US government proposed a canal in a report.

THE FRENCH ATTEMPT TO BUILD A CANAL With the success of the Suez Canal, the French saw a canal as the best solution. They began constructing the canal on January 1, 1880, choosing Panama over Nicaragua because they believed it could best support a sea-level canal, meaning it had no locks (which raise and lower water levels in chambers in order to carry water over uneven terrain). Instead, this canal would maintain the same level all the way through and carve through the terrain. The construction was rushed and poorly planned, and the terrain proved too difficult to cut through with the machinery they had. Harsh weather and tropical fever left an estimated 22,000 people dead, and by 1888, the company funding the construction crashed, ending the building of the canal.

AMERICANS TAKE OVER THE ISTHMUS In 1902, Congress gave the authority to purchase the assets of the French canal company, but it required that the United States and Colombia first form a treaty for the control and use of the canal. As negotiations with Colombia failed, the United States supported Panama's fight for independence. In the Hay-Bunau-Varilla Treaty, Panama gave the United States exclusive rights to the area of the canal without having a Spanish translation. President Theodore Roosevelt backed a lock-based model for the canal, and in 1906, the area was cleared of yellow fever.

CONSTRUCTION OF THE PANAMA CANAL Lieutenant Colonel George Washington Goethals was chosen to become the canal's chief engineer, and he split the work up into thirds: the Atlantic Division, the Central Division, and the Pacific Division. The Panamanian Railroad was a great help for the Americans, as were rock drills, steam shovels, and dynamite, without which the job would have been impossible. The extreme climate and horrible accidents gave it the name "Hell's Gorge." The three-part lock division that Goethals created allowed for two-way traffic; the locks are powered by electricity.

THE PANAMA CANAL TODAY In 1979, the Panama Canal Treaty went into effect, granting Panama complete control of the canal after twenty years, which occurred on December 31, 1999. Because of the age of the canal, the volume of traffic, and the tropical climate, the Panama Canal Authority must perform regular maintenance and repair on the locks and machinery, and stabilization of its banks. The Third Set of Locks project, which was begun in 2007 and completed in 2016, involved construction of new chambers and water-saving basins that are the largest in the world.

THE RUSSIAN REVOLUTION

A CENTURY OF REPRESSION Following the Napoleonic wars, ideas of democracy began to spread throughout Europe. Russians, under the rule of Czar Alexander I, began calling for a constitution guaranteeing basic rights. Though Alexander I granted Poland a constitution, he never made his mind up about Russia. Following Alexander's death, there was great chaos as Nicholas I, the czar's younger brother, came to power. The reign of the son of Nicholas I, Alexander II, brought heavy police repression, creating resentment among the people.

THE FEBRUARY REVOLUTION Throughout 1916 and 1917, as Russia suffered greatly in World War I; due to food shortages, there were many strikes and protests, often leading to violence. The International Women's Day Festival, on February 23, 1917, turned into a citywide protest of men and women from factories and industries. As Czar Nicholas II ordered the military to attack, many in the military, no longer loyal to the czar, joined the protesters. Chaos broke out in the city. By February 27, over 80,000 troops had mutinied. Nicholas II abdicated, giving power to his brother; however, his brother wouldn't accept unless chosen by the representative assemblies. The next day, he resigned, and Russia did not have a head of state.

THE BOLSHEVIKS Vladimir Lenin, an intellectual who had been known as a revolutionary and socialist, had been living in exile in Switzerland. Lenin saw the political unrest in Russia as the perfect opportunity for him and his party, the Bolsheviks. Lenin negotiated with Germany to be brought back to Russia, and in April of 1917, he returned to great applause. Lenin delivered the April Theses, in which he advocated that the Russians withdraw from World War I, not cooperate with the Provisional Government, and give control of all land and the production and distribution of goods to the workers' councils, or "Soviets."

THE SUMMER OF 1917 During the summer of 1917, Lenin attempted to overthrow the Provisional Government. The coup failed, and many Bolsheviks were arrested as Lenin fled to Finland. However, when it was feared that the minister of war was trying to create a military dictatorship, the Bolsheviks, who had created a military force, the Red Guard, were needed for support. By the fall, the Bolsheviks were gaining popularity, and Leon Trotsky was elected as president of the Petrograd.

THE OCTOBER REVOLUTION Lenin planned a coup d'état to overthrow the Provisional Government, which was increasingly ineffective, and replace them with the Bolsheviks. Lenin met with twelve party leaders to persuade them that revolution was necessary. With only ten backing him, Lenin began plotting the revolution. On October 24, 1917, troops that were loyal to the Bolsheviks began taking over government buildings. On October 26, the Provisional Government was arrested and a new provisional government was created with only Bolshevik members.

THE AFTERMATH Lenin's peace policy with Germany was widely unpopular and ended in Russia ceding large territories to the Germans. Following the October Revolution, a civil war broke out between the Whites (the anti-Bolsheviks) and the Reds (the Communists). The Reds eventually won after four years, and in 1922, the Soviet Union was established. When Lenin died in 1923, Joseph Stalin came to power.

WORLD WAR I

THE ASSASSINATION OF ARCHDUKE FRANZ FERDINAND On June 28, 1914, Archduke Franz Ferdinand, heir to the Austro-Hungarian Empire, was assassinated by a member of the Serbian terrorist group known as the Black Hand. This event would lead to the beginning of the "Great War," World War I. In the wake of the murders of the archduke and his wife, the government of Austria-Hungary had to impose their authority on Serbia, calling on Germany for support. On July 23, an ultimatum was delivered to Serbia to wipe out terrorist groups and anti-Austrian sentiment or encounter military action. Serbia called on Russia for support, and on July 28, Austria-Hungary declared war on Serbia. On August 1, Russian forces began mobilizing in support of Serbia, and Germany declared war on Russia. Russia's allies, Great Britain and France, then joined in.

THE FIRST BATTLE OF THE MARNE The First Battle of the Marne was the first significant battle fought that proved that the war would not be short and introduced the fighting style most characteristic of World War I: trench warfare. By the end of August 1914, three of Germany's armies were moving toward Paris to take control of the city and conquer France. By September 3, 500,000 French civilians had left the city. The commander-in-chief of the French forces planned an attack on the German 1st Army, attacking on September 6. By splitting the German armies, the French and the British were able to advance, and German forces couldn't break through. On September 9, the Germans retreated, and by September 10, the battle was over.

THE BATTLE OF TANNENBERG The Battle of Tannenberg was fought from August 26 to August 30, 1914. It is considered

Germany's greatest victory and Russia's worst defeat. Two Russian armies, one led by General P.K. Rennenkampf, the other by A.V. Samsonov, planned on attacking East Prussia. Contact between the two armies was lost, and the Germans took advantage of Samsonov's isolated army. Within the next few days, half of his army was lost, and on August 29, Samsonov shot himself. The Germans took 92,000 Russian prisoners.

THE BATTLE OF CAMBRAI The Battle of Cambrai began on November 7, 1917, and continued through December. It was the first large-scale battle in World War I where tanks were used. Following the failure at the Third Battle of Ypres (with conditions less than suitable), the popularity of tanks dwindled, and they were seen as prone to malfunctioning and had limited use. Though the British would lose the Battle of Cambrai, the use of tanks during this particular battle showcased the strengths of these machines.

THE UNITED STATES ENTERS THE WAR When the war broke out, the United States remained neutral and encouraged isolationism, even though there was pro-British propaganda spreading throughout the nation. On May 7, 1915, the *Lusitania*, a British passenger ship that transported people between the United States and Britain, was sunk by a German U-boat. The sinking of the ship, which had American citizens aboard, outraged the people of the United States. As wishes of neutrality started to wane, the British government intercepted a secret message, the Zimmermann Telegram, sent from the German foreign secretary Arthur Zimmermann to the German minister in Mexico, asking Mexico to attack the United States if the United States declared war on Germany. On April 6, 1917, the United States declared war on Germany.

THE TREATY OF VERSAILLES The Great War ended in 1918 with the Treaty of Versailles. Drafted during the Paris Peace Conference in the spring of 1919, the treaty was crafted mainly by David Lloyd George, the British prime minister; Georges Clemenceau, the French prime minister; and President Woodrow Wilson. Terms of the treaty were severe: Much of the land that Germany had acquired over the war had to be given back; the German army and navy had to be dramatically cut down in size; Germany would not be allowed to have an air force; Germany was forced to pay $33 billion in war reparations; and the country had to take complete blame for the war. The League of Nations, an organization for international cooperation, was created at the Treaty of Versailles in order to prevent the destruction and suffering of any further conflicts.

THE GREAT DEPRESSION

ECONOMIC BOOM Following World War I, America experienced a period of economic expansion. The stock market became increasingly popular as many saw it as a safe and easy way to invest and to get rich. Stocks were being purchased on margin, meaning people didn't have enough to actually buy the stock. They would pay 10 to 20 percent, and the broker would pay the rest. Not only did individual people put their money in the stock market, but even companies and banks invested money in the stock market.

BLACK TUESDAY On October 24, 1929, what would become known as Black Thursday, the New York Stock Exchange crashed and large numbers of people began selling their stocks. Black Thursday is considered the beginning of the Great Depression. Five days later, Tuesday, October 29, was the worst day in the history of the stock market. Panic spread and people could not sell fast enough. With everyone selling and nobody buying, stocks plummeted. On that day, known as Black Tuesday, more than 16.4 million shares of stock were sold. The next day, the stock market was closed.

HOOVERVILLES The Great Depression led to widespread poverty. From 1929 to 1933, over 100,000 businesses failed and many people were left homeless with nowhere else to stay but in shantytowns or Hoovervilles (after President Hoover), which formed coast to coast in the cities of the United States. The largest Hooverville was established in New York City's Central Park. When Hoover's term ended in 1933, unemployment was at 13 million.

THE DUST BOWL During World War I and afterward, the farms of the Southern plains in the United States were extremely profitable. Demand for wheat and corn was high, with farmers producing food for the homeland and abroad. In the 1930s, however, a combination of events led to the creation of the Dust Bowl, the name given to the southern plains area of the United States hit hard by drought. Farming practices, in which much of the land was deeply planted, plowed, and farmed, began to take their toll on the soil. This heavily plowed land, combined with the worst drought in the history of the United States (which lasted years), devastated the once-prosperous agriculture of the southern plains. Inches of dried soil got swept up by the wind, darkening the skies with dust that engulfed entire towns and driving out families.

THE NEW DEAL When Franklin Delano Roosevelt became president, he focused on reforming the nation and set forth the New Deal (a phrase he coined during his speech accepting the nomination). The New Deal was split up into two phases: The first phase (from 1933 to 1934) concentrated on regulating agriculture and business. During this phase, programs like the National Recovery Administration, the Agricultural Adjustment Administration, and the Federal Communications Commission were established. The second phase of the New Deal (from 1935 to 1941) focused on creating policies to help the working class and social legislation. It was during the second phase that Social Security, a federal safety net for elderly or unemployed citizens the system, was created.

WORLD WAR II Though Roosevelt's New Deal reforms certainly helped, the Great Depression did not come to a complete end until World War II began. Unemployment decreased by 7,050,000 in three years, and the number of people serving in the military increased by 8,590,000. While men fought overseas, women worked in the factories to produce weapons and materials for the war. Manufacturing plants where vacuum cleaners had been made were now producing machine guns. By 1943, over 2 million women were employed in factories.

WORLD WAR II

INVASION OF POLAND On August 23, 1939, German leader Adolf Hitler and Stalin agreed to the Nazi-Soviet Nonaggression Pact, in which Germany and the Soviet Union agreed not to attack each other for ten years. The invasion of Poland was originally set for August 26, but Italian prime minister Benito Mussolini told Hitler that Italy was not yet ready for war, so the deadline was extended. Within a week, on September 1, 1939, Germany invaded and defeated Poland in what was the first military engagement of World War II. Hitler believed this invasion would lead to a quick victory in this war. On September 3, Britain declared war on Germany.

INVASION OF RUSSIA Hitler wished to end the war swiftly and knew an invasion of England was not the best way to go about it. Instead, he broke the Nonaggression Pact with Stalin when the German army invaded Russia on June 22, 1941, with a devastating blitzkrieg code-named Operation Barbarossa. Within one week, 150,000 Soviet soldiers had been killed or wounded. On July 3, Stalin implemented a scorched-earth policy that required all facilities and supplies be destroyed as the Soviets retreated so the Germans could not use them. Roads, bridges, factories, and fields of crops were demolished, slowing the German advance. The campaign lasted much longer than Hitler had anticipated, and the German armies could not withstand the Russian winter, giving the Soviets the advantage.

PEARL HARBOR The attack on the US naval base at Pearl Harbor brought America into World War II. The Imperial Japanese Navy led a surprise attack at Pearl Harbor on December 7, 1941. The Japanese launched two attacks, sinking four US battleships, killing 2,400 Americans, and wounding another 1,200. The next day, on December 8, the United States declared war on Japan. President Roosevelt famously announced to the American people, "Yesterday, December 7, 1941—a date which will live in infamy—the United States was suddenly and deliberately attacked by naval and air forces of the Empire of Japan."

THE HOLOCAUST In 1933, there were more than 9 million Jews living in Europe. As Adolf Hitler came to power, he promoted hatred toward the Jewish people, believing Germans were a superior race and that Jews presented a threat to the community. The Holocaust was Hitler's state-sponsored mass genocide of the Jewish people, in which approximately 6 million Jews were murdered. Jews were placed into ghettos, then concentration camps, and then extermination camps, where they were gassed to death. Toward the end of the war, the Jewish people were placed on trains and made to go on marches, known as "death marches." As the Allied forces approached, the camps were liberated.

THE BATTLE OF NORMANDY (D-DAY) By 1944, Germany knew the Allies would attempt to liberate Europe through an invasion of France. Under the plan code-named "Operation Overlord," the Allied forces intended to land on the northwest coast of France, in Normandy. On June 6, 1944, the Allies landed on five beaches of the Normandy coast. Allied forces were met with heavy resistance from the defending Germans, but eventually, they were able to make it through the German lines of defense. The accomplishment of the Allied forces, and the failure of the Germans, put an end to Hitler's goal of a Nazi-controlled Europe.

END OF THE WAR Germany's control and power began to weaken. As the Soviet Union fought German forces in the Battle of Berlin, Hitler, who had been hiding in a bunker during the battle, committed suicide. On May 1, the German forces surrendered in Italy, and on the next day, the forces fighting in Berlin surrendered to the Soviets. On May 7, the war in Europe was over. On August 6 and 9, the United States dropped two atomic bombs on Japan; on August 14, Japan surrendered.

THE HOLOCAUST

HITLER'S PROPAGANDA One way Adolf Hitler made the mass extermination of Jews possible was by eliciting strong feelings of ill will toward the Jewish community. He did so through propaganda in newspapers, film, art, music, books, radio, and the press. The weekly Nazi newspaper, *Der Stürmer*, meaning "The Attacker," featured ape-like caricatures of Jewish people. Films showed the Germans as superior, with an emphasis on German pride, and depicted the Jewish people as inferior, even subhuman. When Hitler came to power, he ruled with a combination of propaganda and a police state to silence any critics.

CONCENTRATION CAMPS From 1933 to 1939, the Jewish people were placed in concentration camps, where they were detained under horrible conditions. The first concentration camps began appearing as early as 1933 with Hitler's appointment as chancellor. The very first concentration camp was at Dachau. Initially, these camps held political prisoners, but they would later go on to hold Jews, homosexuals, gypsies, and those who were mentally ill, as well as anyone who opposed the regime. There were different types of concentration camps, and in 1939, forced labor camps began to appear. These required inmates to do physical labor under horrible conditions. Death was extremely common in these camps, but nothing would compare to the camps created to carry out Hitler's "Final Solution."

GHETTOS Following the invasion of Poland in 1939, all Polish Jews were to be put in ghettos, areas of cities that were surrounded by guards, brick walls, and barbed wire. Jewish people were forced to leave their homes and belongings and were put into these ghettos. By October, Jewish people from Czechoslovakia and Austria were being deported to Poland to be put in these ghettos as well. The largest ghettos were those of Warsaw and Lodz. The conditions in Warsaw were so horrible that from 1940 to 1942, around 100,000 Jews died from disease and starvation.

POGROMS Pogroms, or violent attacks on Jewish populations, began in Russia in the 1800s. During the Holocaust, with the resentment toward the Jewish people growing, pogroms began appearing once again. Pogroms were encouraged by the Nazi regime, leading to entire communities killing all of the Jewish people in their towns. Even when the war ended, pogroms still persisted. The most famous postwar pogrom was the Kielce Pogrom of July 4, 1946, in Poland. The surviving Jewish citizens were met with angry mobs, with forty-two Jews killed and fifty injured.

THE "FINAL SOLUTION" In June of 1941, Germany began to enact the "Final Solution." Mobile killing groups gathered up all of the Jews in the towns, lined them up, and shot them one by one. By 1942, six death camps, or killing centers, were established near railway lines so that the Jewish people from concentration camps could be easily transported. The Jewish people, who at this point were forced to wear yellow stars on their clothing so they could be identified, were gathered up and taken to these death camps where they would be gassed to death. Around 3.5 million Jewish people were killed in these camps. The largest of these camps was Auschwitz.

LIBERATION As the Allies advanced through Germany, the concentration camps were gradually liberated. In total, an estimated 5 to 7 million Jewish people were killed as a result of the Holocaust. Around 50,000 to 100,000 remained in the Allies' zones of occupation, many refusing to ever go back to their homes, later being transported to the United States, Israel, and Palestine. The Nuremberg Trials began in October of 1945 and were presided over by American, British, French, and Russian judges. The first trial prosecuted twenty-one members of the Third Reich, including many of those responsible for the Holocaust.

THE COLD WAR

THE IRON CURTAIN The Warsaw Pact of 1955 was a military treaty between the Soviet Union, Poland, Czechoslovakia, East

Germany, Romania, Albania, Bulgaria, and Hungary agreeing that should any of them be attacked, military aid would be provided by the other countries. The Warsaw Pact was initiated by the Soviet Union as a counter to the formation of NATO. The term *Iron Curtain* was used in reference to this division within Europe, both literally and figuratively. An actual metal fence separated the West from the East in some areas, cutting off all contact.

THE MARSHALL PLAN Following World War II, Europe was left completely devastated industrially, economically, and agriculturally, and the United States was the only major power that had not been left in ruins. In 1947, the Marshall Plan was created by US Secretary of State George Marshall to provide aid, and restore political and economic stability to the Western countries. Marshall believed this plan could both rebuild the Western countries and blunt the Communist advancements. A total of sixteen nations were involved in the program, and nearly $13 billion dollars was received in financial aid.

THE CUBAN MISSILE CRISIS The Cuban Missile Crisis is considered the closest the United States ever came to a nuclear war. By the 1960s, the United States had missiles that could reach the Soviet Union, while the missiles of the Soviets could only reach as far as Europe. In 1962, the Soviets set their attention on Cuba, and began putting their intermediate-range missiles there. Photographs of the Soviet missiles in Cuba surfaced, and a naval quarantine was deployed around Cuba. Tension grew as communication between the United States and the Soviet Union continued. Finally, the Soviet Union agreed to dismantle the installations in hopes that the United States would not invade Cuba.

THE SPACE RACE With the arms race and threat of nuclear war, fear of the Soviet Union grew. On October 4, 1957, the Soviets launched the first artificial satellite into space, *Sputnik* 1. The launch was a surprise to Americans, who believed they were the leaders in technology, and many feared *Sputnik* was a weapon. The United States launched the *Explorer* 1, the first US satellite, only four months after *Sputnik*. The Soviet Union originally led in the space race. In April of 1961, the Soviet Union was the first to launch a man into orbit (twenty-three days later, the United States sent their first man into orbit), and in June of 1963, the Soviet Union sent the very first woman into orbit. Ultimately, the United States won the space race, however. In 1961, President Kennedy announced the goal of sending a man to the Moon. Eight years later, that goal was achieved.

THE BERLIN WALL The Berlin Wall was more than just a division between West and East Germany. It was symbolic of the division between Democracy and Communism. The split had also occurred in the capital, Berlin. West Berlin was actually encircled by the rest of East Germany. While West Germany experienced economic growth, East Germany, under the Soviet Union's Communist influence, had a dragging economy, and individuals' rights were severely restricted. By the 1950s, many residents of East Germany were fleeing to West Berlin. Once there, they were able to fly to West Germany. By 1961, 2.5 million people had left East Germany, and several attempts, with the help of the Soviet Union, were made to control West Berlin, until finally a wall was built that stretched hundreds of miles.

THE DISSOLUTION OF THE USSR In 1985, Mikhail Gorbachev became president of the Soviet Union, and as reform was being promoted and was desperately needed in the Soviet Union, Gorbachev introduced perestroika, a restructuring of the economy, and glasnost, which allowed for political freedom. As reforms continued throughout 1986–1990, Soviet states gained new autonomy, and Gorbachev's power and ability to hold the union together weakened. In 1991, a coup was attempted against Gorbachev. The coup failed, but Gorbachev lost support, and Boris

Yeltsin came to power. The USSR was dissolved and the Russian Federation was created.

US MOON LANDING

APOLLO 1 The Cold War led the United States and the Soviet Union toward a new frontier: space. The *Apollo* program was created with the specific intention of having a human land on the Moon. On January 27, 1967, the launch and flight crew of *Apollo* 1 were conducting a simulation a month before their intended launch. The day was met with problems and delays, and at 6:30 p.m., a spark ignited inside the spacecraft, and the closed compartment was engulfed in flames. The three astronauts in the spacecraft died of asphyxiation. The cause of the spark is still unknown; however, the flammable materials within the spacecraft, combined with an oxygen-rich atmosphere and exposed wiring, were a recipe for disaster. The fire led to several changes in procedures and management for the rest of the *Apollo* program.

APOLLO 7 *Apollo* missions 4, 5, and 6 were successful unmanned flights. On October 11, 1968, *Apollo* 7 tested the manned command module in orbit for the first time. While in orbit, the crew of three practiced lunar-mission maneuvers. Not only was *Apollo* 7 the first manned *Apollo* flight, but it was also the first time such a flight was broadcast on live television. The spacecraft was able to exit Earth's orbit and re-enter the atmosphere successfully, and the capsule was recovered in the Atlantic Ocean.

APOLLO 8 On December 21, 1968, *Apollo* 8 was launched. Close to three hours after the launch, translunar injection occurred, meaning that the ship was maneuvered into a trajectory that would bring it to the Moon. After sixty-nine hours and eight minutes, the spacecraft entered elliptical lunar orbit, the first manned mission to do so. After a little over eighty-nine hours, on December 25, trans-Earth injection occurred, setting the ship into the trajectory headed toward Earth. On December 27, the capsule landed in the Atlantic Ocean and the mission was a success.

APOLLO 9 On March 3, 1969, the *Apollo* 9 was launched. The manned mission successfully used all of the *Apollo* lunar hardware in orbit. It was also the first manned flight to use the lunar module, a separate vehicle that would eventually ferry the astronauts to the lunar surface. The operations lasted ten days, and the crew was able to demonstrate all of the mission maneuvers. While in orbit, the crew simulated a landing using the lunar module and safety maneuvers. One of the safety maneuvers, in which the command module is inoperable and the lunar module is used as a lifeboat, was actually used during the recovery of *Apollo* 13.

APOLLO 10 Launched on May 18, 1969, the *Apollo* 10 mission was to perform a staging of what the *Apollo* 11 mission would be like, without actually landing on the Moon. The *Apollo* 10 mission was the first time that the complete spacecraft traveled to the Moon, making it to around 8.5 miles above the surface of the Moon, and it was the second mission that orbited the Moon. The mission lasted a total of eight days, and the crew was recovered in the Pacific Ocean.

APOLLO 11 *Apollo* 11 was launched on July 16, 1969. On July 20, Neil Armstrong and Edwin "Buzz" Aldrin landed on the Moon and took their very first steps there. The lunar module spent twenty-one hours and thirty-six minutes on the surface of the Moon, and the crew spent two hours and thirty-one minutes outside the craft. Two days after arrival, the crew departed, taking with them 46 pounds of soil and lunar rocks. The mission lasted eight days and landed in the Pacific Ocean. *Apollo* 11 was the first manned spacecraft to land on another planetary body and return home safely.

THE CULTURAL REVOLUTION IN CHINA

MAO ZEDONG Mao Zedong was born in 1893. He founded the People's Republic of China, and when he was younger, he was one of the original members of the Chinese Communist Party. Mao was elected chairman of the Soviet Republic of China in 1931 and became one of the most important Communist leaders of the time. Following the Second Sino-Japanese War, the Communists and a nationalist political party called the Kuomintang fought in a civil war, and by 1949, the Communists had taken most of mainland China. The People's Republic of China was established, and Mao became chairman.

GREAT LEAP FORWARD In 1958, Mao Zedong attempted to modernize the economy of China so that it could rival that of the United States. Mao believed industry and agriculture were to be the focus of the development project, and his plan was called the Great Leap Forward. Mao concluded that in order for industry to grow, workers must be well fed, and in order for agriculture to grow, new tools must be provided. Mao believed the best way to make this happen was by making China into a series of many communes. By 1958, 700 million people had been organized into 26,578 communes. The Great Leap Forward was a dismal failure, however. Poor implementation of the plan, lack of Soviet support, and a series of natural disasters seriously damaged Chinese agricultural output and economy. It is believed that 20 to 30 million people died from famine partly as a result of the policies of the Great Leap Forward.

BREAK FROM THE SOVIETS Following the failure of the Great Leap Forward, Mao Zedong temporarily withdrew from public life. In the 1950s, Mao's People's Republic of China and Stalin's Soviet Union were the largest Communist states, and they supported one another. When Stalin died, Nikita Khrushchev came to power, and began to steer away from Stalin's policies. Mao Zedong believed that Khrushchev's policies were betraying Marxism, and with the Great Leap Forward taking a horrible turn for the worse, Khrushchev stopped funding the People's Republic of China. Mao Zedong was then replaced as chairman in 1959 by his opponent; however, he retained his position with the Politburo of the Communist Party.

THE CULTURAL REVOLUTION From 1966 to 1976, in an effort to prevent the bureaucratization and capitalization of Communism that the Soviet Union was implementing, Mao Zedong created what would be known as the "Great Proletarian Cultural Revolution." The Cultural Revolution is considered one of the darkest periods in China's history. All schools were closed, and the students were encouraged to join the Red Guard, which was responsible for persecuting intellectuals and teachers. The Red Guard turned increasingly more violent (over a million people died from the purges) and split into factions. Mao then ordered the People's Liberation Army to suppress the factionalism of the Red Guard. During this time period, Mao's ideology was harshly enforced. Youths were taken out of cities and forced to work on farms in rural areas. Artists who made antisocialist work and ethnic minorities were highly persecuted.

TIANANMEN INCIDENT Zhou Enlai, the premier who founded the People's Liberation Army, died on January 8, 1976. The Gang of Four forbade anyone to take part in any of the activities honoring his death, creating great uproar. On April 4, 1976, the eve of a festival that paid homage to the deceased, an estimated 2 million people gathered in Tiananmen Square to memorialize Zhou Enlai and express their anger over the Cultural Revolution. The next day, the people were outraged to discover that their wreaths and items for Zhou Enlai had been removed. A violent riot began, police cars were set ablaze, and thousands of people forced their way into government buildings.

END OF THE CULTURAL REVOLUTION By 1968, the Chinese economy was close to collapsing, and the factionalism in the Red Guard was creating havoc. In 1971, the chaos of the Cultural Revolution had died down with the People's Liberation Army. From 1972 to 1976, with both Chairman Mao and the premier in deteriorating health, there was a great struggle over whether to continue the Cultural Revolution in the succession phase. Mao's propagandists blamed the chaos of the Cultural Revolution on four people, known as the "Gang of Four" (one of whom was Mao Zedong's wife). In October of 1976, the Gang of Four was arrested, thus ending the Cultural Revolution. Mao Zedong died on September 9, 1976.

VIETNAM WAR

VIETNAM FOLLOWING THE GENEVA PEACE ACCORDS After 100 years of colonization by the French, the Vietnamese fought and defeated the French in the First Indochina War, forcing them to leave. The French and Vietnamese met in Geneva to sign a treaty in the summer of 1954. According to the Geneva Accords, elections would be held in 1956, eliminating the division between North and South Vietnam at the seventeenth parallel. The United States, believing this would give too much power to the Communist Party in Vietnam, supported the creation of the Southeast Asia Treaty Organization (SEATO) to act as a counterrevolutionary alternative. With the help of the United States and SEATO, South Vietnam established a new government, the Republic of Vietnam (DRV).

A SPLIT IN VIETNAM Ngo Dinh Diem became president of the government of the Republic of Vietnam in 1956, and quickly declared that the Communists of the North were attacking to reclaim the South. In 1957, Diem, with the aid of the US military, counterattacked the North. Diem's presidency was oppressive and corrupt, and was opposed by the Vietnamese people. From 1956 to 1960, the North attempted to peacefully unite the two Vietnams; however, following Diem's attacks, it was understood that a more violent overthrow was necessary. In 1960, the Communists created the National Liberation Front (NLF).

THE KENNEDY YEARS President Kennedy sent a team to Vietnam in 1961 to report on what was happening there; they responded that there was a need for military, economic, and technical aid, as well as advisors to stabilize President Diem's regime and destroy the NLF. Kennedy agreed to send advisors and machines, but not troops. The plan did not work, and the NLF became more successful. Another plan, called the Strategic Hamlet Program, that would place villagers into hamlets to isolate them from the NLF, also backfired. In 1963, Diem's brother raided a Buddhist pagoda, which led to massive protests during which Buddhist monks performed self-immolation. When photos of the monks sparked outrage around the world, the United States decided to support a coup. On November 1, 1963, Ngo Dinh Diem and his brother were captured and executed.

THE JOHNSON YEARS When Lyndon B. Johnson became president after Kennedy was assassinated, he was convinced that more needed to be done in Vietnam. In 1964, in the Gulf of Tonkin, two American ships were attacked by North Vietnam. The attack was used by the Johnson administration to get Congress to pass the Gulf of Tonkin Resolution, which allowed Johnson to order the bombing of North Vietnam. By 1968, North Vietnam had continued success launching attacks on southern cities, with the intention of forcing the United States to make a bargain. That year, Johnson decided not to run for re-election.

ANTI-WAR MOVEMENT Johnson had hoped that going to war in Vietnam would have little effect on everyday life back home. The Vietnam War, however, was met with a great anti-war movement. In major cities and college campuses across the United States, anti-war protests erupted. One of the most famous events occurred during the 1968 Democratic National Convention, where hundreds of thousands of people came to Chicago to protest the war, leading to a police riot.

THE END OF THE VIETNAM WAR When Richard Nixon became president, he had a plan, known as Vietnamization, to end the war by encouraging the South Vietnamese to take control of the war and bring American troops back home, shifting the fighting to air attacks. During the Nixon years, the United States expanded the war into Laos and Cambodia, violating their international rights, in an attempt to crush Communist supply routes and sanctuaries. In December of 1972, the United States launched bombing raids in the largest cities of the DRV. The bombings were condemned by the international community, and Nixon had to reconsider his strategy. In 1973, the Nixon administration and South Vietnam signed a peace accord, and hostilities between the DRV and the United States ended. The war in Vietnam continued until April 30, 1975, when the Communists captured Saigon.

KOREAN WAR

ORIGINS OF THE WAR Following World War II, the Soviet Union began moving into Korea. The United States did not want Korea to become another Communist state and moved in as well. The 38th parallel was chosen as the division between the part controlled by America (South Korea) and the part controlled by the Soviet Union (North Korea). During this time, the Korean people created an interim government known as the People's Republic of Korea (PRK), which became increasingly more Communist. The Soviet Union recognized the new government, but the United States would not, and the PRK became pro-Soviet. The United States tried to bring a free market to South Korea, but it led to elevated prices and famine. The United States handed the issue over to the UN, and elections were held throughout all of Korea. Following the elections, the North cut off all power to the South.

SURPRISE ATTACK FROM NORTH KOREA By 1949, most of the US military had moved out of South Korea, and the United States was afraid to provide too much weaponry, with Syngman Rhee, the leader of South Korea, often talking of attacking the North. On June 25, 1950, the North Korean army crossed the 38th parallel and attacked South Korea, stunning the United States, who had no sort of plan ready. South Korea had very little weaponry (as a result of the US withdrawal), while North Korea entered South Korea in Soviet tanks. The UN condemned the actions of North Korea, and in the United States, there was talk of sending General Douglas MacArthur to lead an attack.

INCHON INVASION North Korea's capture of most of South Korea alarmed the United States, who persuaded the United Nations to support South Korea by sending 300,000 UN troops

(260,000 of which were American) to Korea in July of 1950. General MacArthur led an amphibious attack on the port of Inchon, driving the North Koreans back and recapturing South Korea. UN troops then attacked North Korea and advanced north of the 38th parallel, reaching as far as the Chinese border. Worried that the proximity of UN troops to their border would mean that the US would likely bomb Chinese cities in retaliation for China's involvement in the Korean War, the Chinese began to attack. Using nighttime "human wave tactics," they were able to drive back the Americans, recapture North Korea, and head for South Korea. In response, MacArthur wished to use the atomic bomb, but Truman would not have it, and instead sent more troops, which eventually drove the Chinese army back.

DISMISSAL OF MACARTHUR Without telling anyone else, General MacArthur sent an ultimatum to China to withdraw their troops or he would attack. When Truman found out about MacArthur's actions, he was outraged and knew he had to fire MacArthur. Truman waited, however, and when Congress approved NATO, Truman needed to find another reason. News spread that MacArthur wanted to go against Truman's policies and use the Chinese Nationalist forces to anger the People's Republic of China. When a congressman read MacArthur's plan before Congress, Truman began to discuss dismissing MacArthur, which he did on April 11, 1951.

END OF THE "ACCORDION WAR" Following the dismissal of MacArthur, Matthew Ridgway controlled the US effort. On April 22, 1951, the Chinese attempted to recapture Seoul, but failed. Following another failed attack, the United States believed a counterattack would be successful. By May 30, the UN/US/ROK forces were back at the 38th parallel, and both sides were at a stalemate. Truman began to push for an end to the war, and the United States contacted the Soviet Union, which was willing to negotiate. Peace talks began on July 8, 1951.

THE END OF THE WAR No real progress had been made in the negotiations by the time Dwight Eisenhower had become president in 1953. On June 8, both sides came to an agreement called the "Terms of Reference," a document that provided for Chinese and North Korean prisoners of war who refused to be repatriated or returned to Communist North Korea. Once the POW issue was resolved, the sides focused on a peace treaty. On July 27, 1953, China, North Korea, and the UN signed an armistice (South Korea refused). A buffer zone or demilitarized zone called the "DMZ," where each side pulled back 1.2 miles on either side of the 38th parallel, was created between the North and South. North Korea and South Korea remained separate, and because the treaty was never signed by the South, they are technically still at war with one another.

US CIVIL RIGHTS

BROWN V. BOARD OF EDUCATION On May 17, 1954, the Supreme Court announced one of the most important verdicts relating to a change in civil rights. The case revolved around Linda Brown, an African-American third-grader, who, in order to get to her elementary school, had to walk a mile, even though a white school was closer to her. Brown was denied access by the school principal, and the case went to the Supreme Court. The Supreme Court ruled that "separate but equal" was, in fact, not equal at all, and that segregation of public schools was unconstitutional.

ROSA PARKS On December 1, 1955, Rosa Parks boarded a bus in Montgomery, Alabama. A white passenger told her to give up her seat and move to the "colored section," which was in the back of the bus. Parks refused and, as a result, was arrested.

In response to her arrest, the African-American community of Montgomery, led by Baptist minister and social activist Martin Luther King Jr., boycotted the city's public transportation. The boycott lasted for 381 days and reduced revenue by 80 percent. On December 21, 1956, the buses were desegregated.

PROJECT C Martin Luther King Jr. and the Southern Christian Leadership Conference created a plan known as "Project C" (for *confrontation*) to protest the segregation of Birmingham, Alabama. Their strategy involved sending a message about the horrors of segregation through nonviolence, with boycotts, rallies, and peaceful demonstrations. The police reacted to these nonviolent protests with police dogs, violence, and fire hoses. On April 12, 1963, Martin Luther King was arrested. While in prison, King wrote his famous "Letter from Birmingham Jail."

DESEGREGATION OF THE UNIVERSITY OF ALABAMA In 1963, George Wallace, who had run his political campaign with a slogan of "segregation now, segregation tomorrow, segregation forever," became governor of Alabama. In June of that same year, the state government was barred from interfering with the admission of two African-American students attending the University of Alabama. Wallace temporarily appointed himself the registrar of the university, and stood at the door of the building, refusing to let the African-American students come in to register. President Kennedy called in the Alabama National Guard, and 100 members of the National Guard escorted the two students. The commander, General Henry V. Graham, ordered Wallace to move, telling him to "step aside."

THE MARCH ON WASHINGTON On August 28, 1963, a massive interracial march was held in Washington, DC, to pressure the government to enact civil rights legislation more quickly. Around 250,000 demonstrators, including civil rights supporters as well as regular citizens, peacefully marched for the end of segregation in public schools, the right to vote, protection from police brutality, and a law that prohibited segregation in the workplace, among other things. The event included performances from such artists as Bob Dylan and Joan Baez and readings by celebrities Paul Newman and Sidney Poitier. Most importantly, the march featured an address by Martin Luther King, who delivered his "I Have a Dream" speech at the Lincoln Memorial.

CIVIL RIGHTS ACT OF 1964 In 1963, President Kennedy proposed a new Civil Rights Act. When Kennedy was assassinated, the bill was still being worked on in Congress. On July 2, 1964, the bill was signed into law. The Civil Rights Act of 1964 made it illegal to racially discriminate in public places like restaurants, hotels, and movie theaters, and required that employers provide equal opportunities for employment. Any project that received federal funding would have funding cut if it was found that there was employment discrimination based on race, color, or nationality. It also prohibited unequal application of voter registration qualifications, thereby enforcing the constitutional right to vote.

GULF WAR

INVASION OF KUWAIT From 1980 to 1988, Iraq and Iran engaged in an extremely bloody conflict that left Iraq deep in debt. On August 2, 1990, the president of Iraq, Saddam Hussein, sent 100,000 troops to Kuwait. Saddam believed that Iraq was losing much-needed oil revenue because Kuwait exceeded its quota in oil production, driving down oil prices in the global market. There were two days of intense fighting, which resulted in the Kuwaiti Military Forces being overrun or fleeing to Bahrain and Saudi Arabia. Iraq occupied Kuwait for seven months, during which time there were looting and human rights abuses in Kuwait.

~~~~~~

OPERATION DESERT SHIELD AND OPERATION DESERT STORM

The United States considered Saddam Hussein's actions a threat, especially relating to the oil production in the Persian Gulf. With the approval of Saudi Arabia, President George H.W. Bush sent ground troops and warplanes to Saudi Arabia as Iraqi troops began approaching the borders of Saudi Arabia, indicating an interest in the oil fields. The US deployment sent out to defend Saudi Arabia was known as Operation Desert Shield. It was the largest deployment since the Vietnam War. Thirty other nations joined the United States. On January 17, 1991, with the understanding that Saddam Hussein would not withdraw, Desert Shield turned into Desert Storm, and US-led forces unleashed a massive aerial bombardment on Iraq.

~~~~~~

SCUD MISSILE ATTACKS

Iraq had Scud missiles, tactical ballistic missiles developed by the Soviet Union that were designed to carry chemical and nuclear warheads. Casualties from Scuds ranged from extensive to very little. On January 17, Iraq fired a total of seven Scud missiles at Israel, which the Israelis were prepared for. The United States pleaded with Israel to not counterattack, and Israel agreed because the United States promised to target and destroy all Scud missile sites in Iraq.

~~~~~~

BATTLE OF KHAFJI

On January 29, the Battle of Khafji was fought, lasting for a total of three days. Four days prior to the battle, the US forces noticed the Iraq forces building up behind the border of Kuwait, reinforcing artillery and bunkers. On the night of January 29, the US marines were in position, ready for an attack, and Soviet-built tanks approached. A convoy of Iraqi tanks followed, giving the international sign of surrender—their cannons faced the opposite direction. The cannons suddenly swung around and began firing, and the Iraqis gained control of Khafji for the time being. The Allies attacked with air support and a barrage of fire, which proved to be too powerful for Saddam's forces. By January 31, Iraq's offensive was finished.

END OF THE WAR The war ended with a series of ground attacks that lasted three days, in combination with constant bombing from above. On February 24, Allied troops entered Iraq, targeting Kuwait City, west of the Iraqi flank and then past the Iraqi lines. The next day, marines reached Kuwait City, and the retreat route of the western flank was cut off. On the third day, in one of the largest tank battles ever, American armored forces were able to destroy the Iraqi tanks without losing a single one of their own. On February 26, as Iraqi troops retreated, they set fire to around 700 oil wells. A large convoy of Iraqi troops formed along a major highway, which was bombed from above. On February 27, 1991, President Bush declared that Kuwait was liberated and that the war was over.

THE IMPACT ON THE SOLDIERS When US soldiers returned home, many began experiencing unexplained chronic symptoms such as nausea, rashes, cramps, memory problems, difficulty breathing, headaches, and even birth defects. This came to be known as "Gulf War Syndrome" and, more officially, "Gulf War Illness." In 1994, a panel created by the National Institutes of Health ruled out biological and chemical warfare as the cause. In 2008, it was declared that the evidence suggested that nerve gas, an anti-nerve-gas agent, and pesticides that were used for sand flies might be what caused the syndrome. In an environmental research and public health journal article from 2019, a study showed that Gulf War veterans who reported exposure to chemical weapons suffer from a significantly higher risk of chronic conditions such as high blood pressure, diabetes, arthritis, and chronic bronchitis.

WAR ON TERROR

9/11 On September 11, 2001, a series of attacks would change the course of United States history. Four commercial passenger jet airliners were hijacked by nineteen al-Qaeda terrorists. Two of the planes crashed into the Twin Towers of the World Trade Center in New York City. Within two hours, both of the towers collapsed (killing 2,753 people, including 343 firefighters and 60 police officers). The third plane crashed into the Pentagon (killing 184 people). After hearing about the other attacks, passengers and crew aboard the fourth flight attempted to retake the plane, which eventually crashed near Shanksville, Pennsylvania (killing all forty people on board). In 2004, Osama bin Laden took responsibility for the attacks.

THE WAR ON TERRORISM Following the attacks of September 11, the Bush administration declared a war on terrorism. The objectives of the war were to defeat terrorists and their organizations (including Osama bin Laden and Abu Musab al-Zarqawi), strengthen the international efforts in combating terrorism, deny any forms of support or sanctuary to terrorist organizations, reduce conditions that terrorists can exploit, and defend US interests at home and abroad. In October of 2001, Operation Active Endeavour was launched by NATO with the purpose of preventing any movements of weapons of mass destruction or terrorists.

WAR IN AFGHANISTAN On October 7, 2001, the War in Afghanistan began with the launch of Operation Enduring Freedom, a US-led combat mission whose purpose was to dismantle the al-Qaeda organization, end its use of Afghanistan as its base, remove the Taliban, and find Osama bin Laden. The first phase of Operation Enduring Freedom saw the Taliban get thrown out of power in Kabul. In 2002, Operation Anaconda was launched to destroy any al-Qaeda and Taliban that remained in Afghanistan. The Taliban came together in Pakistan and unleashed offensives on the coalition forces. Fighting between the Taliban and coalition forces is still ongoing, though peace talks are underway.

IRAQ WAR In March 2003, the Iraq War began when US aircraft bombed a bunker rumored to house the Iraqi president and his senior staff. US air strikes against government and military installations followed, and then ground forces went in. Though the reasons for the Iraq War have been questioned, the Bush administration claimed that it was part of the war against terrorism and that Iraq housed terrorists and weapons of mass destruction. In April 2003, Baghdad fell, and soon after the government of Saddam Hussein dissolved. Although President Bush announced the war was over, an insurgency occurred that actually led to more casualties than the initial invasion. No weapons of mass destruction were found. In December 2003, Saddam Hussein was captured, and in 2006, he was hanged. US combat officially ended on September 1, 2010, with Operation New Dawn.

FIGHTING IN PAKISTAN After the attacks of September 11, Pakistan sided with the United States following an ultimatum given by President Bush. The president of Pakistan, Pervez Musharraf, said he was against Islamic extremism and pledged that Pakistan was committed to fighting terrorism. In 2002, Pakistan made some very important arrests within jihadi organizations, including al-Qaeda officials of high rank. In 2004, the Pakistan Army launched 80,000 troops to remove al-Qaeda and the Taliban. When the Taliban in Afghanistan fell, many fled to Pakistan, where they were subsequently killed and captured. Currently, there is still a Taliban Pakistani resistance fighting in Pakistan.

DEATH OF OSAMA BIN LADEN On May 2, 2011, ten years after the attacks of September 11, Osama bin Laden was killed. The operation, ordered by President Obama, was called Operation Neptune Spear. A team of United States Navy SEALs from the United States Naval Special Warfare Development Group (or SEAL Team Six) raided the compound in Pakistan where bin Laden had been living. After the raid, bin Laden's body was taken to Afghanistan to be identified and then was buried at sea following Muslim practices. On May 6, his death was confirmed by al-Qaeda.

ISRAELI-PALESTINIAN CONFLICT

HISTORY OF THE LAND The history of Israel and Palestine is a very complex one. In ancient times, the land was known as Judea and it was the land of the Jewish people. When the Romans conquered the land, it was renamed Palestine, which was then conquered and inhabited by Arabs for more than 1,000 years. The Zionist movement, a nationalist movement that began in the nineteenth century, advocated for the creation and support of a Jewish national state in Palestine, the Jewish homeland. The Balfour Declaration of 1917 stated Britain's support and wish to turn Palestine into a national home for the Jewish people, antagonizing the Arabs who lived there. Riots broke out, and the British stopped immigration of the Jewish people to Palestine. After the Holocaust, the British once again began allowing Jewish people to move to Palestine. In 1947, the land was partitioned into a Jewish state and an Arab state.

PALESTINIAN STATE The Arab people did not accept the division of the land, and the Arab-Israeli War broke out in 1948.

After Israel and Palestine reached an armistice agreement that ended the war in 1949, the Jewish people expanded their territory, leaving hundreds of thousands of Palestinian refugees to flee or be expelled from the area. The two-state solution was finally agreed upon in 1988. Violence and land settlement continued, however, and in September of 2000, there was open conflict. The Road Map for Peace is a plan that was issued by the Bush administration to create a Palestinian state in peace.

TERROR FROM PALESTINE Many Palestinian parties and underground groups were created with the sole intention of destroying Israel through violence. The Palestine Liberation Organization is the only group that has renounced this and honors the right of Israel to exist. As a result, Israel allowed the Palestine Liberation Organization to enter the Gaza Strip and West Bank, leaving most of the area independently controlled by Palestinians. Palestinian terrorism has continued, however, perpetrated by militant Islamic groups such as Hamas who object to the agreements made by the PLO. The violence and resistance of the Palestinians against the Israelis became known as "intifada."

REPRESSION FROM ISRAEL In response to Palestinian violence, Israel limited the number of Palestinians who could enter Israel. They instituted strict border checks at checkpoints that became sources of violence on both sides, with attacks by Palestinians and killings of Palestinians by the border control. In 2002, Israel began construction of the West Bank Barrier, a chain-link fence and concrete security wall that runs near the "Green Line" between Israel and the West Bank to control Palestinian traffic into Israel. In the process, Israel reoccupied land in the West Bank that had been relinquished to Palestinians. Israel Defense Forces created more checkpoints, destroyed homes, and killed thousands of Palestinians in an effort to discourage suicide bombings.

HAMAS Hamas (short for Harakat Al-Muqawama Al-Islamia) is a group of radical Islamic fundamentalists who mostly operate in the Gaza Strip. Hamas wishes to create an Islamic Palestinian state and destroy Israel, and uses politics and terrorism in pursuit of their goal. Many large-scale suicide bombings and attacks on military targets have been conducted by Hamas. Attacks are only aimed at Israel and its territories; Hamas has not turned any of its violence toward the United States.

RECOGNIZING ISRAEL Many Palestinians want Hamas to recognize Israel so that peace can be negotiated. Though Hamas recognizes that Israel exists, they refuse to recognize the land as a Jewish state and do not plan on making peace. Leaders from the United States and Europe have refused to work with Hamas or provide any aid to Palestine until Hamas has recognized Israel and disarms. Even though a large majority of Palestinians want peace, Hamas has refused to listen to them, and will not recognize Israel and will not give up on an Islamic Palestinian state.

PART 2

Language

THE ALPHABET

THE PHOENICIAN ALPHABET By 3000 B.C., there was the cuneiform of Mesopotamia and the hieroglyphs of ancient Egypt. The Phoenician alphabet, however, was quite a different writing system from either of these. Instead of using pictographs, the Phoenician alphabet was an abjad, a non-pictograph consonantal alphabet that showed symbols representing sounds. This writing system quickly spread throughout the Mediterranean and was adapted by many cultures.

THE ARAMAIC ALPHABET The Aramaic alphabet was an adaptation of the Phoenician alphabet, and all Middle Eastern alphabets can be traced back to it. Much like the Phoenician alphabet, letters in the Aramaic alphabet only represented consonants, but it did also have certain places where long vowels were to be pronounced. To this day, the Hebrew alphabet is the closest relative to the Aramaic script of the fifth century B.C. The inventory of the letters and the shapes of the letters are practically identical.

THE GREEK ALPHABET The Greeks adopted the Phoenician alphabet, and, by the eighth century B.C., had modified it and created the first true alphabet, meaning both consonants and vowels were represented. The Greeks even used the Phoenician consonant symbols to represent vowels; they did not have the same sounds the Phoenicians did and needed the symbols for the vowels. The Greek alphabet heavily influenced the Latin alphabet, which is the most widely used alphabet today.

THE LATIN ALPHABET The Latin alphabet, or the Roman alphabet, was taken from the Greek alphabet and then modified by the Etruscans and Romans. The Latin alphabet consisted of twenty-one letters:

A, B, C, D, E, F, Z, H, I, K, L, M, N, O, P, Q, R, S, T, V, X

This was the alphabet used when writing Latin, and as the Roman Empire spread, so, too, did the language and the letters. As the Romance languages started to evolve, the languages adapted with these letters.

OLD ENGLISH ALPHABET The first alphabet for the English language was the Anglo-Saxon futhark runic alphabet of the fifth century. It was used by the Anglo-Saxons in what is now England. In the seventh century, Christian missionaries introduced the Latin alphabet to the Anglo-Saxons, and over time, the Latin alphabet began incorporating some of the Anglo-Saxon futhark alphabet into it. The Old English alphabet was made up of twenty-four letters from the Latin alphabet and five letters from the English alphabet.

MODERN ENGLISH ALPHABET Established around 1550, the Modern English alphabet is the current alphabet used in the United States. With the advent of printing, the Old English alphabet evolved into the Modern English alphabet, dropping many of the Anglo-Saxon letters while maintaining the Latin alphabet. The Old English alphabet looked like this:

$$A\ B\ C\ D\ E\ F\ G\ H\ I\ K\ L$$
$$M\ N\ O\ P\ Q\ R\ S\ T\ U\ X\ Y\ Z$$
$$\&\ \urcorner\ P\ \þ\ \eth\ \mathit{Æ}$$

The Modern English alphabet distinguished between the letters *i* and *j*, as well as *u* and *v*, and it is believed the *w* was added at a later time.

PUNCTUATION

HOW IT STARTED Use of punctuation dates back to Ancient Greece and Rome. Orators placed marks in their speeches to indicate where and when to pause. These marks were given names such as period, comma, and colon, correlating to the kind of pauses needed. Punctuation was used infrequently; it was not until the fifteenth century, with the introduction and rise of printing in England, that the punctuation that we know today began being used.

THE PERIOD A period is used at the end of a sentence, creating a statement and completing a thought. A period can also be used at the end of a command, such as, "When you've finished the last part of the exam, put your pencils down." It is also used to end an indirect question, as in, "Her boss asked her why she didn't come to work on Monday."

THE COMMA A comma should be used when separating any independent clause that is joined by the conjunctions *and, yet, so, but, for, nor, or*. It is also used to separate items in a list or series, and after an introductory adverb clause. The comma can also be used to interrupt a sentence to add extra information. For example, "Her dog, which had jumped in the puddle, was soaking wet."

THE SEMICOLON A general rule is you can use a semicolon instead of a period when joining two sentences without a conjunction in between them. For example, "Give me your number; I'll call you when I get home." A semicolon should also be used before introductory words like *however, therefore,* and *namely*. One can also use a semicolon when, if writing a series, one or more of the items contain a comma, or when two sentences are joined by a coordinating conjunction and there are commas in the first sentence.

THE COLON A colon is used if one wishes to emphasize the second clause when writing two independent clauses. For example, "The time had passed: His date never showed up." A colon can also be used when introducing a list, a quotation, an appositive (in which two phrases are placed next to each other, with one serving to define or change the other), or another idea related to the independent clause.

THE DASH An em dash places emphasis on or sets content apart from the rest of the text. Named because it is the width of the letter *M,* this dash is longer and gives more importance to text than parentheses do. For example, "A lot of people were in the crowd—Tom and Scott among them." The en dash, which is the width of the letter *N,* is shorter and used to indicate a span of values between two numbers. For example, "For ages 3–5."

COMPOSITION

PARTS OF SPEECH Words are classified into nine main categories or parts of speech; knowing these categories is critical to understanding how composition works. The nine parts of speech are nouns (such as people, places, or things); pronouns (words like *he, she,* and *it* that can replace nouns); adjectives (words that describe nouns); verbs (actions); adverbs (words that modify adjectives, verbs, or nouns by describing when, where, how, why, how much); conjunctions (words that connect phrases or sentences); articles (words that define whether a noun is specific, like *the,* or general, like *a* and *an*); prepositions (words that link nouns, pronouns, or phrases to other parts of the sentence); and interjections (words that show emotion and are not linked to the rest of the sentence).

BASIC PARTS OF A SENTENCE There are three main parts in a sentence: the subject, the verb, and the object. The subject is usually the noun, and it is who or what the sentence is about. The verb then follows the subject, indicating what action takes place. Lastly, the object follows the verb and is what receives the action. In the sentence, "Tom threw the ball to Sally," Tom is the subject because the sentence is about him. The throwing of the ball is the verb, and Sally is the object. She receives the ball that the subject threw toward her.

MODIFIERS A modifier is any word, clause, or phrase that adds meaning to another word or part of a sentence. There are two types of modifiers: pre-modifiers and post-modifiers. The head is any word that determines the nature of the sentence. A pre-modifier goes before the head, and a post-modifier goes after the head. For example, "history book" is an example of a pre-modifier, and "a book on history" is an example of a post-modifier.

PREPOSITIONAL PHRASES A prepositional phrase adds meaning to the verbs and nouns in a sentence. It is composed of two parts: a preposition (a word that expresses the relationship between a noun or pronoun and the other words in the sentence) and the object of the preposition. For example, when looking at the phrase "In the building," the word *in* is the preposition because it indicates the location, and *the building* is the object of the preposition.

ADJECTIVE CLAUSES Adjective clauses help indicate which part of a sentence is more important than the rest of the sentence, a process known as subordination. The adjective clause is a dependent word group that modifies the noun. These usually include words such as *which, who, whose,* and *that.* For example, in "The dog that ate everyone's lunch wanted seconds," *that ate everyone's lunch* is the adjective clause.

PARTICIPLE PHRASES A participle is a verb form that is used as an adjective. For example, *cooked, cooking,* and *having cooked* are participles of the verb *cook.* A participle phrase is a sentence that consists of a present or past participle, with any modifiers, objects, and complements. For example, in "Running down the aisle, she knocked over the soup display," The phrase, *running down the aisle* is the participle phrase.

HUMAN LANGUAGE

WHY HUMANS ARE DIFFERENT Human language is truly unique, and much different from languages of other animals. Humans can make an extremely wide variety of sounds to create languages, and in fact, the sounds and words we make are arbitrary. For humans, language is something that is learned through social interaction. Other animals, however, have only a very limited set of sounds they can produce, and those are genetically transmitted.

LINGUISTICS Linguistics is the study of human languages, and it can be broken down into three categories: grammar (the rules used when speaking the language), meaning (how a language uses references to process and assign meaning), and context (the evolution of language). Linguists believe the ability to learn and communicate with language is an innate process for humans, similar to our ability to walk.

SEMANTICS
Language assigns a meaning to a sign. The lexicon is the array of signs, which are arbitrary and connected to specific meanings. In other words, the lexicon is the words you know in a language. A lexeme is a single sign that is representative of a particular meaning. For example, *dog* only means one thing. A dog can never be mistaken for a cat or an elephant.

PRAGMATICS
Pragmatics studies how the context of an utterance leads to meaning. It is used to explain how humans are able to overcome the ambiguities of language that are so closely related to time, space, manner, and so on. An utterance is a concrete example of speech with a specific context, and pragmatics aims to understand how the specific context affects the meaning of the utterance.

PHONETICS
Phonetics is the study of sounds found in human speech. There are three basic areas of study in phonetics: articulatory phonetics, which studies the production of speech from the articulatory and vocal tract of a speaker; acoustic phonetics, which studies the transmission of speech as it goes from speaker to listener; and auditory phonetics, which studies the reception and perception by the one listening.

SYNTAX
Syntax is the study of the rules and principles for constructing sentences. There are many theories relating to syntax. One of the most well-known theories is Noam Chomsky's transformational grammar, which recognizes the relationship between the different elements of a sentence and the variety of sentences in a language, and then uses rules to express the relationship.

DIALECTS

WHAT IS A DIALECT? A dialect is a variety of a particular language that is characteristic within a certain group of speakers of that language. It refers to differing speech patterns within the same language, and is often representative of social, geographic, and economic factors, as well as background. Dialects are distinguished by the use of grammar, syntax, morphology, and vocabulary.

STANDARD DIALECTS A standard dialect, also known as a standard language, is a dialect that begins to be used in other ways, rather than just by the small group of people who speak it. Standard dialects appear in literature and administrative work, for example, and also have support from institutions. Standard English, Standard Australian English, and Standard Canadian English are all dialects of the English language.

SOCIAL DIALECTS Difference in dialects is directly related to social status. Those that are highly educated tend to belong to a higher social class and use the standard dialect, whereas the lower classes, which tend to be less educated, preserve the original dialect of the region. Innovations in the dialect tend to be made in urban areas, whereas the dialect spoken in rural areas is more of the traditional geographic dialect.

GEOGRAPHIC DIALECTS The widespread differentiation in dialects is mostly due to geographical factors. Speech in one locality will always differ in some way from that of another locality. An isogloss is a geographic boundary between regions that shows a difference in linguistic features. Isoglosses are frequently grouped together in bundles, the result of migration and political borders. An example of an isogloss is the La Spezia-Rimini line, which divides the Central Italian dialects from the Northern Italian dialects.

INTERLINGUA From 1937 to 1951, Interlingua was developed as a language that would use the languages of Western civilization as its dialects. Realizing that many words in different languages are similar, linguists used words from English, Spanish, Portuguese, Italian, French, Russian, and German to create a spoken and written language that would be able to be understood by all. Interlingua is known as an international auxiliary language.

FOCAL AND RELIC AREAS Focal areas are locations where innovations in dialect occur. They usually coincide with urban areas or areas with great cultural and economic activity. Relic areas are locations that the innovations from focal areas spread to but haven't arrived yet. Relic areas also have innovations; however, they do not spread as widely geographically as focal areas. Boston is an example of a focal area, while Cape Cod is an example of a relic area.

FIGURES OF SPEECH

WHAT IS A FIGURE OF SPEECH? Figures of speech are a literary device used to add interest, emphasis, freshness, or special meaning to words. A figure of speech can also be referred to as a rhetorical device or locution. Figures of speech are used in figurative (meaning not literal) language, allowing for imagination and more creative ways to describe something.

SIMILE A simile is one of the most common figures of speech. In similes, one thing is described to be like another thing. The important part about similes is their use of the words *like* or *as*. For example, "He eats like a pig" and "It's as light as a feather" are both examples of similes. Other forms of similes can be found in sentences with *as if* and *than*. For example, "I completely forgot how to work the machine, as if it were my very first time" and "larger than life."

METAPHOR Metaphors are very similar to similes, only they do not include the words *like, as, as if*, or *than*. Instead, they simply state that one thing is another thing. In the sentence "Her home is a pigsty," we understand that this does not mean her home is a literal pigsty, but rather a very messy place. The differences between metaphors and similes is that even though they mean the same thing, they are worded differently. For example, "He is a snake" is a metaphor, but the same idea expressed as "He is like a snake" is a simile.

HYPERBOLE Hyperbole is a form of exaggeration used to elicit a strong response. Hyperboles are not to be taken literally and are often used for humor. For example, "He is older than the dinosaurs" and "I'm a million times smarter than you" are both hyperboles. There is great exaggeration in these sentences. Hyperbole is very common in media and advertising.

OXYMORON An oxymoron pairs two opposite or contradicting ideas together to create a new meaning or paradoxical image. For example, in "bittersweet chocolate," *bitter* and *sweet* are opposites of each other, and yet when put together, they take on a whole new meaning. Other examples of oxymora include *deafening silence, jumbo shrimp*, and *freezer burn*.

OTHER COMMON FIGURES OF SPEECH Other common examples of figures of speech include alliteration, where there is a repetition of the beginning consonant; anaphora, the repetition of a single word or phrase in a sentence; onomatopoeia, words that imitate the sounds they are referring to; and antithesis, which juxtaposes opposite ideas in a single, balanced sentence.

LITERARY TERMS

GENRE In literature, a genre is a specific category that literature follows. It is instantly recognizable and follows common conventions pertaining to that genre. Types of genres include nonfiction, in which everything written is true; mystery, in which all stories follow a crime or event that is not solved until the end; and fantasy, which features elements that are not realistic.

ALLEGORY In literature, an allegory is a narrative that is symbolic of something else. With allegories, behind the literal translation of the story, a second, more meaningful story or idea can be found. For example, the literal story of *Lord of the Flies* is about children stranded on an island where chaos ensues; however, the allegory is about civilization as a whole and the evil of humankind.

CATHARSIS In literature, a catharsis is a point in the narrative when there is a release of negative emotions, which in turn ends up either helping the character or helping the audience in understanding the character. The term comes from the Greek *katharsis*, which means "to make clean or purify." Use of the term applied to literature first appeared in Aristotle's *Poetics*, in which he describes the impact of drama on a viewer.

MOTIF A motif is a recurring image, phrase, element, expression, word, action, or object that has symbolic significance to the story. Motifs can help produce the theme of the narrative. A motif can also be a situation, character, image, idea, or incident that is found in other literature. For example, a love triangle or the corruption of power are both examples of motifs.

AMBIGUITY Ambiguity leaves room for different interpretations. It creates an openness in the text. Ambiguity can sometimes be considered a flaw in literature due to a lack of detail or vague characterization; however, it can also be used skillfully and can work to the advantage of the story.

METANOIA Metanoia, which comes from the Greek *metanoiein*, meaning to change one's mind, is when a character goes through a complete breakdown, and then begins the process of healing or experiences a change of mind or transformation. Metanoia is one form of catharsis.

LITERARY ELEMENTS

PLOT Simply put, the plot is the story found in literature, film, television, or other narrative work. It is the sequence of events that make up the story. German novelist Gustav Freytag considered the plot to any story to be composed of five parts: exposition, which introduces the main characters and their stories and relationships; a rising action, which begins with a conflict of some sort (this generally involves the character striving for a certain goal); the climax, which is the turning point of the story; the falling action, where loose ends are tied up; and lastly, the resolution or denouement.

PROTAGONIST The protagonist is the main character found in the story. It is who the entire plot of the story revolves around.

For example, even though in *The Wizard of Oz* the story is about finding the Wizard of Oz, whose name is the title of the book, the story's protagonist is actually Dorothy, because the story is about her journey, not that of the Wizard. The protagonist can sometimes be the narrator of the story. A false protagonist is a dramatic device where the protagonist is disposed of unexpectedly. A famous example of this can be found in Hitchcock's *Psycho*, where halfway through the movie, the main character is killed.

ANTAGONIST The antagonist is the character in opposition to the protagonist. The antagonist may also represent a threat or opposing idea to the protagonist. For example, if the superhero is the protagonist, the evil villain is the antagonist. A classic example of an antagonist is Voldemort or Snape from the Harry Potter series. Harry is the protagonist, and they are his antagonists.

FORESHADOWING Foreshadowing is used to suggest developments that will be found later in the plot. Formal patterning is a form of foreshadowing where certain events, actions, and gestures let the reader anticipate the plot. A red herring is a hint that intentionally misleads the reader.

POINT OF VIEW The point of view is the perspective from which the story is being told. A story can be told in the first-person point of view by the narrator who is experiencing it (using the word *I*), and sometimes is limited to the information in the moment. In the third-person point of view, the narrator is objective, an unattached observer who does not take a character's perspective. An omniscient narrator can relate multiple characters' perspectives, knowing all, including characters' thoughts. A limited omniscient narrator knows all, like an omniscient narrator, but only about one or two characters.

SETTING The setting of a story is more than just a backdrop for the actions to occur. It also sets the mood and tone of the entire story, as well as any context that needs to be understood. The setting establishes the time period, the culture, and the geography; in some cases, the setting can be just as important as the characters.

DEVELOPING A PARAGRAPH

WHAT IS A PARAGRAPH? A paragraph is a group of sentences that are related to the subject being discussed. Good paragraphs are crucial to being a good writer or just having your writing make sense to the reader. Paragraphs organize sentences so that the main idea can get across in an easy and coherent way. A good rule of thumb is to always keep one idea for every paragraph.

THE TOPIC SENTENCE The topic sentence tells the reader what the rest of the paragraph will be about. Though the topic sentence does not need to be the very first sentence in the paragraph, it certainly is a good approach to take. The idea is that one would be able to summarize from the topic sentence what that paragraph is about. The sentence doesn't have to blatantly state the topic at the beginning, as long as the paragraph is understandable.

SUPPORTING SENTENCES Supporting sentences do just that; they support. If the topic sentence is the main idea of the paragraph, then the supporting sentences should provide the necessary information (images, data, analysis) to back up that statement. Generally, paragraphs should be five to seven sentences long to provide enough support for the main idea you are trying to get across.

THE CONCLUDING SENTENCE The concluding sentence is like the reverse of the topic sentence. Instead of beginning a topic for discussion, this is meant to conclude the main idea of the paragraph. One type of concluding sentence would be to summarize all that was said in the topic sentence and supporting sentence. Not every paragraph needs a concluding sentence, but if the paragraph is long or contains lots of information, a concluding sentence can be very useful.

MAKING SURE YOUR PARAGRAPH IS WELL DEVELOPED It can be hard to know when a paragraph has enough information or perhaps too little information. To make sure your paragraph is well developed, here are some helpful tips. Make sure you describe the topic you're going to talk about, analyzing it and citing any information that helps get your idea across. Cite facts and details, talk about causes and effects, use stories or anecdotes, define terms, and compare and contrast when you can.

WHEN TO START A NEW PARAGRAPH There are a couple of ways you know to start a new paragraph. The most obvious is to begin discussing a new topic or a new idea. Similarly, if content contrasts to the material before it, that should be a new paragraph. Even if the idea of your content is continuing, however, if the paragraph goes on for too long, it can make it hard to read. Use another paragraph to give the reader's eyes a break. Lastly, begin a new paragraph when writing your introduction and your conclusion.

POETRY

RHYTHM Rhythm, also known as measure, is the equivalent of beat in music. In poetry, certain words may be held longer or pronounced with more force than other words. A rhythmic effect is produced from this pattern of emphasis. Sometimes rhythm is obvious, but it can also be more muted and subtle.

METRICAL PATTERNS Meter is the recurring pattern of stressed and unstressed syllables in lines of verse. For example, if a line of poetry contains fifteen syllables, the first syllable is unstressed, the second stressed, the next unstressed, and so on. A foot is a set combination of unstressed and stressed syllables. Different meters are used for different types of poetry. Iambic poetry has unstressed and then stressed syllables, while a dactylic meter consists of a stressed syllable followed by two unstressed syllables.

STANZA A stanza is a series of two or more lines of a poem arranged together. They are usually the same length and follow the same patterns of meter and rhyme. Couplets are examples of stanzas that are only two lines and that rhyme. Tercets are made of three lines of poetry that may or may not rhyme. If they do rhyme, that is known as a triplet. Quatrains have four lines and are written in any type of rhyme scheme.

NARRATIVE POETRY Narrative poetry is like a story because it has a plot, but it is told in verse form. These include epic poems, ballads, and idylls. Narrative poems can be long or short, intricate and complex, or more simple. They usually are nondramatic and have a regular meter. One example of a narrative poem is *The Canterbury Tales* by Geoffrey Chaucer.

EPIC POETRY Epic poems are longer narrative poems, and are usually centered around a hero and details of his heroic journey and deeds. Epics have a history in oral poetry, but even as far back as ancient Greece, these types of poems have been written. One of the most famous epic poems is the *Odyssey* by Homer, which follows Odysseus's journey back home following the Trojan War.

SONNETS One of the most common forms of poetry is the sonnet, perhaps most famously written by William Shakespeare. Sonnets must be fourteen lines and written in iambic pentameter with one of the various rhyme schemes. The first quatrain of the poem must be expositional and discuss the main theme and metaphor. The second quatrain complicates or extends the theme. The third quatrain introduces a twist, and then finally a couplet summarizes the poem, leaving the reader with a new image to end on.

HORROR

GOTHIC HORROR Gothic fiction is one of the most famous genres of horror fiction. It began with Horace Walpole's *The Castle of Otranto, A Gothic Story* published in 1764, and became incredibly popular during the eighteenth and nineteenth centuries. Gothic fiction combines elements of horror, romance, and emotionalism, with an emphasis on atmosphere. Gothic fiction also focuses on monsters, and it is from this genre that some of the most famous horror books ever written are descended.

ROBERT LOUIS STEVENSON Robert Louis Stevenson wrote many famous books, one of which was a horror novella by the name of *The Strange Case of Dr. Jekyll and Mr. Hyde*, published in 1886. The book, which tells the tale of a doctor who takes a new drug he had been testing and turns into a horrible monster, deals with the dual nature of humanity and the human capacity for good and evil.

BRAM STOKER Bram Stoker is responsible for introducing one of the most famous horror creatures of all time: Count Dracula. Vampire novels had been around before Stoker's *Dracula* of 1897; however, none has left as much of an impact as Stoker's gothic novel. The book follows Jonathan Harker, who travels to Transylvania to help Count Dracula with a real estate transaction and soon witnesses the horrors of the famous vampire. The book touches on sexuality, religion, and superstition, and introduces the world to famous characters like Professor Van Helsing.

MARY SHELLEY In 1818, Mary Shelley brought to life a monster who is still one of the most well-known creatures to this day with her book, *Frankenstein; or, The Modern Prometheus*. *Frankenstein* fuses elements of gothic horror and romance, and is one of the earliest forms of science fiction. Shelley began the book at eighteen years of age as a bet with other writers about who could write the better horror novel. Three years later, the tale of Dr. Frankenstein's monster was published.

H.P. LOVECRAFT H.P. Lovecraft is not as well known as Mary Shelley or Bram Stoker, but he has become a cult figure, often compared to the likes of Edgar Allan Poe. He is most widely known for his "Cthulhu Mythos," a shared literary universe about which he and fellow authors wrote horror stories. One of his most well-known books is *The Call of Cthulhu*.

STEPHEN KING Of the past forty-five years, one name in horror fiction has stood out above the rest, and is forever associated with horror novels: Stephen King. King has won six Horror Guild awards, twelve Bram Stoker awards, nineteen World Fantasy awards, forty-seven Locus awards, and a Lifetime Achievement Award. Some of his most famous works include *The Shining, Carrie, 'Salem's Lot,* and *It*.

HUMOR

MARK TWAIN Mark Twain is one of the most well-known American humorists. He is the author of such classic books as *The Adventures of Tom Sawyer* and *The Adventures of Huckleberry Finn*. The latter is regarded as one of the greatest books in American literature. Even to this day, Twain's influence as a humorist and a social commentator can be seen. Every year since 1998, the Kennedy Center has awarded the Mark Twain Prize to those comedic voices that have had an impact on the world. Past winners include Carol Burnett, Eddie Murphy, David Letterman, and Julia Louis-Dreyfus.

JOHN KENNEDY TOOLE John Kennedy Toole lived from 1937 to 1969. He wrote one of the most well-known comedic novels of the twentieth century, *A Confederacy of Dunces*. The book was published posthumously in 1980, eleven years after Toole committed suicide at the age of thirty-one. When Toole had finished writing the manuscript of *A Confederacy of Dunces*, the publisher he sent it to rejected the book. After his death, Toole's mother insisted that author Walker Percy read the book. He finally did, and fell in love with it. The book was published, and the next year, John Kennedy Toole was posthumously awarded the Pulitzer Prize.

P.G. WODEHOUSE Sir P.G. Wodehouse lived from 1881 to 1975. His first comedic book, *Something New*, came out in 1915. Of the more than ninety books that he wrote in his career, Wodehouse is most known for the Jeeves and Wooster stories, which feature eccentric characters and multilayered plots. Also a playwright and lyricist, Wodehouse wrote lyrics for musicals such as *Anything Goes*.

TERRY PRATCHETT Sir Terry Pratchett was born in 1948. Pratchett's work combines humor and fantasy, and his first novel, *The Carpet People*, was published in 1971. Pratchett's most well-known books are from his Discworld series, of which there are currently forty-one different titles. In 1990, he collaborated with Neil Gaiman on the book *Good Omens*, a parody of the film *The Omen* and the apocalyptic genre of fiction.

DOUGLAS ADAMS Douglas Adams is the creator of the popular Hitchhiker's Guide to the Galaxy series. Adams, who was discovered by Graham Chapman of Monty Python fame, started his career writing for BBC radio programs. *The Hitchhiker's Guide to the Galaxy* began as a radio show on the BBC, which Adams eventually developed into a series of five books. Since its conception, *The Hitchhiker's Guide to the Galaxy* has been immensely popular, and has been turned into a television series, a video game, a major motion picture, and a comic book series.

DAVID SEDARIS David Sedaris (whose sister is comedian Amy Sedaris) is one of the most prolific humorists writing today. His books usually consist of short essays full of biting, absurdist, and slightly neurotic commentary based on his life. One of his most famous pieces, "Santaland Diaries," is a memoir of his seasonal job working as an elf for Macy's during the holiday season. He has published many books of his essays, one of his most well-known being *Me Talk Pretty One Day*.

MYSTERY

EDGAR ALLAN POE Perhaps more widely known for his dark poetry such as "The Raven" or his horror stories like "The

Tell-Tale Heart," Edgar Allan Poe is actually considered the father of the mystery genre. His story "The Murders in the Rue Morgue," published in 1841, is considered the very first mystery story. It focuses on detective C. Auguste Dupin, as he tries to solve the murders of two women by gathering and analyzing clues. Many elements of modern mysteries can be found in such works by Edgar Allan Poe as "The Purloined Letter" and "The Gold Bug."

SHERLOCK HOLMES Sherlock Holmes is one of the names that immediately comes to mind when thinking about mystery fiction. Created by Sir Arthur Conan Doyle, Holmes's first case was featured in the book *A Study in Scarlet*, published in 1887, and Doyle's most well-known book was *The Hound of the Baskervilles* of 1902. When creating the character, Doyle actually used Poe's C. Auguste Dupin as an influence for Sherlock. Sherlock Holmes was featured in four novels and countless stories, and the Holmes story is still adapted for film and television to this day.

THE GOLDEN AGE OF DETECTIVE FICTION The period from 1920 to 1939 is referred to as the Golden Age of Detective Fiction. During this time, such prolific mystery writers as Dorothy L. Sayers, Agatha Christie, and Freeman Wills Crofts produced their most notable work. While Poe and Doyle brought the mystery genre to life, the writers of this time polished the genre. These books were meant to engage the reader and make the reader try to work along with the detectives. For this reason, certain rules were set in place: The criminal should be mentioned early in the book, detectives were not allowed to be helped by intuition or accident, no supernatural solutions were allowed, and no clues could be concealed from the reader. By World War II, the genre had begun to decline in popularity.

DOROTHY L. SAYERS Dorothy L. Sayers published her first novel, *Whose Body*, in 1923. In *Whose Body*, Sayers introduces the detective that she would use for eleven more novels and twenty-one stories: Lord Peter Wimsey. In 1929, Sayers founded the Detection Club, a group of British mystery writers including members such as G.K. Chesterton and Agatha Christie. In the 1930s, Sayers stopped writing mystery novels, focusing on writing radio plays and theological dramas.

AGATHA CHRISTIE Agatha Christie lived from 1876 to 1976, and is one of the most well-known and prolific mystery writers. Her protagonist, Hercule Poirot, the Belgian private detective, appeared in forty-two of her seventy-eight books, including one of her most famous novels, *The Murder of Roger Ackroyd*, which was published in 1926. Much like Dorothy L. Sayers's mysteries, Christie's novels took place in Britain's upper- and middle-class country houses, in villages, and even on trains. Agatha Christie was able to produce work that was intricately detailed, complex, slightly humorous, and carefully researched (she was even an expert on poisons).

LOUISE PENNY The detective novel did not die when the Golden Age of Detective Fiction ended. Today, there are still great mystery writers who uphold the traditional detective stories. Louise Penny's first book, *Still Life*, came out in 2005 to rave reviews, winning several awards, including the Dagger Award, the Arthur Ellis Award, and the Barry Award. Her work follows Chief Inspector Armand Gamache, head of Quebec's homicide department. Though set in Quebec, the Gamache novels feature many elements of the English mystery novels. Penny has published thirteen books so far and has won the Agatha Award for best mystery novel of the year six times.

FANTASY

THE EPIC OF GILGAMESH *The Epic of Gilgamesh*, which dates back to ancient Sumer, is not only the oldest fantasy story ever written, but it is the oldest story ever written. *Gilgamesh* was actually found inscribed on clay tablets. The story revolves around Gilgamesh, a king who embarks on a journey to slay a horrible beast, Humbaba, and searches for immortality. Gilgamesh was, in fact, based on a king of that time, the king of Uruk, who ruled during the twenty-first century B.C.

THE CHRONICLES OF NARNIA The Chronicles of Narnia series comprises seven books written by C.S. Lewis. Included in that series are some of the best-known fantasy books of all time, such as *The Lion, the Witch and the Wardrobe, Prince Caspian*, and *The Magician's Nephew*. The books, written from 1949 to 1954, are set in the fictional world of Narnia and cover the entire history of Narnia, from its beginnings to its end. The books often have children as the central characters, talking animals, magic, and good versus evil as a common theme.

HARRY POTTER One of the most successful and popular fantasy series of today is Harry Potter, written by J.K. Rowling. These seven books chronicle the story of a wizard, Harry, and his two friends as they go to Hogwarts School of Witchcraft and Wizardry, and Harry embarks on a quest to defeat the evil wizard, Lord Voldemort. One noticeable difference between the Harry Potter series and other fantasy novels is that the world Harry lives in is actually the present day. Unlike C.S. Lewis's Narnia, Harry's world takes place in present-day London.

THE LORD OF THE RINGS In 1937, Oxford professor J.R.R. Tolkien wrote a book called *The Hobbit*, which was set in a fictional Middle Earth where wizards, elves, trolls, and hobbits lived. In 1954, The Lord of the Rings, a trilogy and a sequel to *The Hobbit*, was published. The trilogy focuses on the events following those found in *The Hobbit* and a journey to destroy a powerful ring that could destroy the world if in the wrong hands. Frodo Baggins is the main character, and he is joined by his friend and two cousins as they embark on a journey to save the world.

A SONG OF ICE AND FIRE A Song of Ice and Fire is an ongoing series of books written by George R.R. Martin, first published in 1991. The books take place on a continent called Westeros, and a land mass east of Westeros called Essos. The main stories of each of these books relate to a civil war in Westeros, the threat of a race of creatures known as the Others, and the quest of an exiled daughter of a murdered king to reclaim the throne. The books are told through the third-person point of view of several characters. The first five of seven books of the series were turned into a television show for HBO, *Game of Thrones*.

INHERITANCE CYCLE The Inheritance Cycle is a series of ongoing books written by Christopher Paolini. The first book in the series, *Eragon*, was written by Paolini when he was just fifteen years old. After spending a year working on it, Paolini self-published the book, which was discovered and republished by a major publishing company. The Inheritance Cycle series is set in Alagaësia, with the main characters being Eragon, a teenage orphan, and his dragon, Saphira. The books follow Eragon as he becomes a member of the Dragon Riders and attempts to defeat the evil king who had killed past Dragon Riders fearing they would take the throne.

SCIENCE FICTION

JULES VERNE Jules Verne is one of the most well-known and celebrated science fiction authors of all time, and he is generally regarded as the "father of science fiction." His works include the classics *Twenty Thousand Leagues Under the Sea*, *A Journey to the Center of the Earth*, and *Around the World in Eighty Days*. Verne, a Frenchman, lived from 1828 to 1905, and the first English-language translations of his work appeared in the 1870s.

H.G. WELLS H.G. Wells was dramatically influential in the world of science fiction literature. Among his most famous works are *The Invisible Man*, *The Island of Dr. Moreau*, *The Time Machine*, and *The War of the Worlds*. Written in 1895, *The Time Machine* is considered one of the first modern science fiction novels. Wells's *The War of the Worlds* was so influential that in 1938, Orson Welles and the Mercury Theatre on the Air adapted it as a radio program. The program, about an alien invasion, produced panic in listeners who feared an actual alien invasion was occurring.

ROBERT HEINLEIN Robert Heinlein lived from 1907 to 1988 and is considered one of the most controversial authors of science fiction. Heinlein began his career writing for pulp magazines. He is credited with turning science fiction into a serious field within literature. His work contains political messages and deals with the hypocrisy of religion. He wrote many short stories and thirty-two novels, including well-known works such as *Stranger in a Strange Land*, *Starship Troopers*, and *The Moon Is a Harsh Mistress*. His 1948 novel *Space Cadet* featured nuclear weapons and even cell phones.

ARTHUR C. CLARKE Arthur C. Clarke lived from 1917 to 2008. During World War II, Clarke was involved in working with British radar. In 1945, Clarke published an article in which he proposed placing three satellites in orbit that would facilitate global communications. His surprisingly successful proposal led to his invention of the communication satellite. Clarke published many stories throughout his lifetime; his short story "The Sentinel" was actually the inspiration for the Stanley Kubrick film, *2001: A Space Odyssey*.

ISAAC ASIMOV Isaac Asimov lived from 1920 to 1992, and he is considered one of the greatest writers of science fiction. He wrote around 500 books, publishing in genres such as science, horror, comedy, and even poetry. The best-known works of Asimov are his short story "Nightfall," the Robot series of novels (of which *I, Robot* is one), and the Foundation novels. Asimov's work even inspired the creation of the *Star Trek* character, Data.

RAY BRADBURY Ray Bradbury, an American author who lived from 1920 to 2012, wrote more than 500 works, the most famous of which is also perhaps one of the most controversial science fiction books ever: *Fahrenheit 451*. The novel is set in a dystopian world where hedonism is celebrated and the reading of books is prohibited. Bradbury is also the author of other famous books, including *Dandelion Wine, The Martian Chronicles, The Illustrated Man*, and *Something Wicked This Way Comes*.

FAIRY TALES

AESOP'S FABLES Even though Aesop's Fables (of which there are currently 725) are some of the most popular fairy tales ever written (*e.g.,* "The Tortoise and the Hare"), very little is known about the actual man, Aesop. Aesop was Greek and born in Thrace in the sixth century B.C. It is believed that he spent most of his life living as a slave on the island of Samos and that, though he was a slave, he was allowed many freedoms and used his fables to argue in court. It is not known how many of the fables were actually told by Aesop and how many were just attributed to him later on.

CHARLES PERRAULT Charles Perrault was born in Paris on July 12, 1628, and lived until 1703. At the age of sixty-seven, Perrault lost his job as secretary to the king's finance minister. It was then that he decided to pursue writing. He is the author of some of the most well-known fairy tales that still exist today, including "Little Red Riding Hood," "Cinderella," "Puss in Boots," and "Sleeping Beauty." These stories and four others were published in his book *Stories or Tales from Times Past*; or *Tales of Mother Goose*. Though these stories and plots had existed before Perrault wrote them, he was the first to turn them into a work of literary art through a combination of wit and style.

HANS CHRISTIAN ANDERSEN Hans Christian Andersen was a Danish author who lived from 1805 to 1875 and is considered the father of modern fairy tales. Andersen wrote over 150 fairy tales, of which his most famous include "The Little Mermaid," "The Ugly Duckling," "The Emperor's New Clothes," and "Thumbelina." Not only did Andersen's work break through previous traditions of Danish literature by using idioms and spoken language, but it was also almost completely original; only twelve of his 156 fairy tales were based on folklore. His work came to influence authors such as Charles Dickens (with whom he was friends) and Oscar Wilde.

THE BROTHERS GRIMM Jakob Grimm and Wilhelm Grimm were born in 1785 and 1786, respectively. Intrigued by the Romantic movement occurring in Germany, the two brothers began collecting fairy tales in the early 1800s. In 1812, the first volume, consisting of eighty-six stories, was published, and two years later, another volume of seventy stories was published. The stories were told to the brothers by peasants and villagers, and the brothers edited these stories and added footnotes to many. The work of Jakob and Wilhelm Grimm brought stories like "Cinderella," "The Frog Prince," "Hansel and Gretel," and "Rapunzel" to the masses, and their work became incredibly popular.

GABRIELLE-SUZANNE BARBOT DE VILLENEUVE

Gabrielle-Suzanne Barbot de Villeneuve was a French author who lived from 1695 to 1755. She is most widely recognized as the author of "Beauty and the Beast," a story that was featured in a collection called *La jeune américaine et les contes marins* (told by an old woman during a long sea voyage), published in 1740. Her version of the "Beauty and the Beast" story was much longer (a total of 362 pages), and the Beast was much more ferocious than later versions. A French aristocrat, Madame Jeanne-Marie Leprince de Beaumont, rewrote the story, dramatically cutting it down to size and creating the "Beauty and the Beast" that we know today.

CARLO COLLODI

Carlo Lorenzini, who would come to be known as Carlo Collodi, was an Italian author who lived from 1826 to 1890. Originally working as a satirical journalist, Collodi left journalism and began working as a magazine editor and theatrical censor. It was during this time that he began translating the works of Charles Perrault, which inspired Collodi to start working on his own fairy tales. He wrote "The Story of a Puppet," which would later be retitled and published as the popular "The Adventures of Pinocchio." Two years after his death, the story was translated into English.

JOURNALISM

JOHANN CAROLUS Johann Carolus lived from 1575 to 1634, and is responsible for publishing the very first newspaper, called *Relation aller Fürnemmen und gedenckwürdigen Historien* (meaning "collection of all distinguished and commemorable news"). Carolus made his living writing newsletters by hand and selling them to subscribers at high prices. He realized that he would make more money if he printed a lot and sold them cheaper. In 1604, Carolus bought a printing shop and began printing his newsletters in Strasbourg when it was part of the Holy Roman Empire.

THE OXFORD GAZETTE One of the most important milestones in the history of journalism was the publication of *The Oxford Gazette* in 1665. *The Oxford Gazette* is considered to be England's first legitimate newspaper. It was available to every class, and, most significantly, its text was separated into columns. The *Gazette* was printed twice a week under the same name, unlike other newspapers during this time that were published with alternate titles. The *Gazette*, the official publication of King Charles II, was printed in two locations: London and Oxford. *The Oxford Gazette* later changed its name to *The London Gazette*, and it still exists today as *The Gazette*.

THE CIVIL WAR AND NEWSPAPERS By the American Revolution, newspapers were fairly common. By 1800, there were more than 200 newspapers in the United States. These newspapers, however, were not independent journals featuring objective pieces, but publications put out by political parties to get their messages across to the public. The Civil War, however, changed the way newspapers were written. Reporters were hired as war correspondents to report on what was happening. Due to the rail system and the telegraph, information could travel faster. But given the high cost of sending telegraph messages, the writing had to be concise, which influenced the way stories are written to this day.

~~~~~~~~~~~~~~~~~~~~~~~~~~~~~~~~~~~~~~~

HENRY STANLEY The daily newspapers produced in New York continued to redefine journalism. Henry Stanley became a special correspondent for the *New York Herald* in 1867. In 1866, the famous Scottish missionary and explorer of Africa, David Livingstone, went to Africa once again to study the Nile River. When Dr. Livingstone vanished and was not heard from for a long time, the *New York Herald* sent Henry Stanley to Africa to search for Dr. Livingstone in 1871. There, in November of 1871, Stanley found Dr. Livingstone, and said the famous line, "Dr. Livingstone, I presume?" This was the beginning of investigative reporting.

~~~~~~~~~~~~~~~~~~~~~~~~~~~~~~~~~~~~~~~

WILLIAM RANDOLPH HEARST William Randolph Hearst lived from 1863 to 1951. The son of a self-made millionaire, Hearst studied journalism at Harvard. While he was still at Harvard, Hearst told his father he wanted to run the *San Francisco Examiner*, and on March 7, 1887, William Randolph Hearst became its owner. In 1895, Hearst bought the unsuccessful *New York Morning Journal* and changed it to the *New York Journal*, competing for readership against his fellow Harvard classmate and mentor, Joseph Pulitzer and his newspaper, the *New York World*. These two rival newspaper publishers are credited with printing the first yellow journalist articles—sensationalized news and lurid stories—to attract readers and to goad the US into going to war with Spain in the late nineteenth century.

~~~~~~~~~~~~~~~~~~~~~~~~~~~~~~~~~~~~~~~

MUCKRAKING After World War I, muckrakers were investigative journalists who exposed abuses and corruption in businesses and within the government. Theodore Roosevelt praised the ideas behind this activity, but believed the journalists' methods were irresponsible. One of the most famous muckrakers was Upton Sinclair, whose 1906 novel, *The Jungle,* portrayed the horrible working conditions and unsanitary practices in the food and drug industry. After President Roosevelt read the book, he ordered an investigation into the meat-packing industry in 1906; the Meat Inspection Act and the Pure Food and Drug Act were passed that same year.

BIOGRAPHIES

THE IMMORTAL LIFE OF HENRIETTA LACKS Henrietta Lacks, an African-American woman who was a poor tobacco farmer, died from cervical cancer in 1951 at the age of thirty-one. Lacks's cells were removed from her body during a biopsy and cultured without her permission. Though Lacks has been dead for almost seventy years, her cancer cells, known as an "immortalized" cell line, or the first population of cells to reproduce on their own, are still alive today. They are called the "HeLa cell line" and are considered one of the most important tools that exist in the medical world. *The Immortal Life of Henrietta Lacks,* by Rebecca Skloot, tells the story of Henrietta's suffering, the celebrity of her cells, the birth of a multimillion-dollar industry, and the Lacks family, who, up until forty-three years ago, never knew about Henrietta's cells.

INTO THE WILD Jon Krakauer's *Into the Wild* tells the story of Chris McCandless, an honors graduate from Emory University, who traveled across the United States renouncing society and living as a vagabond. McCandless ultimately hitchhiked to Alaska to live in the wilderness. After surviving for two years on his own, McCandless starved to death. Krakauer chronicles, as best he can, McCandless's journey through interviews with people he met along his journey, his friends and family, and authorities. Though exact details are unknown, Jon Krakauer goes to great lengths to describe the events that may have led to Chris McCandless's unfortunate death.

BONHOEFFER: PASTOR, MARTYR, PROPHET, SPY

Eric Metaxas's *Bonhoeffer: Pastor, Martyr, Prophet, Spy* tells the story of Dietrich Bonhoeffer, a Lutheran pastor who lived in Germany during the reign of Adolf Hitler. While other churches embraced Hitler's hatred toward the Jewish people, Bonhoeffer believed the role of the churches was to help the victimized Jewish people. Bonhoeffer created an illegal seminary with the purpose of training pastors, and was involved in a plot to assassinate Hitler. The assassination attempt would ultimately lead to his death only three weeks before Hitler committed suicide. Metaxas's book focuses on the personal life of Bonhoeffer and his theological ideologies and spirituality.

THE DIVING BELL AND THE BUTTERFLY

In 1995, Jean-Dominique Bauby, an editor, author, and journalist for the French *Elle* magazine, suffered a devastating stroke that left him in a coma for three weeks. When he awoke from his coma, he suffered from locked-in syndrome, where his mind still functioned but his body was left completely motionless. The only thing he could move was his left eyelid. In 1996, as a person recited the alphabet to him, he would blink at the letter he wanted. The result was his memoir, *The Diving Bell and the Butterfly*.

A BEAUTIFUL MIND: THE LIFE OF MATHEMATICAL GENIUS AND NOBEL LAUREATE JOHN NASH

John Nash (1928–2015) was a mathematical genius. He founded game theory, worked for RAND during the Cold War, won the Nobel Prize in Economics in 1994, and even challenged Albert Einstein about a theory of quantum mechanics when he was just twenty years old. He also suffered greatly from paranoid schizophrenia. Sylvia Nasar's book, *A Beautiful Mind: The Life of Mathematical Genius and Nobel Laureate John Nash*, explores Nash's life as he suffered with his illness, becoming entangled in his own thoughts and creating amazing mathematical accomplishments.

THE AUTOBIOGRAPHY OF MALCOLM X Malcolm X (1925–1965) was one of the most important and controversial leaders during the civil rights movement. In his autobiography, he describes his childhood growing up in Boston as the son of a Baptist minister, how his life turned to the streets and prison, and, finally, how he embraced Islam. He discusses his education, which he says he got from the schools, the streets, the prisons, and his mentor. The book was written by Alex Haley transcribing interviews he did with Malcolm X; though Malcolm read drafts, he never lived to see it in print. Haley would later go on to write the 1977 television miniseries, *Roots*.

NONFICTION

A PEOPLE'S HISTORY OF THE UNITED STATES *A People's History of the United States* by Howard Zinn tells history like never before, offering the historical context of events from different perspectives. For example, his first chapter deals with Columbus and the New World. He begins the chapter by telling the perspective of the Arawak Indians who met with Columbus. Zinn then provides details about the murders committed by Columbus's men, and how this is a detail that is not widely talked about in traditional history. Within every chapter of the book, Zinn goes over a major event, retells the event from new perspectives, includes events and information that mainstream history has left out, and interprets how the elite attempted to maintain control of that information.

HELTER SKELTER: THE TRUE STORY OF THE MANSON MURDERS

In August of 1969, over the course of two days, a series of horrible murders occurred in Los Angeles that shook the world. The murderers were a group of young men and women who followed the leadership of Charles Manson. Written by Vincent Bugliosi, the prosecutor in Charles Manson's case, and Curt Gentry, *Helter Skelter: The True Story of the Manson Murders* describes how Manson was able to coerce people into following him, details the murders and other horrible escapades of Manson's, and brings to light Manson's idea of Helter Skelter, an apocalyptic war between the blacks and the whites.

IN COLD BLOOD

Up until 1966, Truman Capote had enjoyed celebrity due to his writing and his colorful personality. His best-known work had been the romantic novel *Breakfast at Tiffany's* (1958). After ten years abroad in Europe, Capote decided to turn to nonfiction. In 1966, he published *In Cold Blood*, which is considered by many to be the first nonfiction novel. The subject of his book was the 1959 murders of Herbert Clutter and his wife and children in Holcomb, Kansas. Capote researched the book for five years, interviewing the two murderers and becoming very close to them. *In Cold Blood* tells the stories of both the murderers and the victims.

FAST FOOD NATION: THE DARK SIDE OF THE ALL-AMERICAN MEAL

Fast food is part of our everyday life. If we are not eating it, then we are seeing it on television, or our children are playing with toys from fast-food restaurants. Eric Schlosser's *Fast Food Nation* examines the ever-growing industry of fast food in the United States. Schlosser goes into great detail, from the creation of fast food to its marketing, and provides plenty of interesting information on a wide variety of topics. Besides simply taking a look at what the food is made of, Schlosser looks at the industry. He discusses, for example, how fast-food companies have moved their operations to anti-union states, like Kansas, Iowa, Texas, and Nebraska, to take advantage of low wages that would not be allowed in areas like New York or Chicago.

THE EDUCATION OF HENRY ADAMS Henry Adams, the great-grandson of John Adams and grandson of John Quincy Adams, wrote *The Education of Henry Adams* himself; however, it is written in the third person. The book describes Adams's early life growing up in Boston, his education at Harvard, his introduction to the world of the South, and the horrors of slavery. As Adams recounts the events of his life, he describes a realization that his formal education did not prepare him for the world at large.

MIDNIGHT IN THE GARDEN OF GOOD AND EVIL John Berendt's *Midnight in the Garden of Good and Evil* is the true story of a murder trial in Savannah, Georgia, in 1981. Similar to Capote's *In Cold Blood, Midnight in the Garden of Good and Evil* is more like a novel than just an account of events. The crime, however, only sets the scene for the book's true focus, which is the city of Savannah, with its rich history and its quirky and colorful residents.

EXISTENTIALISM

WHAT IS EXISTENTIALISM? Existentialism is the philosophical study of the meaning of existence. There are several key ideas that existentialism touches on: free will, the idea that human nature is influenced by the choices one makes in life; the idea that decisions create stress and have consequences; and that a person is at their best when struggling for life. Existentialism is very much about understanding the meaning of life on a personal level without touching on factors like wealth, social values, or other external forces.

THE ORIGINS OF EXISTENTIALISM

Gabriel Marcel was the first to coin the term *existentialism* in the mid-1940s. However, he was certainly not the first to write on the topic. Existentialist ideas can be found in the work of Henry David Thoreau and Voltaire, and even the teachings of Buddha and in William Shakespeare's *Hamlet*. Although he was not well regarded in his time, Søren Kierkegaard is considered the first existentialist; it is a major theme found in his work related to human existence and free will. In the 1920s, Martin Heidegger, influenced by Kierkegaard's thought, worked on what he referred to as *Dasein*, or being.

EXISTENTIALIST LITERATURE

The ideas of existentialism were featured not only in philosophical theory, but also in literature. In fact, some of the most acclaimed existentialist work is actually found in novels and plays. Existentialist literature focuses on attempting to find meaning and make sense of a world that is filled with chaos. As a result, existentialist literature often features themes such as absurdism, alienation, and isolation.

FYODOR DOSTOYEVSKY

One of the most important existentialist novelists was the Russian essayist and novelist Fyodor Dostoyevsky, who lived from 1821 to 1881. Dostoyevsky is perhaps best known for his novels *Crime and Punishment*, *The Brothers Karamazov*, and *The Idiot*. Dostoyevsky's most important work relating to existentialism, however, is his *Notes from the Underground*. His work focused on the problem of freedom. To Dostoyevsky, humans were limited by everything, including society, the economy, the church, and God. Though Dostoyevsky had extreme political and social views, he was a devout Christian.

SØREN KIERKEGAARD Søren Kierkegaard was a Danish philosopher who lived from 1813 to 1855 and was one of the founders of existentialism, though much of his work was based on his faith in God. His book *Fear and Trembling* is key to the origins of existentialism. Kierkegaard attempted to comprehend Abraham's anxiety when God told him he had to kill Isaac, his only son, to show his faith. To understand this, Kierkegaard creates the "Knight of Faith" and the "Tragic Hero." To Kierkegaard, the Tragic Hero commits acts within social or ethical codes, which Abraham, Kierkegaard claimed, did not do. Instead, Abraham was a Knight of Faith who knew killing his son was wrong, but would be going against God if he didn't do it. Ethics now turns into temptation, and the Knight of Faith shows that faith is a reason to rise above ethics.

JEAN-PAUL SARTRE Jean-Paul Sartre was a French existentialist who lived from 1905 to 1980. Among other things, Sartre wrote novels, screenplays, and plays. One of his most famous works was *Being and Nothingness*, a book that focuses on the consciousness of being. Sartre suggests that appearance is the only reality, and that there are two kinds of being: in-itself and for-itself. In-itself refers to inanimate objects that just exist without any active or passive consciousness; for-itself refers to something that is cognizant of its awareness. When a person gazes at another person, that person goes from a being-for-itself to a being-in-itself.

VICTORIAN LITERATURE

STYLE OF VICTORIAN LITERATURE The Victorian era is the transitional period between the Romantic period and the twentieth century, during the reign of Queen Victoria in Britain (1837–1901). Literature produced in this time examined the issues of daily life. The rise of industrialism, reform movements battling child labor, women's rights, emancipation, and the concept of evolution heavily influenced the work; as a result, the Victorian age is considered one of pessimism and doubt. Works had moral purposes, and featured ideals like love, justice, and truth.

THE ENGLISH NOVEL During the nineteenth century, the novel became the most popular form of literature. Novels focused on portraying the difficulty of real life, where ultimately it is love, perseverance, and hard work that win out. An especially important part of the novel during this time was the depiction of the emerging and expanding middle class, a break from the portrayal of aristocratic characters found in earlier novels. Most of the novels were published serially in journals; the latest chapter or section appeared with each new issue and featured intricate plots and plot twists to keep readers interested.

CHILDREN'S LITERATURE Children's literature changed during the Victorian era. By 1848, the work of Hans Christian Andersen was translated into English, sparking a great interest in fairy tales. It was during the Victorian era, for example, that Lewis Carroll's *Alice in Wonderland* books came out and became popular. The rise in children's literature is a direct result of shifting views on children and child labor, and the education of children came to the forefront of social issues during the Victorian era. As more children began reading, an industry based on producing literature for them began to grow.

POETRY The most highly regarded poet during the Victorian era was Alfred, Lord Tennyson. His poetry reflected the feelings of the era, expressing melancholy and doubts about religion, yet conveying confidence in class. In the middle of the nineteenth century, the Pre-Raphaelite movement focused on reviving the work of medieval and classical times. The greatest example of this movement was Tennyson's *Idylls of the King*, which combined the story of King Arthur with ideas and issues of the modern day.

SCIENTIFIC AND PHILOSOPHICAL WRITING

During the Victorian era, Charles Darwin's 1859 book *On the Origin of Species* shook the world with its ideas about evolution and writings about nature. Evolution became widely popular. It was also during this time that some great philosophers began to write. The Victorian era saw the work of John Stuart Mill, John Henry Newman, and Henry Edward Manning. Karl Marx and Friedrich Engels, the two founders of Communism, wrote their books during this time in Victorian England.

LATE VICTORIAN PERIOD

The Victorian era can be divided into two parts: the early Victorian period (which ended around 1870), and the late Victorian period (which lasted from 1890 to 1918). In the late Victorian period, the principles that followed throughout the Victorian era were rejected. There was a return to fantasy, with such works as Robert Lewis Stevenson's *The Strange Case of Dr. Jekyll and Mr. Hyde*, and the emergence of the "problem novel." Problem novels focused on the institution of marriage, the role of the sexes, and sexual identity.

WILLIAM SHAKESPEARE

SHAKESPEARE'S EARLY LIFE

William Shakespeare lived from 1564 to 1616 in England. Very little is known of his childhood, including the exact date of his birth. Shakespeare did not attend university, which was reserved for the wealthy, and by the time he was eighteen in 1582, he was married. By 1589, Shakespeare was living in London pursuing acting and playwriting, and had begun writing his first play, *Henry VI, Part I*. By 1590, Shakespeare had become a popular playwright, and in 1593, his poem *Venus and Adonis* was published and achieved great success. From 1594 until his death, Shakespeare was associated with a theater company called the King's Men.

HIS WORK

William Shakespeare wrote some of the world's most famous comedies, tragedies, and histories, as well as sonnets and poems. The number of plays he wrote is still up for debate. The general consensus is that he wrote a total of thirty-seven plays; however, some scholars believe that, including possible lost works and collaborations, the number is closer to forty. He also wrote countless poems, including 154 sonnets and two long-form narrative poems. Shakespeare wrote sonnets all of his life, and a collection of them was published in 1609 by publisher Thomas Thorpe. As the sonnets were printed without Shakespeare's consent, it is believed that they were actually private pieces not intended for publication.

SHAKESPEARE'S WRITING STYLE

Shakespeare's plays featured blank verse, a metrical pattern that consisted of lines of iambic pentameter that did not rhyme. When passages deviated within the plays, Shakespeare would use a different poetic form or simple prose. With one exception, his sonnets were written in iambic pentameter. Shakespeare also invented words and phrases (of which there are at least 1,500). Among the many words he invented or made popular are *assassination, bump, submerge, frugal, gnarled, dishearten, obscene, generous,* and *monumental.*

THE GLOBE THEATRE

Shakespeare's most well-known plays were performed at the Globe Theatre in London. The theater was built by the brother of Richard Burbage, one of the actors who worked with Shakespeare, who wrote for the troupe the King's Men. From 1592 to 1593, an outbreak of the plague caused the theater to shut down, and it is during this time that William Shakespeare turned to poetry. The Globe Theatre reopened in 1594, and Shakespeare and the troupe became extremely popular. The Theatre could seat two to three thousand people, and performances were held in the afternoon to take advantage of the daylight. During a performance of *Henry VIII* on June 29, 1613, a cannon was fired, which set fire to the roof, burning the Globe Theatre to the ground.

SHAKESPEARE'S SEXUALITY Though William Shakespeare married at the age of eighteen, the issue of his sexuality is much debated. It is believed that Shakespeare had several affairs with women and showed an interest in men, but the only evidence, gleaned from analysis of his sonnets, is circumstantial. His book of sonnets, which was supposed to be private, was a collection of love poems about a young man he referred to as "Fair Lord," in which he expressed his love for him. This book was dedicated to "Mr. W.H."

AUTHORSHIP CONTROVERSY Since the 1700s, there have been anti-Stratfordians, people who question whether William Shakespeare actually wrote all of his plays or whether they had been written by contemporaries of his. There are three main candidates who could have been the true authors of the plays Shakespeare takes credit for: Edward de Vere, Francis Bacon, and Christopher Marlowe. Many believe that the life of Edward de Vere, the seventeenth Earl of Oxford and a courtier of Queen Elizabeth I, paralleled content found in Shakespeare's plays. Perhaps the strongest candidate is Francis Bacon, whose personal and private book *Promus of Formularies and Elegancies* contains 4,400 terms and phrases that parallel words in Shakespeare's plays. Christopher Marlowe was a playwright who was stabbed to death in a bar fight in 1593. Some believe that he was actually a spy and that he faked his own death, and continued to write plays under the pen name William Shakespeare.

EDGAR ALLAN POE

POE'S EARLY LIFE Edgar Poe was born on January 19, 1809, in Boston, Massachusetts. Poe's mother had left his father, taking the children with her. When Poe was only two years old, his mother died. Edgar was taken in by Frances and John Allan. Poe spent five years studying in England, and in 1826, he attended the University of Virginia. Less than a year later, Poe quit school due to drinking and being in heavy debt. The next year, he joined the army. By 1835, Poe was living in Baltimore and working as an editor of a newspaper. In 1836, Poe married his thirteen-year-old cousin and moved to New York City. In 1845, his wife died of tuberculosis two years after "The Raven" was published.

THE AMERICAN ROMANTIC MOVEMENT Poe's writing belongs to what is known as the American Romantic movement, one of the great literary genres to come out of America. Literature of American Romanticism focused on nature, the power of one's imagination, and individuality. Edgar Allan Poe's life was dark and extremely emotional, and his writings reflected this. His work featured mystical, magical, and mysterious elements in ways that set it apart from more realistic writing. Other writers of American Romanticism include Henry David Thoreau, Walt Whitman, Emily Dickinson, Washington Irving, and Herman Melville.

"THE RAVEN" "The Raven," arguably Edgar Allan Poe's most famous poem, was first published on January 29, 1845, in the *New York Evening Mirror* to rave reviews. The poem tells the story of a man who desires a love who has died. He is visited by a talking bird that says only one word: "Nevermore." So caught up in his imagination, the man believes the bird is telling him that he will never be reunited with his love. Poe has said "The Raven" discussed man's proclivity to torture himself.

HIS DEATH

It is unknown what caused Edgar Allan Poe's death. What is known is that Poe died on October 7, 1849, in Baltimore. Days earlier, he had been discovered outside of a bar, lying on a wooden plank, and brought to the hospital. Records of his hospitalization indicated that he was delirious, hallucinating, and was having tremors up until he slipped into a coma. When he came out of the coma, he was at first calm, but then became increasingly delirious and combative. Four days later, he would be dead. The cause of death on his death certificate reads "congestion of the brain." Many believed this to be alcohol related; however, Poe had not had any alcohol six months prior to his death. Researchers today believe the cause of death was from rabies.

GRISWOLD'S OBITUARY

Rufus Wilmot Griswold was an anthologist, journalist, editor, and critic who worked with Poe and had a long-standing feud with the writer. When Poe died, Griswold wrote an obituary printed in the *New York Daily Tribune* signed with the pseudonym "Ludwig." The obituary claimed Poe was a reckless drunk, friendless, and a madman, and that he would be missed by few. After Poe's death, Griswold claimed to be his literary executor and wrote a memoir about his relationship with Poe. The book is famous for its terribly inaccurate depiction of Poe as a drug addict and madman, and much of it was fabricated.

THE POE TOASTER

Beginning in 1949, 100 years after the death of Edgar Allan Poe, a mysterious man dressed in black with a white scarf started bringing three roses, a bottle of French cognac, and sometimes a note to the tombstone of Edgar Allan Poe on Poe's birthday. He did this every year until 1998, when it is believed he died and his son took over. Though there were attempts to discover the identity of the Poe Toaster, they never succeeded, and 2010 was the first year the Poe Toaster did not show up. It is believed that he, too, has passed away. In 2016, the Maryland Historical Society revived the tradition by holding a competition for a new Poe Toaster, who now performs the annual tribute in public.

CHARLES DICKENS

ABOUT CHARLES DICKENS Charles Dickens, who lived from 1812 to 1870, is one of the Victorian era's best-known writers. Dickens's work, much of which drew upon his own life experience, depicted hypocrisy, injustice, and social evils, and featured comical characters and social commentary. Like other Victorian works, his writing was often serialized, and in total, Dickens wrote fifteen novels. Some of his most famous novels include *Oliver Twist, Nicholas Nickleby, A Christmas Carol, A Tale of Two Cities, Great Expectations*, and *The Pickwick Papers*. Dickens began his career as a journalist at the age of sixteen and continued working in journalism for the rest of his life.

OLIVER TWIST *Oliver Twist* was published serially in 1837. The story was his second novel (the first being *The Pickwick Papers*, which was a great success), but it was the first of his stories that focused on social commentary and critiquing how public institutions dealt with the poor. Dickens revisited this theme again in *Nicholas Nickleby*. One reason Dickens wrote *Oliver Twist* was because of the Poor Law Amendment Act of 1834, which stripped citizenship rights from the poor, who had to give up their political rights for financial aid and work in factories.

A CHRISTMAS CAROL Though Dickens's *A Christmas Carol* is a celebration of Christmas, at its heart, the novel is a social commentary on the division of the rich and poor in Victorian England. It is Dickens's criticism of the rich and celebration of the selflessness of the poor. It was published in late 1843, at a time when the British government enacted new, harsher Poor Laws, which stipulated that the poor live in workhouses or in debtor's prisons, and labor in factories under horrible conditions. When Dickens was twelve years old, his own family was moved to a debtor's prison, and Dickens was forced to work in a shoe polish factory.

DAVID COPPERFIELD Charles Dickens's eighth novel was *David Copperfield*, published in 1849. The book is considered the closest Charles Dickens ever got to writing an autobiography. In July of 1948, Dickens's sister, who was a model for Scrooge's sister Fan in *A Christmas Carol*, became terminally ill and died in September. Dickens intended to write an autobiography, but the process proved too painful for him, so instead, he fabricated a character and told his story through David Copperfield. In the book, many of the events that David Copperfield (whose initials are the inverse of Dickens's) goes through are dramatizations of Dickens's life.

A TALE OF TWO CITIES Published in 1859, *A Tale of Two Cities*, Dickens's twelfth novel, was a departure in many ways for the author. The story is historical, with the backdrop being the events of the French Revolution, and is less character-driven and more focused on political events. Dickens shows both the cruelty of the French aristocracy and the suffering of the poor, justifying the need to revolt, but he also depicts the heinous deeds of those revolutionaries as they rise to power.

THE MYSTERY OF EDWIN DROOD Dickens was writing a murder mystery, *The Mystery of Edwin Drood*, when he died, leaving the book unfinished and the mystery unsolved. Since his death, there have been numerous attempts to finish the book. Perhaps one of the most famous was *Drood*, a Broadway musical based on Dickens's story that makes up for the lack of ending by asking the audience to vote on the answers to the various mysteries. The musical debuted in 1985 and won five Tony Awards, including Best Musical.

VIRGINIA WOOLF

ABOUT VIRGINIA WOOLF Born Adeline Virginia Stephen in 1882, Virginia Woolf was educated at home by her father, Leslie Stephen, who was the first editor of the *Dictionary of English Biography*. Woolf suffered from depression and severe mental illness all of her life. Her first series of nervous breakdowns started after her mother's death, when she was just thirteen. When her father died in 1904, she had to be hospitalized. Her novels, short stories, and essays are considered to be some of the best feminist and modernist work of the twentieth century.

THE BLOOMSBURY GROUP Following Virginia's second nervous breakdown, her sister Vanessa and brother Adrian bought a house in Bloomsbury. Woolf became friends with several intellectuals of the time, such as Roger Fry and Duncan Grant, and they formed what was known as the Bloomsbury Group, an artistic and literary circle of intellectuals. The Bloomsbury Group gained notoriety from the Dreadnought Hoax of 1910, in which they tricked the Royal Navy, making them believe they were Abyssinian royals. Virginia participated, dressed as a man. The Bloomsbury Group was very liberal regarding sex, and Virginia started a relationship with a fellow female writer.

THE VOYAGE OUT Virginia Woolf's first published novel, *The Voyage Out*, appeared in 1915. The book was written at a time when Virginia was seriously struggling with her depression; she had even attempted suicide at least once during the process. Her feelings of domestic repression and the influence of the Bloomsbury Group can be found in the book. *The Voyage Out* also contains the beginnings of a focus on sexuality, female consciousness, and death, themes that would later become prevalent in her work.

MRS. DALLOWAY One of Virginia Woolf's most well-regarded novels, *Mrs. Dalloway,* was published in 1925. The book examines a single day in the life (and inner life) of a woman, Clarissa Dalloway, in post–World War I England. The narrative structure jumps in and out of the character's mind, and travels forward and back in time. The book features themes of mental illness, depression, homosexuality, feminism, and existentialism.

TO THE LIGHTHOUSE *To the Lighthouse* is considered one of Virginia Woolf's greatest works and a modernist masterpiece. The structure of the narrative is less concerned with plot and more focused on character introspection and consciousness. There is no narrator in the story; instead, the story is told through shifting from one consciousness to another. The existence of God is discussed and questioned.

VIRGINIA WOOLF'S DEATH After Virginia Woolf completed another manuscript, she once again became greatly depressed. Her emotional condition deteriorated as World War II worsened and her London home was destroyed by a bomb. On March 27, 1941, Virginia's husband took her to see a doctor, where she told the doctor that everything was normal, even though she had been hearing voices. The next day, Virginia wrote two notes to her husband and one note to her sister, placed stones in the pockets of her coat, and walked into the River Ouse, drowning herself.

JANE AUSTEN

ABOUT JANE AUSTEN'S LIFE The biography of Jane Austen is not fully known. Jane Austen was born on December 16, 1775, in Hampshire, England, and by 1787, Jane began writing plays, poetry, and stories. By the time she was twenty-three, she had already completed the original versions of *Pride and Prejudice, Sense and Sensibility*, and *Northanger Abbey*. Her sense of humor was evident from the beginning, and she keenly watched the interactions of the social classes. Jane Austen's work was known for its realism, humor, and social commentary.

THE SENTIMENTAL NOVEL The sentimental novel was a popular literary genre of the eighteenth century that celebrated emotions and sensibility. These novels focused on the emotional response of both the reader and the characters. Plots were created to further the emotions of the story rather than the events. Jane Austen's *Sense and Sensibility* was a satire of this type of literature.

SENSE AND SENSIBILITY *Sense and Sensibility* was Jane Austen's first published novel. The book came out in 1811, and Austen credited herself with the pseudonym "A Lady." Jane Austen would continue to publish anonymously until the day she died, with only her family knowing it was she who was writing the books. The book follows two sisters who relocate to a new home after their father's death, and experience romance and heartbreak. The book sold out all 750 copies in its first edition.

PRIDE AND PREJUDICE *Pride and Prejudice* was published in 1813. The book, like much of Austen's work, uses free indirect speech (meaning in the third person with the essence of first person) to tell the story. The book focuses on the importance of one's environment and how it affects upbringing, and the fact that wealth and a high social status do not necessarily mean one has an advantage.

EMMA *Emma* was published in December of 1815. Once again, the book depicts misconstrued romance among genteel women. When starting the novel, Austen said, "I am going to take a heroine whom no one but myself will much like." The character Emma Woodhouse is a spoiled young woman who overestimates her matchmaking abilities; she is the first heroine of any of Austen's books who does not have to worry about her finances. *Emma* is a major shift away from themes common in Austen's work (such as finding a husband and attaining financial security).

REACTIONS THEN AND NOW When Austen's books first came out, they were well received. Reviews praised the realism and narrative qualities of her novels. In the nineteenth century, as Victorian and Romantic literature appeared, Austen's work became less popular, and those who still liked her considered themselves the elite. When her favorite nephew, James Edward Austen-Leigh, published *A Memoir of Jane Austen* in 1869, Austen's work was reintroduced and once again grew in popularity. By the twentieth century, Austen's work became a major focus of academic studies, as well as a source for media adaptations (e.g., the 1995 movie *Clueless* is a modernization of *Emma*).

FRANZ KAFKA

ABOUT FRANZ KAFKA Franz Kafka is considered one of the most important existentialist writers. Kafka, a Jewish man from

Prague, lived from 1883 to 1924. Kafka grew up studying at German schools, which was considered the language of the elite at the time, and worked for a large insurance company. Kafka's work often explores themes of alienation and the absurdity of life. The only works published during Kafka's lifetime were his articles and short stories. His three novels, which are considered masterpieces, were unfinished when he died, and Kafka had wished them to be destroyed. However, Kafka's friend Max Brod did not comply with his wishes and had them published.

KAFKA AND EXISTENTIALISM Kafka's writing explores the concepts of absurdity, dread, cruelty, pity, and injustice. He wrote about characters in a surreal world who only wanted to be recognized and accepted by those around them. His work depicts rationality in an irrational world, showing that there is nothing a person can do to give meaning to his or her relationship with the world.

"THE METAMORPHOSIS" One of Kafka's most well-known stories is "The Metamorphosis." The plot revolves around Gregor Samsa, who one day wakes up to discover that he has turned into a large insect (it is never mentioned what kind). We follow Gregor as he and his family deal with this absurd situation. Ultimately, the family cannot stand to look at Gregor and feels great relief when he dies. The story deals with the absurdity of life, the disconnect between one's body and one's mind, alienation, and the limitations of sympathy.

THE TRIAL *The Trial* tells the rather pessimistic story of Joseph K., a young man who, on his thirtieth birthday, is visited by two guards and arrested, even though he has not done anything. K. is told to stay at home and wait for instructions. The novel then follows K.'s process of dealing with the law and the untouchable court. On Joseph K.'s thirty-first birthday, he is once again visited by two guards, who bring him to a quarry and tell him to kill himself. Though K. does not fight them, he cannot do it, and they kill him.

THE CASTLE *The Castle* tells the story of K., a land surveyor, who arrives at a village to do work. The village's government office is found in a castle above the village. The task of doing the work he was hired to do becomes increasingly more difficult for K. as he interacts with the village and its bureaucracy. *The Castle* is Kafka's only novel that expresses close relationships between characters. Instead of portraying an unattainable quest, such as those found in Kafka's other works, *The Castle* is really about the lives of the villagers.

AMERIKA Kafka's last novel, *Amerika,* was published three years after his death by his friend and editor, Max Brod. It follows the journey of Karl Rossmann, an innocent seventeen-year-old European emigrant who is forced to go to New York after having sex with a family servant. Unbeknownst to Karl, his uncle, Senator Jacob, is also on board the ship that Karl takes to America. Senator Jacob recognizes Karl and has him stay with him, but later abandons Karl. The book then follows Karl as he interacts with people and gets various jobs, until ultimately, Karl decides to join a traveling theater in Oklahoma. The book was never finished, but Kafka told Max Brod that it would end on that chapter and its theme of reconciliation.

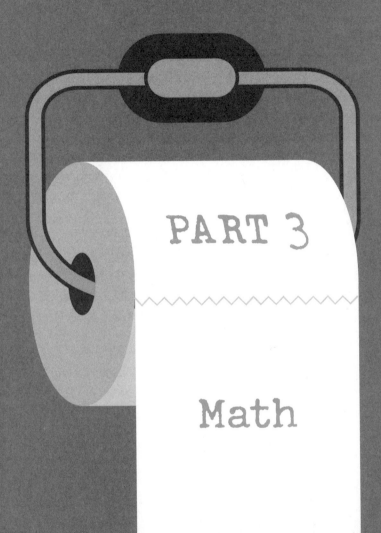

PART 3

Math

NUMBERS

BABYLONIAN NUMBERS The Babylonians, another civilization of Mesopotamia, created a number system 5,000 years ago. The Babylonians used the cuneiform writing system, and their number system, based on a set of tally marks, was extremely complex. The Babylonians divided the day into twenty-four hours, sixty minutes per hour, and sixty seconds per minute. Their system was sexagesimal rather than decimal, meaning all numbers are based on the number 60 and powers of 60. Decimal, or base ten, is the number system we use today.

THE GREEK NUMBERS The Greek numbers were based on the Greek alphabet, which came from the Phoenicians circa 900 B.C. The Greeks borrowed some of the symbols created by the Phoenicians and also created new symbols. By using the alphabet, they were able to have a more condensed version of their original number system, Attic, a technique that was based on putting symbols in rows. By using letters instead, these numerical values took up less space on clay tablets and were able to fit stamped on coins.

THE EGYPTIAN NUMBERS The number system of Ancient Egypt was made up of hieroglyphs. By using this system of writing, where values and words are depicted with images, the Egyptians were able to note numbers all the way to 1,000,000 and perform addition, subtraction, multiplication, and division. The ancient Egyptians also had a very good understanding of fractions: The use of fractions was so important that scribes would create tables for temple personnel referencing the division of supplies and food.

ROMAN NUMERALS Roman numerals were somewhat influenced by the Greek's alphabet-based number system. Many believe Roman numerals were based on the shape of the finger and the hand. One finger represents the number 1 as I, and the whole hand spread out is represented by V, meaning 5. Reading Roman numerals is fairly simple, as they are read from left to right, with the larger number at the beginning and other numbers added as you move to the right. To subtract, the smaller number is placed in front of the larger number.

ARABIC NUMERALS Arabic numerals were developed in India in A.D. 600, and it is the current system we have today. However, until A.D. 952, before this system was brought to Europe, these numerals were actually written backward. The shape of the numerals is actually derived from the number of angles in the shape of the number. The numeral 1 has one angle, the numeral 2 has two angles, and so on.

REAL NUMBERS Real numbers are whole numbers, such as 1, 2, 3, etc. Rational and irrational numbers as well as positive and negative numbers are also real numbers. Real numbers get the name "real" because they are not "imaginary." An imaginary number is any number that becomes negative when squared. Imaginary numbers were at one time believed to be impossible, but they are actually useful in calculating things such as electricity.

ZERO

A PLACEHOLDER The zero has many functions. One very important function zero has is as a placeholder. The difference between 500, 50, and 501 is the placement and amount of zero digits.

Even though the value zero is nothing, the digit zero means something. We understand that 501 is not the same thing as 51. The notion of the placeholder was first used by the Babylonians.

A NUMBER THAT MEANS NOTHING Zero precedes the number 1, meaning it represents an absence of value. It is an even number; however, it is neither prime nor composite and neither positive nor negative. The use of zero as a number, meaning a symbol representing a value of nothing, was first found in India around the eighth century A.D.

THE FIRST USE OF ZERO In A.D. 825, Persian scientist Al-Khwarizmi used the zero for the first time as a number in an arithmetic book that combined Greek and Hindu mathematics. Also included in the book was an explanation by Al-Khwarizmi on how to use zero as a placeholder.

THE ORIGINS OF THE SYMBOL Originally, the Babylonians put a space between numbers and didn't have a symbol representing zero. (For instance, 303 would have been 3 3.) By 300 B.C., the notion of the placeholder was represented by two slanted wedges. In A.D. 130, Greek astronomer Ptolemy represented the zero placeholder as a circle with a long overbar.

THE RULES OF BRAHMAGUPTA Rules governing how the zero should be used as a value and not a placeholder first appeared in a book written by the Indian mathematician Brahmagupta in A.D. 628. Though he states some things that conflict with modern science, he also laid down much of the groundwork for how zero is applied in mathematics. Such examples are:

- The sum of a positive number and zero is the positive number.
- The sum of a negative number and zero is the negative number.

- The sum of zero with zero equals zero.
- The sum of a positive number and a negative number equals their difference, and if their absolute values are equal, then the result is zero.

OTHER RULES OF ZERO When using zero in math there are several basic rules beyond those mentioned in the Rules of Brahmagupta section. When a number is multiplied by zero, the answer will always be zero. A number cannot be divided by zero; this makes the solution undefined. When discussing exponents, x^0 equals 1, unless the quality of x is zero. In that case, the answer is zero.

PRIME NUMBERS

WHAT ARE PRIME NUMBERS? A prime number is a whole number greater than 1 that can only be divided by 1 and itself. Examples of prime numbers are:

$$2, 3, 5, 7, 11, 13, 17, 19, 23 \ldots$$

There is an infinitude, or infinite set, of prime numbers, and this concept was first demonstrated by Euclid in 300 B.C. A whole number that can be divided by numbers other than itself and 1 is known as a composite number. Furthermore, any whole number that has a value greater than 1 is either composite or prime.

THE FUNDAMENTAL THEOREM OF ARITHMETIC The Fundamental Theorem of Arithmetic states that all integers that are positive and larger than 1 can be written as the product of one or many primes so that it is unique—except, perhaps, for the order of prime factors. This theory says that primes are the building blocks of numbers that are natural or composite. Prime factorization is the process of finding out which prime numbers make up a natural number. For example, if you wanted to find the prime factors of 18, you would do:

$$18 \div 2 = 9$$
$$9 \div 3 = 3$$
$$18 = 3^2 \times 2$$

EUCLID'S THEOREM As previously stated, prime numbers are infinite. This is actually known as Euclid's theorem. There are many proofs that show Euclid's theorem to be true. Euclid showed this with his own proof. His proof states that if you have a list of prime numbers, there will always be another one after the last number you've written. If P is the product of the prime numbers and $q = P + 1$, the answers produced will be either prime or not prime. Though this doesn't only give prime answers, it proves the number of primes goes on infinitely.

THE LARGEST KNOWN PRIME Since Euclid has proven that prime numbers go on infinitely, mathematicians have been trying to discover the existence of larger prime numbers. The Electronic Frontier Foundation even awards prizes for those who find the next largest prime numbers. Many of the largest prime numbers are called Mersenne numbers, named after the seventeenth-century monk who created the formula $M_P = 2^P - 1$. Of the ten highest prime numbers found, the top nine are Mersenne primes, and the tenth is the highest non-Mersenne prime. Currently, the largest prime is $2^{82,589,933} - 1$.

TRIAL DIVISION Trial division is an extremely complex process based on a very simple idea. The basic concept of trial division is to see if a number that is going to be factored (n) can be divided by a number greater than 1 but less than that number (n). This means that one has to test whether n is divisible by a number that is not itself. You begin by 2 and work your way up. If a number is not divisible by 2, it will not be divisible by 4 (because 4 is divisible by 2). This rule applies for any multiples. So from that, we can determine that the only numbers worth testing are prime numbers.

PRIME GAPS

When there are no prime numbers that show up in a sequence of numbers, it is called a prime gap. Another way to think of prime gaps is that it is the difference between two successive numbers that are prime. For example:

Primes:	2	3	5	7	11	13	17 ...
Gaps:	1	2	2	4	2	4 ...	

Mathematically, this is written as: $g_n = P_{n+1} - P_n$

In this formula, g_n is the nth prime gap, and P_n represents the nth prime number.

OPERATIONS

ADDITION

Addition is literally the process of adding, or combining, one thing to another thing. So in the problem $3 + 6$, you are adding or combining the two numbers together, leaving you with an end result of 9. The plus sign ($+$) is actually derived from an abbreviation of the Latin word *et*, which means "and." The plus sign first appeared in print in 1489 in Johannes Widmann's *Mercantile Arithmetic,* or *Behende und hubsche Rechenung auff allen Kauffmanschafft.*

SUBTRACTION Subtraction, the inverse of addition, is the process of taking one number away from the original value. For example, if we subtract 3 from 10 (expressed as 10 − 3), then we are left with 7. The first time the minus sign appeared in text was also in Johannes Widmann's *Mercantile Arithmetic,* or *Behende und hubsche Rechenung auff allen Kauffmanschafft.* It is believed that the minus sign may have come from the tilde (~), which was used with the letter *m* to represent the Latin word *meno,* meaning "minus."

MULTIPLICATION Multiplication is the process of repeated addition. For example, 5 × 4 is simply saying 5 added to itself 4 times, or 5 + 5 + 5 + 5. There are many ways to represent multiplication. The first and most common is by using the multiplication sign ×. Multiplication can also be expressed as a dot, such as 5 • 4, or by placing numbers side by side with parentheses between them, such as 5(4).

DIVISION Division is the opposite of multiplication. It is the process of splitting something into equal parts. Division can be represented in several ways. The most common symbol is ÷, but it can also be expressed with / between two numbers or with a bar between two numbers like in a fraction. So, if 5 × 4 = 20, then 20 ÷ 5 = 4. That problem can also be expressed as 20/5 or $\frac{20}{5}$.

SQUARING AND THE SQUARE ROOT Squaring a number is multiplying that number by itself. It is represented by having a small 2 as the exponent next to the number that you are going to multiply. So, 4^2 is equal to 16, because 4 × 4 = 16. The square root is the inverse of squaring and is represented by $\sqrt{}$. Perfect squares are squares of whole numbers. For example, $\sqrt{100} = 10$ because $10^2 = 100$, and that is a perfect square. However, $\sqrt{105} = 10.246951$, and that is not a whole number, and therefore, not a perfect square.

FACTORIALS Factorials are a simple concept to understand. It is expressed by having an exclamation point following a number (for example, 5!). Factorials are the product (meaning result from multiplication) of all of the positive integers less than or equal to that number. So, 5! is really saying $5 \times 4 \times 3 \times 2 \times 1 = 120$.

DECIMALS

NAMING NUMBERS WITH DECIMALS Decimals are another way of expressing a fraction. The fraction $\frac{8}{10}$ is equivalent to 0.8. Each number after the decimal is based on the number 10. Therefore, 0.8 is actually eight-tenths. A number in the next spot to the right would make it hundredths, and the next spot to the right would make it thousandths. For example, 0.54 is the same as saying fifty-four-hundredths, and 0.986 is the same as saying nine-hundred eighty-six-thousandths.

ADDITION AND SUBTRACTION WITH DECIMALS When adding decimals, it is important to line the decimals up. The numbers are then added in their respective rows starting from the right, and the decimal is carried over. So for example:

$$
\begin{array}{r} 3.4 \\ +1.4567 \\ \hline 4.8567 \end{array}
\quad \text{and} \quad
\begin{array}{r} 4.5 \\ -3.2 \\ \hline 1.3 \end{array}
$$

When subtracting decimals with multiple places, be sure to add zeros to the number with fewer digits. For example:

$$
\begin{array}{r} 4.5 \\ -3.234 \end{array}
\quad \text{can also appear as} \quad
\begin{array}{r} 4.500 \\ -3.234 \end{array}
$$

Now it appears as any other subtraction problem.

MULTIPLYING WITH DECIMALS

Multiplying with decimals requires a few extra steps. Let's take a look at a problem:

$$5.46$$
$$\times \ 0.6$$

The first thing you do is start from the number on the bottom, the 0.6. Starting from the right, take the 6 and multiply it by each of the numbers on top, starting from the right and moving to the left.

$$3$$
$$5.46$$
$$\times \ 0.6$$
$$6$$

6×6 equals 36, so you put the 6 down, and then place the 3 above the 4. After multiplying 6 by 4, you then add that 3. So your problem now looks like this:

$$5.46$$
$$\times \ 0.6$$
$$76$$

Then continue moving to the left until you have:

$$5.46$$
$$\times \ 0.6$$
$$3276$$

Do the exact same thing with the next digit on the bottom row. In this case, because it is zero, the result will be 000. You then add the two numbers you got, leaving 3276, and then count up the numbers that are behind decimals. In this case, there are three total numbers behind decimals, so starting from the end of the number, you move to the left three spaces and your answer will be 3.276.

〰〰〰〰〰〰〰〰〰〰〰〰〰〰〰〰〰〰

DIVISION WITH DECIMALS

The process of dividing a whole number by a decimal is similar to any long division problem. Just remember to bring the decimal over and work it out normally.

For example:

$$9\overline{)0.326}\ \text{would be}\quad \begin{array}{r} 0.0362 \\ 9\overline{)0.3260} \\ \underline{27} \\ 56 \\ \underline{54} \\ 2 \end{array}$$

The answer is 0.0362

When dividing a decimal by a decimal, the process requires one extra step. In order to divide, you need to make the divisor into a whole number by multiplying it by either 10, 100, 1,000, or whatever is needed to make it whole, and whatever you do to the divisor, you must also do to the dividend. So for example:

$$.86\overline{)0.567}\ \text{would become}\ 86\overline{)56.7}$$

and then you would solve it normally.

ROUNDING DECIMALS Rounding with decimals is similar to rounding with any other kind of numbers. If the number in the thousandths is 4 or less, then that number is dropped and the number in the hundredths place remains. For example, 0.983 would be rounded to 0.98. If the number in the thousandths is 5 or higher, then the number is rounded to the nearest hundredth. For example, 0.986 would turn into 0.99. This same rule applies whether you are rounding from the tenths, the hundredths, or the thousandths.

FINDING THE PERCENT OF A NUMBER Finding the percent of a number is very easy. If you are asked, "What percent of 98 is 32?" you must first divide 32 by 98. The answer is 0.32653061. Choose the first four numbers, and remember to round. You now have 0.3265. Then multiply this number by 100, leaving you with 32.65, and then round to the nearest whole number. So, 32 is 33 percent of 98.

MEASUREMENT

THE METRIC SYSTEM Though there are many systems of measurement found throughout the world, the Metric System is one of the most common systems used worldwide, with the notable exception of the United States. The metric system is a decimal system that measures with a base of 10. Weight is measured in grams, volume is measured in liters, dimensions are measured in meters, and Celsius is used to measure temperature.

THE UNITED STATES CUSTOM UNITS There are only three countries in the world that have not adopted the metric system: Myanmar, Liberia, and the United States (though the metric system is used for scientific and medical measurements). The measurement system in the United States is based on the imperial system used in England (though England has since converted to the metric system). The system is not a base ten system.

LENGTH The units of length used every day in the United States are inch, foot, yard, and mile. In this system, 12 inches makes 1 foot, 3 feet equals 1 yard, and 1 mile is 5,280 feet. In the metric system, 1 yard measures to be 0.9144 meters, and 1 inch is measured to 2.54 centimeters.

MASS There have been four systems to measure mass in the United States: tower weight, troy weight, avoirdupois weight, and apothecaries' weight. Today, avoirdupois is the main system used. Troy, apothecaries', and avoirdupois are all based on the same unit of measurement, the grain. In today's system, 1 grain equals 64.79891 mg, 1 dram equals 1.772 grams, 1 ounce equals 16 drams or 28.35 grams, 1 pound equals 16 ounces or

453.59237 grams, 1 hundredweight equals 100 pounds, and 1 ton equals 20 hundredweights.

VOLUME Measurements of volume in the United States are the cubic inch, cubic foot, and cubic yard. Volume is also separated into two categories: volume of dry material and volume of liquids. Measurements of liquid volume and dry material include cups, pints, quarts, and gallons; however, the measurements are different. For example, 1 pint in dry volume is 550.610 mL, but 1 pint in liquid volume is 473.176 mL.

TEMPERATURE Temperature in the United States is measured in degrees Fahrenheit. Both Celsius and Fahrenheit use the same reference points—the boiling point and freezing point of water—to make their measurements. However, in Celsius, the freezing point is 0°, and in Fahrenheit, 32°. In Celsius, the boiling point is 100°, and in Fahrenheit, 212°. To convert from Fahrenheit to Celsius, subtract the number by 32 and then multiply by 5, and divide by 9. To convert from Celsius to Fahrenheit, multiply the number by 9, divide by 5, and then add 32.

GRAPHS

LINE GRAPHS Line graphs are useful for showing data that changes over a period of time. By plotting the dips and peaks on the graph and then connecting them to make a line, you are able to compare, monitor, and analyze improvement and decline of the data. Line graphs use an x axis and a y axis, the x axis going horizontally, and the y axis going vertically.

BAR GRAPHS Bar graphs are excellent for presenting and comparing data. The values are represented by rectangular bars that differ in height according to the values they represent. Whereas line graphs are used to show a change in time, bar graphs are used to show different amounts. Similar to line graphs, bar graphs also make use of the x and y axes, and bar graphs can be presented either horizontally or vertically.

PIE CHARTS Pie charts are very easy to use and do not require an x or y axis. They are used when representing categorical data or values in proportion to the whole. Essentially, a pie chart is a circle that is divided into segments that reflect the values or categories that they are supposed to represent.

FLOW CHARTS Flow charts are used to describe how all of the steps in a process fit together. They represent a progression and are useful in depicting the various stages that go into a project. Flow charts use three symbols that are all labeled according to their description. There are elongated circles, representing the start and finish; rectangles, which show the steps or instructions; and diamonds, which show the decisions that have to be made. Arrows connect the symbols to one another, showing the progression in the process.

ORGANIZATIONAL CHARTS Organizational charts are used to show the formal and informal relationships in an overall structure. They are mostly used in the workforce, showing the ranks and relationships among employees. Organizational charts also show how different departments can be connected. Generally, they are shaped like pyramids, with the top rectangle representing the highest position, such as the president or CEO, and other rectangles descending according to rank. The size of the rectangles relates to the level of authority, and arrows are used to represent the flow.

PICTOGRAPHS Pictographs use picture symbols to represent data and compare trends. The symbols used represent a specific quantity, and are repeated a certain number of times along the chart. Pictographs do not provide precise information but rather give a general representation. An example of a pictograph would be a chart showing the amount of apples four students have eaten. The key on the bottom might say that for every picture of an apple, four apples have been eaten. So on the chart, if the students have three apples pictured by their names, it means they've actually eaten twelve apples each.

PI

THE SYMBOL Pi is a mathematical constant. Pi is always equal to the ratio between the area of a circle to its radius that is squared. Pi is represented by the Greek letter π. This symbol's name is pi, and it is the symbol still used today. The letter stems from the Greek word περίμετρος, meaning "perimeter." The first to use the symbol as the mathematical constant was William Jones in 1706. The mathematical constant is always represented by the lowercase π, because the capital version, Π, has an entirely different meaning.

THE DEFINITION To put it simply, π is the ratio of a circumference of a circle to the diameter of the circle. In other words, the equation looks like this:

$$\pi = \frac{C}{d}$$

Regardless of the size of the circle, this ratio will always equal π. There is another way to define π by using a circle's area, and that is by this equation:

$$\pi = \frac{A}{r^2}$$

In this equation, *r* represents the radius of the circle, which is half of the diameter.

EARLY HISTORY OF PI
The Rhind Mathematical Papyrus, a famous piece of Egyptian papyrus dated around 1650 B.C., shows the use of pi written by the scribe Ahmes. He states: "Cut off ⅑ of a diameter and construct a square upon the remainder; this has the same area as the circle." According to these calculations, pi equals 3.16049. In the nineteenth century B.C., the Babylonians believed the value to be ²⁵⁄₈, which is only 0.5 percent below the actual value of π.

PI GETS MORE ACCURATE
At first, pi was believed to have less than ten digits. Aryabhata, an Indian mathematician and astronomer from the fifth century, came to the realization that pi is in fact an irrational number; that is, the decimals go on forever without repeating. Around 1600, Ludolph van Ceulen, a German mathematician, correctly identified the first 35 decimals in pi. In 1789, a Slovene mathematician calculated to the first 140, though only the first 126 numbers were correct. In 1873, the first 527 numbers were calculated correctly. And in 2019, with the use of a supercomputer, the first 31.4 trillion places were claimed to have been calculated correctly.

AN IRRATIONAL CONSTANT
Pi is an irrational constant, which means that it cannot be expressed as a fraction or ratio of two integers. Pi is also a transcendental number, meaning that it is not the root of any algebraic numbers. When pi is calculated out into numbers, the decimal representation does not repeat or end. For example, the number truncated to 50 decimals is 3.14159265358979323846264338327950288419716939937510. So for basic mathematic equations, many people shorten pi to 3.14.

THE NOT-SO-ACCURATE PI Less accurate depictions of pi can be found in sources as early as the Bible, which states that pi equals 3. More recently, the Indiana Pi Bill of 1897 was an attempt to turn into law the notion that pi equals 3.2 in the state of Indiana. The bill never passed the Indiana General Assembly and never became a law.

SCIENTIFIC NOTATION

WHAT IS SCIENTIFIC NOTATION? Scientific notation is a method of writing numbers that makes them easier to work with. These numbers can be of any value, and this system is typically used because the numbers are too big or too small. By simplifying normal decimal notation, one can then apply them to other equations and formulas with ease. This is a typical example of scientific notation:

$$x + 10^y$$

x is a real number, and y is an integer representing how far you have to move the decimal point.

EXAMPLE OF SCIENTIFIC NOTATION Let's look at a simple example of scientific notation:

$$3 \times 10^4 = 30,000$$

The 3 can also be shown as 3.0 because there are no numbers following it. From there, we then have to move the decimal point an additional four spots. We move to the right, because the exponent is positive.

Similarly, to show the number 5,000 in scientific notation, it would look like this:

$$5 \times 10^3$$

~~~~~~

SCIENTIFIC NOTATION WITH NEGATIVE INTEGERS For negative integers, back the number of spaces the integer indicates. For example:

$$500 \times 10^{-1} \text{ is equal to } 50.$$

You start at 500, which can be shown as 500.0, and you move the decimal point to the left one space, making it 50. No matter how complex the number may appear, to turn a number into decimal notation, you must follow the exponent.

~~~~~~

GOING FROM SCIENTIFIC NOTATION TO DECIMAL NOTATION To turn a number from decimal notation to scientific notation, you must work backward. You are starting with a number in decimal form, and want to end with the $x \times 10^y$ equation. Make x as simple a number as you can between 1 and 10. So, for example:

$$0.003 \text{ would be equivalent to } 3 \times 10^{-3}$$

And if the number is more complex, just remember to make it between 1 and 10. For example:

$$.002345 \text{ is just } 2.345 \times 10^{-3}$$

~~~~~~

ORDER OF MAGNITUDE The order of magnitude is a number rounded to the nearest power of 10. This enables simple comparisons, estimates, and rough calculations to be performed. So, for example, if something is 1.9 and you need to use it in a calculation, that number is closer to 10^0 than it is to 10^1, so when solving your problem, you would use 10^0.

ENGINEERING NOTATION Engineering notation is a form of scientific notation used in civil and mechanical engineering. It is slightly different than scientific notation. In engineering notation, the powers of 10 are restricted to be only multiples of 3. This is because they are actually powers of 1,000, so instead of writing $1,000^2$, it looks like 10^6.

LOGARITHMS

WHAT ARE LOGARITHMS? Maybe the most useful concept in arithmetic that can be used in all sciences, logarithms are ways to express a power that a fixed base, or number, is raised to so that a given answer is produced. Common logarithms have a base of 10, while natural logarithms have a base e. Here are some basic logs:

$\log(10) = 1$
This is because $10^1 = 10$

$\log(100) = 2$
This is because $10^2 = 100$

$\log(2) \approx 0.3$
This is because $10^{0.3} = 2$

The opposite of a log, known as an antilog, looks like this:

$$\text{antilog}(2) = 100$$

With antilogs, you are just raising the base (10) to the power of x (in this case 2).

BASIC RULES OF LOGARITHMS

Just like you can add exponents when there is the same base, logarithms follow a similar rule. Here are the three main rules for logarithms. Note that these only work when the bases are identical:

$$\log_b(m) + \log_b(n) = \log_b(mn)$$

This means that when adding logs with the same base, you multiply the numbers inside of the log:

$$\log_b(m) - \log_b(n) = \log_b(m/n)$$

When subtracting logs with the same base, divide the numbers inside the logs:

$$n \cdot \log_b(m) = \log_b(m^n)$$

When there is a multiplier, it turns into an exponent on everything that is in the log, and vice versa.

~~~~~~

EXPANDING LOGARITHMS

When logs have a lot of information in them, they should be taken apart by using the rules until each log only has one thing inside of it. For example, if you want to expand $\log_3(4x)$, you break it down as this:

$$\log_3(4) + \log_3(x) = \log_3(4x)$$

Your answer is $\log_3(4) + \log_3(x)$. You should not try to then find the value of $\log_3(4)$ in your calculator, but rather leave it as is. Here is another example:

$$\log_5(25/x) = \log_5(25) - \log_5(x)$$
$$\log_5(25/x) = 2 - \log_5(x)$$

SIMPLIFYING LOGARITHMIC EXPRESSIONS Simplifying logarithmic expressions is essentially doing the reverse of expanding logarithmic expressions. Instead of breaking it down into many parts from one large part, you are given many parts and are asked to create one large logarithm. For example, if you were asked to simplify $\log_4(x) + \log_4(y)$, you would do:

$$\log_4(x) + \log_4(y) = \log_4(xy)$$

To simplify $3\log_3(x)$, remember to make the multiplier the exponent inside of the log. It would look like this:

$$\log_3(x^3)$$

No matter how complicated the problem might look, the processes are very simple.

~~~~~~

CHANGE-OF-BASE FORMULA If you wish to calculate a log that doesn't have a base of 10, you have to use what is known as the change-of-base formula. This formula states:

$$\log_b(x) = \frac{\log_d(x)}{\log_d(b)}$$

For example, if you wanted to convert $\log_4(9)$ to base 5, you would do:

$$\log_4(9) = \frac{\log_5(9)}{\log_5(4)}$$

Using the change-of-base formula is helpful for locating plot-points of a graph that is a nonstandard log (that is, a log that does not have a base of 10).

APPLICATIONS OF LOGARITHMS Logarithms have very real applications in both math and non-math subjects alike. The nautilus, for example, is a cephalopod that has a large shell. The chambers of the shell are approximate copies of the last chamber that are scaled by a constant number. This same idea can be found in mathematics, and it is known as the logarithmic spiral. Logarithms are used to measure the strengths of earthquakes (which is known as the Richter scale) and how bright stars are. They are even used in psychology (where Hick's law uses a logarithm to explain the time it takes a person to make a decision as a result of the amount of choices they have).

BASIC ALGEBRA

WHAT IS ALGEBRA? In algebra, equations are given with unknown numbers. These unknown numbers are represented with letters. Based on the equation laid out, one has to figure out the missing value. The letters can be variables, where the value of the letter can change, or they can be constants, which have a fixed value (such as π).

ADDITION AND SUBTRACTION WITH ALGEBRAIC EXPRESSIONS

An example of a single algebraic expression is $6x$, where 6 represents the coefficient and x represents the variable, and these numbers are being multiplied together. You can only add and subtract like terms. For example, in $7x + 9z$, x and z are unlike terms and the problem thus cannot be simplified further; however, with $7x + 9x$, since the variables are both x, we can work the problem out and get $16x$.

MULTIPLICATION WITH ALGEBRAIC EXPRESSIONS With multiplication, it is a matter of following the laws regarding exponents. For example:

$$x^4(x^3 + 6a) = x^7 + 6ax^4$$

This is the simplest answer we can get from a problem like this. With problems with two sets of equations in parentheses, break up the first set as such:

$$(x + 7)(a - 2)$$
$$x(a - 2) + 7(a - 2)$$

You add or subtract the problems based on whether the second part of the problem is positive or negative. So that gives us:

$$xa - 2x + 7a - 14$$

We cannot break it down any further, so that is our answer.

~~~~~~

DIVISION WITH ALGEBRAIC EXPRESSIONS When dividing algebraic expressions, you first write the problem out as a fraction. The next step is to then simplify the coefficient, and then cancel out like variables in both the numerator and the denominator. For example:

$$8ab^4 \div 2ab = \frac{8 \times a \times b \times b \times b \times b}{2 \times a \times b} = 4b^3$$

~~~~~~

SOLVING FOR X When solving for x, you want to get x all by itself. For example:

$$2x = 10$$

To get x by itself, you have to divide $2x$ by 2, and whatever you do on one side, you must do on the other side. So you end up with

$x = 5$. No matter how complex the problem might get, as long as you remember to get x by itself, you will be able to solve the problem.

REARRANGING FORMULAS Rearranging formulas is essentially taking all that you have learned and working backward. It is very similar to solving for x, only you are not limited to just one number. You can solve any part of the problem. For example, if you have a formula that states $2b = c$, and then you are asked to solve for b, you can just divide both sides by 2. So, $b = c/2$.

FIBONACCI SEQUENCE

WHAT IS THE FIBONACCI SEQUENCE? The Fibonacci sequence is a series of numbers that follows the very simple rule that any number in the sequence is the sum of the previous two numbers. The first ten numbers in the sequence are as follows:

$$0, 1, 1, 2, 3, 5, 8, 13, 21, 34$$

The Fibonacci sequence is written as:

$$x_n = x_{n-1} + x_{n-2}$$

THE GOLDEN RATIO The golden ratio, expressed as φ, is a mathematical constant with a value of 1.6180339887. If the ratio between the sum of two quantities and the larger quantity equals the ratio of the larger quantity and the smaller quantity, it is called the golden ratio. In other words:

$$\frac{a+b}{a} = \frac{a}{b} = \varphi$$

Any two successive numbers from the Fibonacci sequence will have a ratio close to the golden ratio.

THE FIBONACCI SEQUENCE IN NATURE Fibonacci sequences appear in the natural world with astounding frequency. The number of petals on a flower, the branching in trees, the arrangements of leaves on a stem, the spirals of a pinecone, and even the scales of a pineapple all show Fibonacci sequences. One particular example of the Fibonacci sequence in nature is with the reproduction of the honeybee. The sequence of honeybee parents and ancestors correlates exactly with the Fibonacci sequence.

THE FIBONACCI SEQUENCE IN MUSIC The Fibonacci sequence can also be found in music. In any octave, thirteen notes can be played. A scale is made up of eight notes, and the third and fifth notes in the scale are the foundation of the chords. These are based on a whole tone, which is two tones away from the root tone, which happens to be the first note.

THE MAN BEHIND FIBONACCI The Fibonacci sequence was named after the Italian Leonardo Pisano Bigollo, who lived from 1170 to 1250. His nickname was Fibonacci, meaning "son of Banacci." Though the sequence was described earlier by Indian mathematicians, it was Leonardo Pisano Bigollo who helped spread the sequence to Western Europe. He also helped introduce Hindu-Arabic numerals (the current system used today) to Europe, replacing the Roman numeral system.

LEONARDO PISANO BIGOLLO'S RABBITS Leonardo Pisano Bigollo first mentioned the sequence in his book *Liber abaci*. In it, he examined the growth of an unrealistic rabbit population. Bigollo wondered how many pairs of rabbits there would be in one year if a male and a female rabbit could mate at one month old. By the end of the second month, the female could produce another pair, the rabbits do not ever die, and a new pair is produced every month from the second month on.

SQUARE ROOTS

SIMPLIFYING SQUARE ROOTS For simplifying square roots, you begin by taking out any perfect squares. For example:

$$\sqrt{25} = \sqrt{5^2} = 5$$

When the number is not a perfect square, there might be a perfect square within the number. First you must factor the problem, and then take out the perfect square. For example:

$$\sqrt{400} = \sqrt{100 \times 4} = \sqrt{100} \times \sqrt{4} = 10 \times 2 = 20$$

If there is no perfect square, you break it down to its simplest form. For example:

$$\sqrt{98} = \sqrt{49} \times \sqrt{2} = 7 \times \sqrt{2} = 7\sqrt{2}$$

MULTIPLYING SQUARE ROOTS When multiplying square roots, simplify the problem into its basic form. For example:

$$\sqrt{10} = \sqrt{5} \times \sqrt{2} = \sqrt{5}\sqrt{2}$$

When working in the other direction, the problem must be simplified by writing no more than one radical. For example:

$$\sqrt{3}\sqrt{12} = \sqrt{3} \times \sqrt{3} \times \sqrt{4} = \sqrt{3} \times \sqrt{3} \times 2 = 3 \times 2 = 6$$

ADDING AND SUBTRACTING SQUARE ROOTS With addition, if the root is the same, you just have to add the numbers before it. For example:

$$3\sqrt{5} + 2\sqrt{5} = 5\sqrt{5}$$

If a square root can be simplified into whole numbers, then they should be, and then continue with the problem. For example:

$$3\sqrt{25} + 2\sqrt{25} = 3(5) + 2(5) = 25$$

Only like radicals can be combined in the end, so if you end with a problem like $2\sqrt{3} + 3\sqrt{7}$, then that is your answer.

DIVISION WITH SQUARE ROOTS Division is very simple. Begin by simplifying the problem from inside the square root. For example:

$$\frac{\sqrt{32}}{2} = \sqrt{16} = 4$$

You can also split the division into radicals and then work from there, simplifying and canceling numbers out. For example:

$$\sqrt{\frac{3}{36}} = \frac{\sqrt{3}}{\sqrt{6\times6}} = \frac{\sqrt{3}}{6}$$

RATIONALIZING DENOMINATORS The denominator can never contain a radical. To fix this problem, you must find the common denominator, the exact same way you were taught to do with fractions. For example, to simplify

$$\frac{8\sqrt{2}}{\sqrt{3}}$$

you must first find the common denominator and multiply it by both the top and the bottom:

$$\frac{8\sqrt{2}}{\sqrt{3}} = \frac{(\sqrt{3})}{(\sqrt{3})} = \frac{8\sqrt{6}}{\sqrt{3\times3}} = \frac{8\sqrt{6}}{3}$$

HIGHER INDEX ROOTS Operations with higher roots such as cube roots, fourth roots, etc., are similar to square roots. With cube roots, take out factors that occur in threes. With a fourth root, take out factors that occur in fours, etc. For example:

$$\sqrt[4]{16} = \sqrt[4]{2 \times 2 \times 2 \times 2} = 2$$
$$\sqrt[3]{54} = \sqrt[3]{3 \times 3 \times 3 \times 2} = 2\sqrt[3]{3} \times 2 = 2\sqrt[3]{6}$$

GEOMETRY

POLYGONS Geometry is the study of shapes and their properties. Polygons are particular types of shapes used in geometry. Polygons have many straight sides. With regular polygons, all of the angles and sides have to be the same. A shape with three sides and angles is called a triangle. A shape with four sides and angles is called a quadrilateral. A shape with five sides and angles is a pentagon, six makes a hexagon, and so on. A shape that has two pairs of parallel lines is called a parallelogram.

AREA The area is the amount of space inside a shape. To find the area of a square or any other plane shape, the formula is simple. You multiply the length by the height of the object. To find the area of a parallelogram, you multiply the base by the height of the object. For trapezoids—shapes with four sides but only one pair of parallel sides—you add the lengths of the two parallel sides, divide by two, and then multiply that number by the height.

PERIMETER Perimeter is a very simple idea with a very simple solution to finding it. The perimeter of an object is the distance around the outside of the shape. The easiest way of finding the perimeter is by adding up all of the sides. For example, if a rectangle has two sides that are 7 inches and two sides that are 3 inches, then the perimeter would be $7 + 7 + 3 + 3 = 20$.

CIRCUMFERENCE Circumference is the same idea as perimeter, only it applies to circles. The formula for finding the circumference requires a little more work, however. To find the circumference, multiply the diameter of the circle by π, which as you may recall is simplified to 3.14. If only the radius is provided, multiply the radius by 2 to find the diameter, and then solve for the circumference.

VOLUME Whereas area deals with two-dimensional figures, volume is the amount of space in three-dimensional figures. To find the volume of a rectangular prism, multiply the length by the width by the height. To find the volume of a triangular prism, you do the same formula and then multiply by ½ . As the shapes get more advanced, so, too, does the formula for volume. For example, the formula for finding the volume of a cone is ⅓ times the area of the base times the height.

SURFACE AREA The surface area is the sum of all of the areas. For rectangular prisms, finding the surface area requires finding the area of each side and adding them together (this of course can be simplified by finding the area of one side and then multiplying it by two because there are two sides, and then doing the same thing for the other sides). To find the surface area of a cylinder, the formula is: $2\pi r^2 + 2\pi rh$.

ANGLES

WHAT IS AN ANGLE? Angles are used in geometry. An angle is formed when two rays, an order of points in a line, share the same endpoint. The size of an angle refers to the value of the arc between the two lines, or the value of the rotation. There are five basic types of angles to know: acute, right, obtuse, reflex, and perigon.

DIFFERENT TYPES OF ANGLES As angles increase, their names change. Acute angles have values that are greater than zero but less than 90 degrees. A right angle is exactly 90 degrees. An obtuse angle is any angle greater than 90 degrees but less than 180 degrees. A reflex angle is larger than an obtuse angle, and it is any angle that is more than 180 but less than 360. A perigon is a full rotation that equals 360 degrees exactly.

COMPLEMENTARY AND SUPPLEMENTARY ANGLES Complementary and supplementary angles involve combining two angles. Complementary angles are any two angles that when added up, the sum is equal to 90 degrees. This means that if you put them together, they will form a right angle. A supplementary angle is the sum of any two angles that equals 180 degrees. This means that when they are added together, they make a straight line.

MEASURING ANGLES The angle is defined by the theta symbol, θ. The length of the arc is represented by the lowercase letter s, and the radius of a circle is represented by the lowercase letter r. The lowercase letter k is used to represent a scaling constant, and that depends on the units of measurement in the problem.

The basic formula for finding the value of an angle is:

$$\theta = k\frac{s}{r}$$

THE TRIGONOMETRIC FUNCTIONS
In trigonometry, sine, cosine, and tangent are used to find the relation of the angles of a triangle to the sides of the triangle. The basic equations are:

$$\sin\theta = \frac{\text{opposite of angle}}{\text{hypotenuse}}$$

$$\cos\theta = \frac{\text{adjacent line}}{\text{hypotenuse}}$$

$$\tan\theta = \frac{\text{opposite of angle}}{\text{adjacent line}}$$

POSITIVE AND NEGATIVE ANGLES
If an angle is counterclockwise, the angle (θ) will have a positive value. If the angle is in a clockwise motion, then the value of θ will be negative. θ equaling -50 and θ equaling 50 do not mean the same thing. Angles have degrees of rotation and directions of rotation. Even though both of those numbers have the same degree of rotation, their directions are the opposite, making them different angles.

CURVES

WHAT IS A CURVE?
A curve is similar to a line in that it is a continuously moving point, but it does not have to be straight. A curve starts out like a straight line then begins to deform in a smooth and continuous formation. The shape the curve takes on

is the result of a particular equation. Closed curves repeat, and open curves have infinite length.

CONICS Conics are algebraic forms that are curved. They are the result of a cone being sliced by a plane. Four common conics are the circle, the ellipse, the parabola, and hyperbola. All conics can be written by using the formula:

$$Ax^2 + Bxy + Cy^2 + Dx + Ey + F = 0$$

CIRCLES The most common curve is the circle. The circle is made up of determinate lines. They do not extend forever but rather have an ending point. When drawing curves on a graph with an x and y axis, a basic formula that tells you the curve will be a circle is $x^2 + y^2 = a^2$. Both values are squared, making them positive, and both have the same coefficient, making them equal distances. Another formula for making a circle is:

$$(x - h)^2 + (y - k)^2 = r^2$$

In this formula, h and k represent the x and y coordinates that are found in the center of the circle, and r is the radius. For example, if you have coordinates $(8,5)$ with a radius of 10, your circle would be $(x - 8)^2 + (y - 5)^2 = 100$.

ELLIPSES An ellipse is another form of a closed curve. Its appearance resembles a circle, only it is squashed and is an oval. Ellipses are defined by two points, known as Focus 1 (F1) and Focus 2 (F2). At any point of the ellipse, if the distances of the focus points are added up, they are constant. The basic formula for an ellipse is:

$$\frac{(x-h)^2}{a^2} + \frac{(y-k)^2}{b^2} = 1$$

PARABOLAS A parabola is a curve that is U-shaped. It is the locus of a point that is always the same distance from the focus and a given line, called the directrix. The standard equations for making parabolas are:

$$y - k = a(x - h)^2 \quad \text{and} \quad x - h = a(y - k)^2$$

If a is greater than zero, the parabola opens upward, and if it is less than zero, it opens downward.

~~~~~~

HYPERBOLAS A hyperbola is kind of like two parabolas put together, making a sort of X shape. There are two types of hyperbolas: vertical and horizontal. The formula for a horizontal hyperbola is:

$$\frac{(x-h)^2}{a^2} - \frac{(y-v)^2}{b^2} = 1$$

The formula for a horizontal hyperbola is:

$$\frac{(y-v)^2}{a^2} - \frac{(x-h)^2}{b^2} = 1$$

PYTHAGOREAN THEOREM

WHAT IS THE PYTHAGOREAN THEOREM? The Pythagorean theorem is one of the most well-known formulas ever written:

$$a^2 + b^2 = c^2$$

The letters a and b represent the sides of the triangle, and the letter c represents the hypotenuse, which is opposite of the right angle. The Pythagorean theorem can only be used when dealing with right triangles (which, as you might recall, means an angle of 90 degrees). There are at least 370 ways to prove the Pythagorean theorem.

PROOF WITH TRIANGLES THAT ARE SIMILAR

The simplest way to prove the Pythagorean theorem is by using similar triangles. In similar triangles, corresponding parts are proportional, regardless of how big or small the two triangles are. This type of proof depends on length and not on area. The equation for this proof is:

$$\frac{a}{c} = \frac{e}{a} \text{ and } \frac{b}{c} = \frac{d}{b}$$

From there, $a^2 = c \times e$ and $b^2 = c \times d$.
If you add them together, you get $a^2 + b^2 = c \times e + c \times d$ which leads to $a^2 + b^2 = c^2$.

EUCLID'S PROOF

In Euclid's proof, a large square is divided into two rectangles, one large, one small. Of the larger rectangle, a triangle is created that is half of the area of the rectangle. The same thing is done with the smaller rectangle, so you have two congruent triangles:

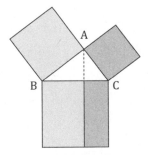

After working through a set of rules, you will end up with $AB^2 + AC^2 = BC^2$.

ALGEBRAIC PROOFS The Pythagorean theorem can also be proven by using algebra. To do so, the equation looks like this:

$$(b - a)^2 + 4(ab/2) = (b - a)^2 + 2ab = a^2 + b^2$$

When solved, this problem simply turns into:

$$c^2 = a^2 + b^2$$

Another proof related to this was actually created by President James Garfield.

PROOF WITH DIFFERENTIALS A proof using differentials employs principles of calculus to prove the Pythagorean theorem. This type of proof involves studying how changes to a side of the triangle affect the hypotenuse. This is considered to be a metric proof, and instead of using areas, the proof is based on lengths.

THE PYTHAGOREAN TRIPLE The Pythagorean triple is a series of three whole numbers, such as 3, 4, and 5, that work when put into the Pythagorean theorem, and can be the sides of a right triangle. Other examples of Pythagorean triples include 5, 12, 13 and 7, 24, 25. To create a Pythagorean triple, take any odd number and square it. Then find two consecutive numbers that add up to that number.

PRECALCULUS

WHAT IS PRECALCULUS? Precalculus was created in math education to better prepare students for calculus. It is a more advanced form of algebra that gives students the information needed for the full transition from algebra into calculus. Some of the most important notions of precalculus are functions, polynomials, quadratics, completing the square, and permutations.

FUNCTIONS Functions are essential to mathematic equations, and even though you might not know what they are called, you have already seen and worked with examples of functions. For example, $7x + 3 = y$. To find y, you need to find x. When y depends on finding x, and only one possible answer can be found, that is a function. No matter what x equals, there can only be one value for y.

POLYNOMIALS Polynomials are expressions that are the sum of exponents and variables. Each section of the polynomial is considered a term. To be considered a polynomial, terms must follow strict rules. There cannot be any square roots of variables, fractions, or fractional powers. There must be variables that are raised to a whole number exponent or a regular number. A polynomial looks like this:

$$7x^2 + 8x - 9$$

And do not be fooled by the $8x$. It still follows the rules of terms because it is just saying $8x^1$.

QUADRATICS Polynomials that follow the pattern $ax^2 + bx + c$ have a special name. These are called quadratics. To factor quadratics, you need to find numbers that when multiplied equal c, but when added equal b. For example:

$$x2 + 6x + 8$$

You first break it down into two sets to multiply:

$$(x + ?)\,(x + ?)$$

Then plug in numbers and test:

$$(x + 4)(x + 2) = x^2 + 2x + 4x + 8 = x^2 + 6x + 8$$

Therefore, your answer is: $(x + 4)(x + 2)$.

COMPLETING THE SQUARE Some quadratic equations cannot be factored. To solve these, a method called completing the square is used. This turns $ax^2 + bx + c$ into $ax^2 + bx + c = (a + b)^2$. For example:

$$x^2 + 2x + 1 = 0$$

Begin by transposing the constant term:

$$x^2 + 2x = -1$$

Then you have to add a square to both sides. To do so, you have to take half of the coefficient of x and then square it. So, half of 2 is 1, and then 1^2 is 1.

$$x^2 + 2x + 1 = -1 + 1$$
$$x^2 + 2x + 1 = 0$$

Now you have $(x + 1)(x + 1) = 0$.
Break up these into two individual problems:

$$x + 1 = 0 \text{ and } x + 1 = 0$$

Solve for x. In both cases, x equals -1. Your answer will go in brackets and look like this:

$$\{-1, -1\}$$

PERMUTATIONS Permutations are all of the possible arrangements you can make of a set. For example:

The permutation of abc is: abc
                            bac
                            acb
                            cba
                            bca
                            cab

There are six permutations. The more letters you have, the more permutations there are. In order to solve these larger problems, this is where you use the factorials you learned about earlier. Permutations are set up like this: $_8P_3$.

The number on the left is the same thing as saying 8!, and the number on the right is how many number places you will go. So that really means $8 \times 7 \times 6 = 336$.

CALCULUS

WHAT IS CALCULUS? Calculus is the study of change over time through using advanced forms of geometry and algebra, and it has many real-world applications. It provides the framework for understanding why things change, how to model things, and learning how to predict change in models. Calculus deals with the concept of infinity. If something is always changing, that means it is changing infinitely.

DERIVATIVES The derivative is one of the core concepts used in calculus. In calculus, derivatives are represented in two ways. In geometric terms, derivatives are the slope of a line. The other way to show a derivative is physically, in which it is the rate of change. In a straight line, the slope indicates the speed at which the function changes. With a curved line, however, the slope changes, and this is where derivatives are used.

RULES OF DIFFERENTIATION
Differentiation is the process of finding the derivatives. There are several rules of differentiation. Among these rules are the constant rule, which states if $F(x) = C$, then $F'(x) = 0$ (for example, if $F(x) = 5$, then $F'(x) = 0$) and the power rule, which states $F(x) = nx^{n-1}$, where n equals the exponent. For example, if $F(x) = X^4$, then $F'(x) = 4X^3$.

LIMITS
Limits are the intended height of a particular function. The formula for limits looks like this:

$$\lim_{x \, à \, c} f(x) = n$$

Limits deal with the process of moving up the graph, and are not concerned with the value of c. For example, if $f(x) = x^2$, we know that $x = 2$, we can just plug it into the formula to figure out the answer and arrive at c. What limits do is figure out where the line is as it moves to the constant.

MAXIMA AND MINIMA
Maxima and minima (known as extrema) are the largest and smallest values a function has within a specific area (local), or as a whole (global or absolute). Local maximum is the height at a point that is greater than or equal to any other points in the interval. The formula for local maximum is $f(a) \geq f(x)$. Local minimum is the opposite, with a formula of $f(a) \leq f(x)$.

INTEGRATION
Integration in calculus deals with two things. The first is to find the antiderivative, which is the inverse transform

of the derivative. The other thing integration does is find the value of the area below the curve. Integration is represented by $\int f(x)\, dx$. And dx equals the difference of x_n and x_{n-1}. Two common equations for integration are:

$$\text{If } f(x) = x^n, \text{ then } f(x)\, dx = x^{n+1}/(n+1)$$
$$\text{If } f(x) = cx^n, \text{ then } f(x)\, dx = cx^{n+1}/(n+1)$$

TRIGONOMETRY

RATIOS *Trigonometry* literally means "measurement of triangles," and that is exactly what it is: the study of triangles. Trigonometry is based on the measurements of right triangles, meaning triangles with right angles, and the ratios of each side. In ratios, you use cardinal and ordinal numbers. Cardinal numbers are the numbers that you use for counting (1, 2, 3, 4, etc.), while ordinal numbers are in the form of first, second, third, fourth, etc. When a large number is a multiple of another smaller number, that smaller number is part of the larger number. For example, 3 is the first multiple of 3, and 9 is the second multiple of 3. A ratio of two numbers is the relationship regarding the relative size. This is expressed in a sentence. For example, if you were asked what ratio has 3 to 9, the answer would be 3 is the third part to 9.

THE LAW OF COSINES When solving triangles that do not have right angles (known as oblique triangles), the laws of sines and cosines are used. If you need to find the third side, and the other two sides of a triangle and the angle are known, then you use the law of cosines. The formula for the law of cosines is:

$$c^2 = a^2 + b^2 - 2ab \cos \theta$$

For example, if we are given a triangle ABC, side $a = 9$ inches, side $b = 11$ inches, and the angle of c is 60°, what is the value of c? The formula would look like this:

$$c^2 = 9^2 + 11^2 - 2(9)(11) \cos 60$$
$$c^2 = 202 - 99$$
$$c^2 = 103$$
$$c = \sqrt{103}$$

THE LAW OF SINES

For the law of sines, we are dealing with triangles where the sides are the same ratio as the sines of opposite angles. So $a : b : c = \sin A : \sin B : \sin C$.

So, side a is to b, is to $\sin A$ is to $\sin B$, and the same with b to c. In other words:

$$\frac{a}{b} = \frac{\sin A}{\sin B} \quad \text{and} \quad \frac{b}{c} = \frac{\sin B}{\sin C}$$

RADIAN MEASURE

One revolution in a circle is measured as 2π. This means that half of a circle is π, and that every right angle in a circle is $\pi/2$. $\pi/4$ is half of a right angle, and thus, it equals 45°. So this means that 2π is actually 360°. To find degrees in radians, follow this equation:

$$\text{Radians} = \frac{\text{Degrees}}{180} \bullet \pi$$

So to convert 90° into radians, you do:

$$\frac{90}{180} \bullet \pi = \frac{\pi}{2}$$

RECIPROCAL IDENTITIES

Identities are true no matter what value the variable is. For example, the problem $(x + 3)(x - 3) = x^2 - 9$ is always true. That makes it an identity. In trigonometry, there are several reciprocal identities one has to know. The reciprocal identities are:

$$\sin\theta = \frac{1}{\csc\theta} \qquad \csc\theta = \frac{1}{\sin\theta}$$

$$\cos\theta = \frac{1}{\sec\theta} \qquad \sec\theta = \frac{1}{\cos\theta}$$

$$\tan\theta = \frac{1}{\cot\theta} \qquad \cot\theta = \frac{1}{\tan\theta}$$

LOGIC

WHAT IS LOGIC? Logic is the study of correct reasoning or inference. The origins of logic can be traced back to Aristotle, who viewed logic as a tool to be used, rather than an actual philosophy. This is still the view mathematicians and philosophers take. In order to establish something as true, such as a philosophy, one needs logic to demonstrate a proof and to have it accepted. And that is exactly what logic is used for.

SHORTHAND SENTENCES An example of logic might be:

> Assuming: The cat is orange.
> And assuming: The cat is a female.
> I conclude: The cat is orange and the cat is a female.

In logic, shorthand sentences are essential. Instead of writing out full-length sentences all the time, a letter is chosen to represent that sentence. So the sentence "The cat is orange" would be represented by the letter *A,* and the sentence "The cat is a female" would be represented by the letter *B.*

CONNECTIVES Connectives are what are used to connect your sentences represented by *A* and *B*. Connectives are the "and, or, if…then, not, if and only if." Connectives have their own symbols. They are:

and	^
or	v
if…then	->
not	~
if and only if	<->

So, now the sentences about the cat look like this:

The cat is orange and the cat is a female. ($A \wedge B$)
The cat is orange or the cat is a female. ($A \vee B$)
If the cat is orange, then the cat is a female. ($A \rightarrow B$)
The cat is not orange. ($\sim A$)
The cat is orange if and only if the cat is female. ($A \leftrightarrow B$)

USE OF PARENTHESES Parentheses play an important part in writing out logical arguments. If we wanted to negate a sentence, we would use the symbol ~. But if we write $\sim A \wedge B$, that does not mean the entire thing is negated, but that only *A* is. Parentheses help us clarify. So, we would write it out like:

$$\sim(A \wedge B)$$

Parentheses also help distinguish the sentences while working. Logic problems can be very complex, sometimes with thirty lines of derivation, so the parentheses keep it all orderly.

THE RULES OF LOGIC These are the twelve rules of logic:

1.		**Assumption:** You can assume anything, but you have to keep track of your assumptions
2.	->	**Introduction:** If you presume A and then obtain B, you can write $(A \rightarrow B)$
3.	^	**Elimination:** If you have $(A \wedge B)$, then you can also have A and you can have B
4.		**Repetition:** If you have A, then you are allowed to have A
5.	^	**Introduction:** If you have A and you have B, then you can have $(A \wedge B)$
6.	->	**Elimination:** If you have A and you have $(A \rightarrow B)$, then you can have B
7.	<->	**Introduction:** If you have $(A \rightarrow B)$ and $(B \rightarrow A)$, then you have $(A \leftrightarrow B)$
8.	<->	**Elimination:** If you have $(A \leftrightarrow B)$, and you have A, then you can have B (and vice versa)
9.	~	**Introduction:** If you have A and find a contradiction, you can have $\sim A$
10.	~	**Elimination:** If you have $\sim A$ and find a contradiction, you can have A
11.	v	**Introduction:** If you have A, you can write $(A \vee B)$ no matter what
12.	v	**Elimination:** If you have $(A \vee B)$ and $(A \rightarrow C)$ and $(Y \rightarrow C)$, then you can have C

MODUS PONENS, MODUS TOLLENS, AND HYPOTHETICAL SYLLOGISM

Modus ponens is a very straightforward law. If you have $(X \to Y)$ and you also have X, then you are allowed to have Y. This is essentially rule number six, $\to$ Elimination. Modus tollens is the reverse of modus ponens. It states if you have $(X \to Y)$ and you also have $\sim Y$, then you are allowed to have $\sim X$. Essentially, this means that if Y is false, X cannot be true. Hypothetical syllogism states that if there is $(X \to Y)$ and you also have $(Y \to Z)$, then you can have $(X \to Z)$.

PROBABILITY

WHAT IS PROBABILITY? Probability is the study of the likelihood or chance of a particular event occurring. With problems regarding probability, identifying all of the different outcomes that can actually happen is crucial to understanding how to solve the problem. When you flip a coin, you want to know what the likelihood is that you'll get heads. When you pick a card from a deck, you want to figure out the probability that the card is a seven, or that the card will be hearts. Probability is about how likely an event is to occur.

PROBABILITY OF AN EVENT In probability problems, the event is the end result. It's what we want to figure out. To figure out the probability of an event A occurring, the formula is:

$$P(A) = \frac{\text{Number of outcomes favorable to } A \text{ occurring}}{\text{Total number of equally likely outcomes}} = \frac{n(A)}{n(S)}$$

For example, every letter from the word *pizza* is written down on a piece of paper and put in a hat. What is the probability that you will pick a *z*?

$$S = \{P, I, Z_1, Z_2, A\}$$
A = event of getting $Z = \{Z_1, Z_2\}$

$$P(A) = \frac{2}{5}$$

~~~~~~

COMPLEMENTARY EVENTS The complementary event is the probability that an event will not occur. This is represented as:

$$1 - P(A)$$

For example:

The probability of getting a green towel from the hamper is $\frac{1}{4}$. What is the probability of not getting a green towel?

$$P \text{ (Towel is not green)} = 1 - \frac{1}{4} = \frac{3}{4}$$

And as you get more complex, it looks like this:

A hamper contains green and blue towels. The probability of getting a blue towel is $\frac{3}{5}$. What is the probability of getting a green towel?

A = Getting a blue towel
B = Getting a green towel
A and B are complementary events.
Another way to say $P(B)$ is to say $P(A')$
$P(A') = P \text{ (Not getting a blue towel)}$
$= 1 - P(A)$

$$= 1 - \frac{3}{5}$$

$$= \frac{2}{5}$$

PROBABILITY AND AREA Problems involving probability can also have to do with finding the area to a particular geometric shape. For example:

If a dart is thrown at this circle, what is the probability it will land on the area that is shaded?

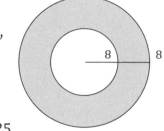

Total area: $\pi \times 16^2 = 804.25$
Area of not-shaded part: $\pi \times 8^2 = 201.06$
Area of shaded part: $804.25 - 201.06 = 603.19$, which rounded equals 603
So:

$$\frac{603}{804} = \frac{3}{4}$$

～～～～～～～～～～～～～～～～～～～～～～～～～～～～

COIN PROBABILITY To solve problems regarding probability with a coin, you have to use tree diagrams. These are very simple because they are a visual way of showing all of the possible outcomes.

If a coin is tossed 3 times, this is what it looks like:

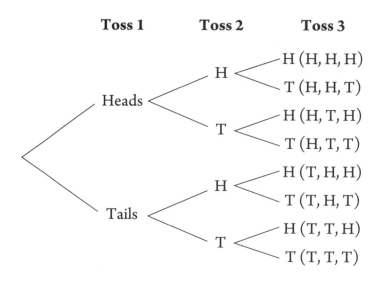

MUTUALLY EXCLUSIVE EVENTS If events cannot occur at the same time, that means they are mutually exclusive. For example, if you toss a coin and get heads, you cannot also have tails at the same time. If events are mutually exclusive, then the probability of having A or B is represented as $P(A) + P(B)$. For example:

What is the probability of rolling a die and getting a 3 or a 4?

$$P(3) = \frac{1}{6}$$

$$P(4) = \frac{1}{6}$$

$$P(3) + P(4) = \frac{1}{6} + \frac{1}{6}$$

$$= \frac{2}{6}$$

$$= \frac{1}{3}$$

So, the probability of getting a 3 or 4 when the die is rolled is $\frac{1}{3}$.

STATISTICS

MEAN In statistics, the mean is another way of saying the average. To find the average, you have to add up all of the numbers and then divide the sum by the amount of numbers that were just added together. For example:

What is the mean of these numbers? 9, 12, 14, 19, 20

First, you add all of the numbers together:
$9 + 12 + 14 + 19 + 20 = 74$
And then, since you added up 5 numbers, you divide 74 by 5:
$74 \div 5 = 14.8$

MEDIAN The median is another way of saying the middle. Before you can do anything, the numbers have to be put in order of value. For example:

> **What is the mean of the following numbers?**
> 6, 8, 10, 13, 16

Since there are five numbers, the number 10 is right in the middle, and that is our median.

However, when you have a median in between two numbers, you then take the mean of those numbers. For example:

> **What is the mean of the following numbers?**
> 9, 14, 16, 17, 19, 21

The median is between 16 and 17, so you take the mean.

$$16 + 17 = 33$$
$$33 \div 2 = 16.5$$

⌁⌁⌁⌁⌁⌁⌁⌁⌁⌁⌁⌁⌁⌁⌁⌁⌁⌁⌁⌁⌁⌁⌁⌁

MODE The mode is the number that appears most frequently. For example:

> **What is the mode of the following numbers?**
> 1, 3, 5, 9, 5, 6, 5

First, you put it in order of value: 1, 3, 5, 5, 5, 6, 9
The mode would be 5 because it appears the most.

You can have several modes in any problem. If there are no modes, then you put the numbers into groups. For example:

> **What is the mode of the following numbers?**
> 1, 3, 4, 11, 13, 21, 22

There are no modes, so you group accordingly:
0–9: 3 values; 10–20: 2 values; 20–30: 2 values

BASIC COUNTING PRINCIPLE The basic counting principle is very simple and is used to determine the number of outcomes. In essence, the principle states that when you have *A* ways to do something, and *B* ways to do another thing, then doing both would equal $A \times B$. For example:

> If there are 5 types of ice cream and 2 types of cones, then there are 10 (5×2) different combinations you can have.

This problem can also be written out with a tree diagram, which was discussed earlier in coin probability. An important thing to note about this rule is that it only works if the objects or things are independent from one another.

STANDARD DEVIATION Standard deviation, represented by σ, is the measurement of how spread out the data is. To find the standard deviation, you take the square root of the variance. The variance is the average of the squared deviations that came from the mean. To find the variance requires a few steps, but it is actually quite simple. You first must find the mean. From there, subtract the mean from each number and then square those numbers. Then, find the average of those squared numbers.

COMBINATIONS For mean, median, mode, and standard deviation, you have had to put numbers in value order. But sometimes the value order is not important. When value order is not important, it is called a combination, and this is represented as $C(n,r)$. The letter *n* represents the number of things selected at *r*. This also equals $P(n,r)/r!$

For example: If four shirts are taken from a group of eight shirts and you want to figure out how many combinations of four there could be, you would do:

$$P(8,4)/4! = (8 \times 7 \times 6 \times 5)/(4 \times 3 \times 2 \times 1) =$$
$$1,680/24 = 70 \text{ combinations}$$

KNOT THEORY

WHAT ARE MATHEMATICAL KNOTS? In mathematics, a knot is a one-dimensional closed curve or loop that does not intersect, and that exists in a three-dimensional world. More than one loop is known as a link, and the separate loops are called components. The area where the loops cross over is known as the crossing. The unknot, or trivial knot, the simplest form of a knot, is a loop with zero crossings. If two knots can move around without cutting and still look the same, these knots are considered the same. This process of moving a knot without cutting is known as ambient isotopy.

THE REIDEMEISTER MOVES In 1932, German mathematician Kurt Werner Friedrich Reidemeister worked with knot diagrams (that is, pictures of knots), and discovered a set of three moves that could make any knot diagram into any other type of knot diagram with the same knot. He came up with three rules: A strand could twist and untwist; one strand could be placed over the other strand (also known as the poke move); and a strand could be moved over or under a crossing (also known as a slide move).

WHY KNOT THEORY IS IMPORTANT Knot theory might not sound very useful at first, but it is very important in understanding some of the most complex parts of our world. Understanding knots is extremely useful in learning about enzymes that act on strands of DNA, because DNA is tangled in knots. In order for DNA to interact with enzymes, the strands must unpack. The enzymes help unpack DNA by slicing through the DNA, allowing the strands to reconnect in a less tangled manner. By thinking of DNA as a knot, one can use knot theory to understand how DNA unknots and how hard the process is, as well as understand more about enzymes.

KNOT POLYNOMIALS
A knot polynomial is an example of a knot invariant—meaning a quantity that is the same value for any equivalent knots—that is a polynomial. The most well-known knot polynomial is the Alexander polynomial, which was discovered in 1928. This was the only known polynomial knot until 1984 when the Jones polynomial was discovered. The Alexander polynomial could not distinguish handedness, meaning the objects are the same unless in a mirror reflection. The Jones polynomial, however, was able to distinguish handedness.

ADDING KNOTS
Knots become more complex through addition. The process of adding knots together is known as knot sum. Two knots can be added by cutting the knots and then joining the pairs of the ends together. The zero knot, which looks like an O, is a very special case. When more knots are added to it, though it is longer, its shape of the O remains.

TABULATING KNOTS
In knots, a crossing number is a knot invariant that is the least amount of crossings in a knot diagram of a particular knot. Knots are cataloged by their crossing number. Tables include the prime knots and one submission for a knot and its mirror image. Prime knots are the knots that cannot be expressed any more simply after knot sum. Tabulation of knots can become increasingly difficult as the number of nontrivial knots of a particular crossing number increases. John Horton Conway did the first major work verifying the process of tabulating knots.

CHAOS THEORY

WHAT IS CHAOS THEORY? Chaos theory is the mathematical study of extremely complex systems; more than that, it is the study of the unpredictable and uncontrollable. For example, the stock market, the weather, ocean currents, even migration patterns of birds are all extremely sensitive to any sort of change, and therefore cannot be predicted like other principles in mathematics and science (such as gravity or chemical reactions). Chaos theory emerged in the early twentieth century when Henri Poincaré determined that any measurement of something (such as an orbiting planet) could never be infinitely precise, even if it can be accurately predicted.

THE BUTTERFLY EFFECT Perhaps the most well-known principle to come out of chaos theory is the butterfly effect. The butterfly effect shows how even one slight change in space-time can change giant systems. For example, there is a link between a butterfly flapping its wings in one part of the world at a precise moment in time and space with a hurricane that happens on the other side of the world. The flapping of the butterfly's wings could alter the movement and strength of the wind, which in turn leads to something else. The butterfly effect proves that large systems are unpredictable.

FRACTALS A major part of chaos theory involves understanding fractals. Fractals are the shapes we see in everyday life. They are complex patterns that never end and are self-similar on other scales. A fractal can be created by repeating a process in a continual loop. Fractal patterns can be seen throughout the natural world, in mountains, trees, rivers, seashells, clouds, and hurricanes. In nature, we do not see a right triangle. We see shapes the mountains and rocks create. Using chaos theory and fractals, scientists try to uncover what makes these shapes.

STRANGE ATTRACTORS

When there is a long-term pattern within a bounded chaotic system, and it is not a simple orbit or periodic oscillation, it is known as a strange attractor. With strange attractors, patterns that are not obvious will appear. The Lorenz attractor is an example of a system that is nonlinear and dynamic. It corresponds to the Lorenz oscillator, a three-dimensional system that evolves over a pattern that doesn't repeat.

MISCONCEPTIONS OF CHAOS THEORY

There are several misconceptions related to chaos theory. Chaos theory is not about proving disorder or disproving determinism. Chaos theory is not used to show ordered systems are not possible. While chaos theory shows that slight changes can have dramatic impacts and that prediction of a state is not possible, chaos theory still states that it is plausible and possible to create a model of a system based on the behavior overall. While systems might be unpredictable, the only way to express this is with representations of a system's behaviors.

APPLICATIONS OF CHAOS THEORY

Chaos theory has many real-world applications, and has even been exploited by companies. In 1993, Goldstar Company created a washing machine that used chaos theory and made clothing cleaner and less tangled. As one large pulsator rotated, another smaller pulsator would rise and fall at random times, stirring the water. Chaos theory is also applied to understanding the stock market, to predicting weather, and even to understanding how the solar system works. Chaos theory has also been applied to learning more about the body, and can be used in attempting to control brain seizures and cardiac arrhythmias.

APPLIED MATHEMATICS

WHAT IS APPLIED MATHEMATICS? Mathematics can be separated into two categories: pure mathematics and applied mathematics. Pure mathematics is the study of completely abstract math. Applied mathematics, however, uses mathematical techniques in very real and specialized ways. It applies math to some sciences (such as physics), engineering, industry, and business. In applied mathematics, mathematical models are used to solve and work with very real problems and applications. Applied mathematics is also used in newer fields, such as computer science.

COMPUTER SCIENCE Computers are an integral part of society. Computer science is more than being able to build computers or write programs. At its simplest, computer science is about solving problems and understanding how information (which, in its smallest form, is known as a bit) is transferred through complex algorithms and algebra, logic, and combinatorics. The field of study began in the 1940s, and since then, has become a fundamental part of everyday life. Computer science can be used to understand the big bang, earthquakes, and even genetics.

SCIENTIFIC COMPUTING Scientific computing, also known as computational science, is different from computer science. Scientific computing involves creating mathematical models and performing quantitative analysis with computers to solve problems. Typically, scientific computing involves computational simulation. Unlike computer science, which studies the processing of information, scientific computing implements models on computers to receive and analyze information. Work in scientific computing is often done with supercomputers, software, and programs. Scientific computing involves numerical analysis, which uses algorithms that feature numerical approximations.

~~~~~~

OPERATIONS RESEARCH In operations research, also known as management science, models and concepts are used to improve problems relating to managerial issues or pertaining to organizations, as well as to see how effectively organizations make use of technology. There are many different techniques that can be applied to operational research, including game theory, probability theory, graph theory, statistics, and simulation. Some of the fields involved in operations research include transportation, financial engineering, marketing engineering, energy, and manufacturing. In the years following World War II, the operations research that was used for the problem-solving work of military planners expanded into the civilian sector.

~~~~~~

ACTUARIAL SCIENCE Actuarial science involves the assessment of risk and the creation of insurance policies to mitigate the risk for finance and insurance industries. Statistics, probability, finance, and economics are all used in actuarial science. Actuarial science also allows actuaries (those who work to assess risk and create insurance policies) to be able to predict income levels that would be needed for specific retirement incomes. In order to become an actuary, you must take several exams and become certified so that you can apply and perform the science.

~~~~~~

STATISTICS Though statistics is the study of organization, collection, and interpretation, it often features applied mathematics (especially when dealing with statistical procedures and research, which get improved through mathematical tests). Probability, algebra, decision theory, scientific computing, and combinatorial design are all used in statistics. Statistics can also be applied to a wide range of topics, including economics, engineering, public health, marketing, biology, education, sports, and medicine.

THE NUMBER *e*

WHAT IS *E*? The number *e*, also known as Euler's number, is one of the most famous and important irrational numbers, and it is the base of the natural logarithms. The number was first introduced in the early 1600s by John Napier, who discovered logarithms. Napier abandoned the concept of natural logarithms, instead focusing on common logarithms that had a base of 10. Leonhard Euler picked up where John Napier left off, and it was Euler who was responsible for discovering the properties of *e*. The number *e* expands infinitely, with the first values of *e* being:

$$e = 2.71828182845904523536\ldots$$

THE NATURAL BASE When looking at the graphs of the exponential functions $y = f(x) = 2^x$ and $y = g(x) = 3^x$, we see a couple of things. The function that equals 2^x begins with a higher value than the function that equals 3^x, but the value of the 3^x function starts to get higher than the 2^x function when $x = 0$. As the values of the function get larger, they grow faster and the curves get steeper. When comparing the average growth rates of the functions, the average rates of f lag behind the value of the function, and the average rates for g are always slightly higher. Both curves do not coincide with the average growth rates; however, 3^x is closer. This means that the base of the exponential function lies somewhere between 2 and 3, which is *e*. The exponential function $y = e^x$ has an equal rate of growth to its value.

NUMERICAL SERIES

The numerical value of e goes on for infinity. To find the values of e, you can use several different equations:

$$e = 1 + 1/1! + 1/2! + 1/3! + 1/4! + 1/5! + \ldots$$

$$\text{or } 1/e = 1 - 1/1! + 1/2! - 1/3! + 1/4! - \ldots$$

$$\text{or } e - 1 = 1 + 1/(1 + (1/(2 + 1/(1 + 1/(1 + 1/(4 + 1/\\(1 + 1/(1 + 1/(1 + 1/(6 + \ldots))))))))))$$

$$\text{or } (e - 1)/2 = 1/(1 + (1/(6 + 1/(10 + 1/(14 + 1/(18 + \ldots))))))$$

DISCRETE ACCUMULATION

The number e is also a very important part of understanding investments and loans. Using e, one can easily compute the limit on the effective rate (or the interest rate that is paid on an investment). For example, if you invest $100 into a bank with an annual rate of 4 percent, and your bank offers a monthly compounding, by the end of the year your investment would be worth $104.08. One can use e to figure out the limit on the effective rate. For example: $100 \times e^{0.04} = 104.08$.

HYPERBOLIC TRIGONOMETRY

The formula for a hyperbole is $x^2 - y^2 = 1$. The x and y coordinates have hyperbolic functions known as hyperbolic cosine and hyperbolic sine, which are written as $x(v) = \cosh v$ and $x(v) = \sinh v$, where v represents the area. An example of this in the real world would be the shape of a hanging necklace, known as a catenary (which can be expressed as $y = \cosh x$). Another way of writing these equations is:

$$\sinh(v) = \frac{e^v - e^{-v}}{2}$$

$$\cosh(v) = \frac{e^v + e^{-v}}{2}$$

DERANGEMENTS Derangements are related to permutations. They are solutions that are "all wrong." For example, 10 guests are about to leave your home; if you wanted to figure out how many random ways the coats could be put on, it would be a permutation of 10. The derangements are the number of times that no person gets their own coat, or everything is wrong. There are 3,628,800 different permutations and 1,334,961 derangements. If you divide those two numbers, you get e. No matter how many people there are, the odds of getting the correct coat is $1 - 1/e$.

DIOPHANTINE EQUATIONS

WHAT ARE DIOPHANTINE EQUATIONS? Named after Diophantus of Alexandria of the third century, Diophantine equations feature indeterminate polynomials, where variables are only allowed to be integers. In other words, the value of variables like x and y have to be whole numbers. Diophantine equations relate to algebraic surfaces and algebraic curves, and involve finding the values of the integers so that the equations work out correctly. Diophantus was one of the first people who introduced symbolism into algebraic formulas. While some equations have a finite solution, others have no solution at all. You've already seen plenty of Diophantine equations throughout this book.

EXAMPLES OF DIOPHANTINE EQUATIONS You have seen countless examples of Diophantine equations. The values of x, y, and z are unknown and represent real values. The Pythagorean theorem is one example of a Diophantine equation:

$$a^2 + b^2 = c^2$$

Pell's equation is another example, where n is a constant:

$$x2 - ny2 = \pm 1$$

The Erdős–Straus conjecture states:

$$\frac{4}{n} = \frac{1}{x} + \frac{1}{y} + \frac{1}{z}$$

This can also be stated as the polynomial equation:

$$4xyz = yzn + xzn + xyn = n(yz + xz + xy)$$

HILBERT'S TENTH PROBLEM In 1900, German mathematician David Hilbert created a list of twenty-three mathematical problems that had not yet been solved. His tenth problem proposed a question as to whether there was an algorithm that existed that could determine if there was a solution to any random Diophantine equation. There is an algorithm that exists for first-order Diophantine equations (meaning the variables do not have any powers greater than 1). A mathematician named Matiyasevich was able to prove in his theorem that it was impossible to create a general algorithm.

LINEAR DIOPHANTINE EQUATIONS A linear Diophantine equation is written in the form: $ax + by = c$. If the value of c is the greatest common divisor of both a and b, then there is an infinite number of solutions. A problem that meets these characteristics is known as a Bézout's identity. This is also the case when the value of c is a multiple of a and b's greatest common divisor. When the value of c is not the greatest common divisor for both a and b or a multiple of a and b's greatest common divisor, then the Diophantine equation does not have any solutions.

EXPONENTIAL DIOPHANTINE EQUATIONS When there are exponents with a variable or additional variables, it is known as an exponential Diophantine equation. For example, the Ramanujan–Nagell equation states $2^n - 7 = x^2$. There is no theory that allows one to solve these types of problems. Thus, in order to figure out the solution, one can try simple trial and error, testing out possible values and working from the solutions to see which number it should be; or one can try methods like Størmer's theorem, which is based on Pell's equation.

GENERAL METHOD TO USE FOR FIRST-ORDER EQUATIONS WITH TWO VARIABLES When given a first-order equation that has two variables, there are several steps you can take to figure it out. Instead of using x, y, and z, simplify it to x, x_2, x_3. The first step is to rewrite the equation so that it appears as $ax_2 + bx_1 = c$, so that a is larger than b. Then divide a by b, creating a quotient and a remainder (q and r). Rewrite a as $q \cdot b + r$. Now, make the equation so that the left side looks like $q \cdot$ term $+$ value $\cdot x_2$. Then replace "term" with x_3.

CATEGORY THEORY

WHAT IS CATEGORY THEORY? Category theory is an extremely complex process that takes mathematical results that already exist and abstracts them even further. Not only does this give perspective for results, but it also unifies mathematics. This can lead to some very important outcomes. Category theory can reveal that unrelated topics in mathematics have common ideas, that a proven result can create many results in other areas of math, and that extremely difficult problems can be translated into problems that are easier and relate to other fields of math. Concepts are viewed as a collection of arrows and objects that satisfy specific conditions.

FUNCTORS Categories can be thought of as even more abstract. A category is a kind of structure, and as such, one can search for processes that preserve this type of structure. Those processes are known as functors. Functors associate an object of a category with another object from another category (and with every morphism in the first, a morphism in the second is associated). Functors allow one to study the relationships among a variety of classes of structures—a fundamental concept in areas such as algebraic topology.

WHAT CATEGORIES ARE MADE OF A category, known as C, is made up of three entities. Class ob(C) features elements that are referred to as objects. Class hom(C) features elements that are morphisms (which are really arrows). The morphism (known as f) features a source object that is unique (known as a) and an object it targets (known as b), so it would be expressed as: f: $a \to b$ (which can be stated as f is a morphism from a to b). The last mathematical entity that a category is made up of is a binary operation (shown as $\circ$). This is known as the composition of morphisms, and can be broken down as follows:

$$\text{hom}(a, b) \times \text{hom}(b, c) \to \text{hom}(a, c)$$
$$f: a \to b \text{ and } g: b \to c \text{ is written as } g \circ f$$

COMPLETENESS AND COCOMPLETENESS Initial objects occur if there is exactly one morphism for every other object f: $S \to X$, while terminal objects occur if there is exactly one morphism for every other object f: $X \to T$. Objects can also go through pushout and pullback. If, in a category, all pullbacks exist and there is a terminal object, it is finitely complete. If there is a category where all pushbacks exist and it has an initial object, then it is finitely cocomplete.

NATURAL TRANSFORMATIONS A relation between two functors is known as a natural transformation. Natural transformations allow for the transforming of one functor into another functor while also respecting the arrangement of morphisms of the categories. Besides the concepts of categories and functors, natural transformation is one of the most basic concepts in category theory.

DUALITY In category theory, every theorem or definition features a dual. The dual can be found by reversing the direction of the arrows. If something is true in category C, then this means that the dual will also be true in C^{op}, or the opposite category. Similarly, if something is not true in C, then its dual is not true in C^{op}. Oftentimes, C^{op} is abstract and does not have to be a category that comes from a mathematical performance. When this is the case, the category D is said to be in duality with C when D and C^{op} are what is known as "equivalent as categories."

INFINITY

THE SYMBOL The symbol for infinity, ∞, is known as a lemniscate. This comes from the Latin word *lemniscus,* which means "ribbon." The symbol is used for the very first time in John Wallis's *Tractatus de Sectionibus Conicis* of 1655. It is unknown why Wallis chose the symbol. Some believe that it was derived from the Roman numeral for the number 1,000. This number was actually derived from the Etruscan numeral and appeared as CIↃ (this was also used at the time to mean "many"). Others believe that the symbol came from the last letter of the Greek alphabet, omega (ω).

ARISTOTLE Aristotle distinguished between two different types of infinity. There was potential infinity and actual infinity. Aristotle believed that natural numbers were potentially infinite due to the fact that they did not have a greatest number. Aristotle did not believe, however, that numbers were actually infinite, but rather that it was impossible to think of all of the natural numbers as complete. He believed that the idea of actual infinity did not make sense, and so only potential infinity was allowable. Aristotle believed actual infinity to be a paradox because it is something that is complete yet consists of an infinite amount of something.

GALILEO'S PARADOX Galileo came up with a surprising paradox relating to infinity. Galileo noticed that if you remove half of the set of equal numbers, there are as many numbers remaining in the set as before. For example, if you remove all of the odd numbers from a set, you will only have the even numbers remaining. If you then pair the natural numbers (n) with $2n$, which is even, the set that has the even numbers is equinumerous (meaning they have the same cardinality) to the set that had all natural numbers. In other words, if you had infinity, you still have infinity.

CANTOR'S SET THEORY Georg Cantor came to the realization that one cannot count to infinity, but one can compare sets to see if they are the same size by finding a one-to-one matching of the elements within the sets. The size of any set is known as cardinality. Sets are known as infinite if elements can be removed without reducing the cardinality. When there is the same cardinality as there are natural numbers, the set is called countable. Cantor's theorem states if there is a set X, there is at least one set that is raised to the power of X, and that is cardinally bigger than X.

FINITISM There is also a field of math that rejects the notion of infinity known as finitism. Finitism states that objects cannot exist unless they are constructed in a finite amount of steps from natural numbers. One of the leading researchers was David Hilbert. A concept even stronger than finitism is known as ultrafinitism. Ultrafinitists deny the existence of infinite sets of natural numbers because they can never actually be completed. Both finitism and ultrafinitism are forms of constructivism, which holds that in order to prove the existence of a mathematical object it must be constructed.

REAL ANALYSIS There are some basic formulas regarding infinity, indicating its limitlessness. For example, $x \to \infty$ and $x \to -\infty$ show that x can grow and decrease without bound. If every t is $f(t) \geq 0$, then:

$$\int_\infty^\infty f(t)\, dt = \infty$$
shows the area under $f(t)$ is infinite.

$$\int_\infty^\infty f(t)\, dt = n$$
shows that the area under $f(t)$ equals n, and thus, is finite.

$$\int_a^b f(t)\, dt = \infty \text{ shows } f(t)$$
doesn't bound an area that is finite from a to b.

PART 4

Science

EVOLUTION

CHARLES DARWIN SAILS TO THE GALAPAGOS In 1831, twenty-year-old Charles Darwin, a failing medical scholar and naturalist, sailed to the Galapagos Islands on a five-year-long trip. When Darwin landed on San Cristobal, one of the easternmost of the Galapagos Islands, he noticed something peculiar about the animals on the island. Not only were the animals different from those on the mainland; also, among the islands, animals of the same species behaved differently due to different environments.

DARWIN'S FINCHES The finches of the Galapagos laid the groundwork for understanding evolution. All of the finches Darwin saw shared many qualities. They were the same size and color and had similar habits. The most noticeable difference was the size and shape of their beaks, which was a direct result of the different eating habits the birds had on the different islands.

NATURAL SELECTION Darwin's most groundbreaking idea was his theory of natural selection, which states that when there is an environmental change, only the organisms with the traits best suited to the new environmental conditions will survive. Those organisms that do not have these desirable traits cannot compete and will die off. If enough traits change, over time, this could lead to an entirely new creature or organism.

ON THE ORIGIN OF SPECIES Darwin published his findings and his theory of natural selection in his book *On the Origin of Species* in 1859. Darwin stated that as a result of natural selection, organisms must have evolved over time, which led to the wide variety of species. He also stated that all of these organisms must have originated from a common ancestor. His beliefs about natural selection were quite controversial at the time, as the British scientific world was closely linked to the Church of England.

GENETIC DRIFT Another important aspect of evolution is genetic drift. However, unlike natural selection, genetic drift does not allow for adaptations. Rather, genetic drift happens by chance. In every generation of an organism, chance plays a key part in who lives and who dies. Some individuals may leave behind more descendants than others, meaning the genes of these organisms will be passed on. The genes will pass on simply because of luck, not because of a genetic advantage.

MUTATION Mutation is the last crucial part of evolution. Natural selection and genetic drift explain why organisms change, but they don't necessarily explain how. A mutation is a change in the DNA of an organism that affects appearance, behavior, and the organism's physiology. These mutations enable the changes that Darwin mentions. Mutations are random, and not all mutations lead to evolution. If a mutation doesn't occur in reproductive cells, it is somatic (*i.e.*, relating to the body) and it will not be passed on to offspring.

EARLY HUMANS

LUCY In 1974, a nearly complete skeleton (a total of forty-seven bones) was found by Donald Johanson in Ethiopia. This skeleton was named Lucy, and it was an absolutely incredible discovery. Lucy, who was named after the Beatles' "Lucy in the Sky with Diamonds," lived around 3.18 million years ago, and was an *Australopithecus afarensis.* She is the oldest-known humanlike hominid that proved to be bipedal, meaning she had the ability to stand up. Lucy was 4 feet tall and weighed only 50 pounds, and it is believed that she died by falling into a river or lake and drowning.

HOMO HABILIS The first real humans lived 2.4 to 1.4 million years ago in Africa and are called *Homo habilis.* The *Homo habilis* still had apelike features; however, they were taller and had larger brains than the *Australopithecus afarensis.* They also had foot and hand bones that were relatively humanlike. Simple stone tools were found along with their remains, which is the first evidence found of tool making. *Homo habilis* marks the beginning of the Stone Age, in which tools of stone were used by early humankind (*Homo habilis* means "handy man"). *Homo habilis* did not know how to make fire, however.

HOMO ERECTUS *Homo erectus* (Latin for "upright man") existed 1.89 million to 70,000 years ago. *Homo erectus* were the first humans to feature the body structure of modern humans, with shortened arms and elongated legs (however, their brains were two-thirds the size of ours). This indicates that humans were no longer tree climbers but were adapting to life on the ground, and could walk and perhaps even run. *Homo erectus* began to travel beyond Africa, migrating to other continents. *Homo erectus* were also the first to make and control fire and were the earliest hunters.

HOMO SAPIENS *Homo sapiens*, literally meaning "wise man," began to appear 250,000 years ago and evolved in Africa. These humans had much larger brains, and as a result, their skulls extended forward. *Homo sapiens,* the genus that we are currently in, is considered the earliest "modern man." *Homo sapiens* were hunters and gatherers, created tools from stone, and even sewed clothing. During this time, *Homo sapiens* lived side by side with another species, *Homo neanderthalensis,* who behaved much like *Homo sapiens.*

HOMO NEANDERTHALENSIS *Homo neanderthalensis* (or Neanderthals) were an entirely separate species from *Homo sapiens.* Neanderthals were much taller and stronger than the *Homo sapiens,* had larger brains than even current humans, and buried their dead (which is considered perhaps the first sign of religion). At around 30,000 B.C., the Neanderthals died off, and no one is certain why. Some believe *Homo sapiens* killed them all, while others believe there was interbreeding between *Homo sapiens* and Neanderthals, and eventually the one species ceased to exist. In 2010, a study discovered that traces of Neanderthal DNA were found in modern human DNA.

HOMO SAPIENS SAPIENS *Homo sapiens sapiens* existed as far back as 300,000 years ago and were spread across the world. In what is now Europe, *Homo sapiens sapiens* were known as Cro-Magnons. *Homo sapiens sapiens* made bows and arrows; constructed homes like huts and tents (used when following herds of animals); created advanced weaponry, clothing, and artwork; and improved languages. It was during the era of Cro-Magnons that the famous cave paintings of Lascaux, France, were created. Anatomically speaking, the Cro-Magnons are almost identical to modern humans of today.

THE EARTH'S LAYERS

THE CRUST The outermost layer of the Earth, the layer we are living on, is called the crust. It is the thinnest layer of the Earth, and is composed of two types of rock: granite (otherwise known as the continental crust) and basalt (also known as the oceanic crust). Basalt is found underneath the oceans, and granite is the crust of the continents. Granite is also older than basalt.

THE UPPER MANTLE The layer underneath the crust and above the core is known as the mantle. Mantle rock makes up around 84 percent of the Earth's volume. The mantle begins about 19 miles below the continental crust and 6 miles below the oceanic crust. It can be divided into two parts: the upper and lower mantle. In the upper mantle is the asthenosphere, which is involved in plate tectonic movement. Part of the lithosphere, the outermost shell of the planet, is also in the upper mantle.

THE LOWER MANTLE The lower mantle plays a key role in controlling the planet's thermal evolution; it can be found 190 to 1,800 miles below the crust, with an average temperature of 5,400°F. The lower mantle is mostly made of perovskite, a magnesium silicate mineral, which can change into a high-pressure form.

THE OUTER CORE The core of the Earth, which is about 15 percent of the Earth's volume, is made of iron-nickel, and is roughly the size of Mars. The outer core is 1,800 to 3,200 miles below the surface and is made of mostly molten iron. The temperature of the molten core ranges from 7,200°F to 9,032°F. The motions of the molten core create the Earth's magnetic field.

THE INNER CORE The inner core is 3,200 to 3,960 miles below the surface and is the hottest part of the Earth, with a temperature of 9,032°F to 10,832°F. There is so much pressure in the inner core that it is actually solid metal, which is believed to be a nickel-iron alloy. The extreme heat of the core directly affects the movement of plate tectonics and the Earth's magnetic field.

THE ATMOSPHERE The final layer is not on the ground but above it. The atmosphere is what surrounds the planet and gives life to the planet. There are several layers in the atmosphere, which is about 500 miles thick. It is composed of various gases, dust, and water. The atmosphere provides warmth and even protection from the Sun's rays and meteorites.

GEOLOGIC PERIODS

CAMBRIAN The Paleozoic era, the time period when life-forms first began to explode in diversity, started with the Cambrian Period. The Cambrian Period occurred 543 to 490 million years ago. Many significant events occurred during the Cambrian Period. The ancient supercontinent Gondwana broke apart and global temperatures began rising. Oceans were considerably higher, and though life on land was sparse, it was during this time that the first invertebrates began to appear in the oceans. While Precambrian life had soft bodies, the Cambrian Period saw the development of creatures with hard shells.

TRIASSIC The Triassic Period occurred 251 to 199 million years ago, and it was the first period of the Mesozoic Era, the time when dinosaurs first started developing. There were two major extinction events in the Triassic Period: one toward the beginning (the Permian-Triassic extinction event, which is considered the most severe extinction event of life on Earth) and one toward the end (the Late Triassic extinction event). This second period is defined by the first appearance of dinosaurs (which were no more than 15 feet tall and walked on all four legs), the first mammals (which were small and lizard-like), and flying reptiles (known as pterosaurs).

JURASSIC The Jurassic Period occurred 206 to 144 million years ago, and it is considered the middle of the Mesozoic Era. In the early part of the Jurassic Period, Pangaea broke up into northern and southern supercontinents. It was during this time that the most commonly known dinosaurs, such as stegosaurus, brachiosaurus, and allosaurus, lived. The dinosaurs that were herbivores were quite large in size, while the carnivores were smaller. Mammals were still relatively small (around the size of dogs), and the first bird, which resembled a dinosaur but had feathers, appeared.

CRETACEOUS The Cretaceous Period occurred 145 to 65 million years ago. It was the longest period found in the current eon, the Phanerozoic Eon. While dinosaurs still thrived and Pangaea continued to separate, flowering plants, new kinds of birds (which still could not fly) and mammals, as well as the first lizards and snakes, began to appear. This period ended with the K-T extinction (or the Cretaceous-Tertiary extinction), one of the largest mass extinctions, in which all of the dinosaurs and large marine reptiles died off.

TERTIARY The Tertiary Period occurred 66 to 2.6 million years ago. This period is divided into five epochs. During the first epoch, the Paleocene Epoch, the first primates started appearing. In the Eocene Epoch, aquatic mammals and modern birds started to appear. The Oligocene Epoch featured toothed whales, cats, and dogs. During the Miocene Epoch, primates, horses, camels, rhinos, and beaver-like animals started to appear. During the Pliocene Epoch, the first ancestors of modern humans, hominids, appeared, and the geography of the planet was similar to what it is today.

QUATERNARY The Quaternary Period, which continues to the present, started 2.6 million years ago and began with a great Ice

Age. This is the age dominated by human beings and mammals. During this time, the woolly mammoth, saber-tooth tiger, and other giant mammals (known as megafauna) roamed. Today, much of the remaining megafauna, such as the elephant and hippopotamus, are found in Africa. It was during the Quaternary Period that the hominids evolved into modern humans (who evolved into their current form around 190,000 years ago).

BIOMES

FRESHWATER Freshwater biomes consist of ponds, lakes, streams, rivers, and wetlands. The freshwater biome has a low concentration of salt (usually less than 1 percent); plants and animals that inhabit these types of locations would not be able to live in bodies of water with higher concentrations of salt. Ponds and lakes are often isolated from larger bodies of water, and as a result have limited wildlife diversity. Streams and rivers flow in one direction and end at the ocean. Wetlands are locations with standing water, such as marshes, bogs, and swamps. Wetlands support specific types of aquatic plants and have some of the highest amounts of wildlife diversity.

MARINE The marine biome includes the oceans, estuaries, and coral reefs. Oceans, which make up 70 percent of the entire planet, are the largest of the ecosystems and have a great variety of wildlife. Estuaries are the locations where the rivers and freshwater streams join the ocean. The ecosystem of estuaries is unique due to the mixtures of the different concentrations of salt. Coral reefs exist around warm and shallow water. These are found along continents and islands, and the most dominant lifeform is coral, which is composed of both animal polyp tissues and algae.

DESERT One-fifth of the surface of the planet is composed of desert, and rainfall is less than 20 inches a year at these locations. There are four types of desert: hot and dry, semiarid, coastal, and cold. Hot and dry deserts feature little humidity, resulting in twice the radiation from the Sun. An example of a hot and dry desert would be the Mojave Desert. Cold deserts, which are found in places like Antarctica and Greenland, are on the opposite end of the spectrum, and have cold winters with a lot of snow.

FOREST There are three types of forests: tropical, temperate, and boreal. The greatest diversity in wildlife can be found in tropical forests. These forests do not experience winter, and have only two seasons: a rainy season and a dry season. Temperate forests grow in areas with well-defined seasons that have a distinct winter (such as Wisconsin or the Adirondacks). The largest of the biomes are the boreal forests. Boreal forests (also known as taiga) are found across North America and Eurasia. There, seasons are short, moist summers are moderately warm, and winters are cold, dry, and long.

GRASSLAND When land is dominated by grass instead of trees, it is known as a grassland. There are two types of grasslands: tropical (also known as savannah) and temperate. Savannahs have trees scattered throughout and make up about half of Africa. In order for savannahs to exist, there must be hot or warm climates and rainfall of about 20 to 50 inches a year. Unlike savannahs, temperate grasslands do not have any trees and there is more variation in temperature from winter to summer. Prairies are temperate grasslands with tall grass, and steppes are temperate grasslands with shorter grass.

TUNDRA The coldest biome is known as the tundra, of which there are two types: arctic tundra and alpine tundra. Tundras are characterized by very low diversity in wildlife, very cold climates, and short growth and reproduction seasons. Arctic tundras encircle the north pole and are desert-like. Though there are several plants that thrive in arctic tundras, they do not have deep root systems. Alpine tundras are found on mountains where the altitude is so high that trees cannot grow. There, the plants and animals are similar to those found in the arctic tundra—able to withstand extremely cold environments.

WEATHER

THE WATER CYCLE   There is a limited amount of water on Earth as it is recycled again and again. This is known as the water cycle. The first step in the process is evaporation, where the Sun heats up the water until it turns into steam or water vapor, which then rises into the air. As the water vapor in the air gets cold, it turns back into water, forming clouds. This process is known as condensation. When there is so much water that the air can no longer hold it, precipitation occurs in the form of rain or snow.

CLOUDS   Clouds are large collections of droplets of ice crystals or water so small that they can float in the air. As warm air rises, it cools down and expands. Moisture begins to condense and forms water droplets. As billions of the droplets come together, they begin to form a cloud. Clouds can be classified into three groups: high-level clouds with the prefix "cirro" (which occur above 20,000 feet); mid-level clouds with the prefix "alto" (which appear between 6,500 feet to 20,000 feet); and low-level clouds with the names "strato" or "cumulo" depending on their features (which appear below 6,500 feet).

THUNDER   The sound of thunder is actually caused by lightning. As a bolt of lightning passes through the cloud, it creates a channel, or a small hole in the air. When the lightning is gone, the air collapses back in again, which creates a sound wave. Because light travels faster than sound, we see the lightning before we hear the thunder.

LIGHTNING In a thundercloud, frozen raindrops hit each other while moving around in the air. These collisions begin to form an electric charge, and soon the entire cloud is full of electrical charges. The protons form at the top while the electrons form at the bottom. A positive charge builds up below the cloud on the ground, and eventually the charges connect, creating a bolt of lightning.

WIND Wind is simply the air put in motion. Because the surface of the Earth is very dynamic and not even, the Sun's radiation is absorbed unevenly. This uneven spread of the Sun's rays makes some areas hotter than others. Warm air weighs less than cold air, and it begins to rise. Cold air then replaces the warm air as it rises, creating wind.

WEATHER FORECASTING By understanding how air masses react, one is able to predict how the weather will turn out. One way of doing this is by looking at fronts. The two basic types of front are cold fronts and warm fronts. A cold front is a mass of cold air moving into a mass of warm air. As the cold air contracts, it becomes heavier and pushes below the warm air. A warm front is the zone where warm air moves into a mass of cold air, replacing the cold air.

CLIMATE CHANGE

GREENHOUSE GASES Of the many different gases in the Earth's atmosphere, greenhouse gases are particularly important. When sunlight meets the Earth's surface, some of it radiates upward toward space as infrared radiation or heat. Greenhouse gases absorb this infrared radiation and trap its heat in the atmosphere, creating a greenhouse effect. The major greenhouse gases in Earth's atmosphere are carbon dioxide, methane, water vapor, ozone, and nitrous oxides. Without the greenhouse gases, life would not be able to survive on Earth.

THE GREENHOUSE EFFECT

The greenhouse effect is a natural process that heats the Earth's surface and atmosphere. As the energy passes through the atmosphere, 26 percent of it is reflected and scattered back into space from the clouds. The clouds absorb 19 percent of the energy and another 4 percent is reflected from the Earth's surface and sent back to space. Fifty-one percent of the Sun's energy that reaches the Earth's surface is used in a number of processes, one of which is heating the surface. The majority of this energy is absorbed by the greenhouse gases and then sent back in a continuous cycle, further heating the planet until it is no longer available for absorption.

THE ROLE OF THE INDUSTRIAL REVOLUTION

When the Industrial Revolution began, not only did it have huge effects down on the ground, in society, but it also had a huge effect up in the atmosphere. The burning of fossil fuels such as coal, gas, and oil pours greenhouse gases like carbon dioxide into the atmosphere. As a result, the Earth absorbs and holds more heat than is being radiated into space.

IMPACTS OF CLIMATE CHANGE

With the increase in greenhouse gases, the average temperature of the Earth begins to increase. Climate change can have serious effects on the planet. Oceans rise, more hurricanes develop as the temperature of the oceans increases, droughts and heat waves occur more frequently, and, in the most well-known result of climate change, the polar ice caps melt, which can throw the Earth's ecosystems completely out of balance.

~~~~~~

THE CLEAN AIR ACT The Clean Air Act, first passed in 1963, is a United States federal law enacted to control air pollution. Since 1963, it has had two significant amendments in 1970 and in 1990. In 2007, in a landmark decision, the US Supreme Court stated that climate change emissions such as carbon dioxide and greenhouse gases are air pollutants and would be subject to regulation by the EPA under the Clean Air Act if it was proven they were an endangerment to the public's health. In 2009, the EPA released its findings, declaring that climate change emissions were a danger to public health. In 2011, the House and Senate voted to block the EPA from regulating greenhouse gases and reverse the EPA's finding that greenhouse gases were an endangerment to human health and the environment. Since 2017, the Trump administration has challenged or diminished Clean Air Act regulations, weakening regulations on carbon dioxide emissions from power plants and rolling back fuel efficiency standards for new automobiles.

~~~~~~

FACT OR FICTION? Even today, debate still rages between those who do not believe climate change is real and those who see evidence that it is real. While climate change skeptics claim there is not enough evidence to prove greenhouse gases are heating the planet or will in the future, 97 percent of climate scientists agree that there is abundant proof that climate change is real and is caused by human activity. Skeptics say that reliable sources of temperature data do not show a trend of climate change; scientists counter that every part of the Earth's climate system has continued warming since 1998, with 2015 shattering temperature records. Analysis of eight years of temperature records, from 2011 to 2018, showed about 2,600 hottest versus 230 coldest temperatures on record. If we were in a stable climate, those numbers would be roughly equal. Climate contrarians say that computer models are too crude to predict the future climates;

scientists say that these models have already predicted many of the phenomena for which we have empirical evidence.

GAS LAWS

PROPERTIES OF GAS Gases have three properties: They are easily compressed, they can easily expand, and they take up more space than any liquids or solids. Gases exert pressure, and because the molecules are spread over a wide area, gas has a low density. Many properties of gas are based on five postulates that make up the kinetic molecular theory. The kinetic theory states:

- Gas is composed of molecules, and the size of these molecules is negligible compared to the distance between molecules.
- Molecules move at random in straight lines, in any direction and at a wide variety of speeds.
- Forces of repulsion and attraction between molecules is weak, except when colliding.
- There is no kinetic energy lost when molecules collide, making the collisions elastic.
- The absolute temperature of a molecule is proportional to its average kinetic energy.

BOYLE'S LAW Boyle's law, named after Robert Boyle, states that if temperature is constant, there is an inversely proportional relationship between volume and absolute pressure. The equation for Boyle's law is represented as:

$$pV = k$$

p is the pressure, V is the volume, and k is a constant, which is found by multiplying the pressure by the volume. Because there is an inverse relationship between volume and pressure, if the volume is doubled, the pressure would be inverted, which means that one-half of the pressure is being used.

CHARLES'S LAW   In the 1800s, Jacques Charles and Joseph-Louis Gay-Lussac studied how gas volume was affected by the gas's temperature. Charles's law, which is also called the law of volumes, shows that when heated, gas expands. Charles's law can be depicted as:

$$V \propto T$$

Other ways of showing this are:

$$\frac{V_2}{V_1} = \frac{T_2}{T_1} \quad \text{or} \quad \frac{V_1}{T_1} = \frac{V_2}{T_2} \quad \text{or} \quad V_1 T_2 = V_2 T_2$$

V represents the volume, and T represents the absolute temperature. In each formula, the volume of the gas increases proportionally when the absolute temperature increases.

GAY–LUSSAC'S LAW   Gay-Lussac's law builds upon Boyle's law and Charles's law, and actually represents two ideas. The first part is known as the law of combining volumes. This law states that gases combine in simple proportions (for example, water is simply two parts hydrogen and one part oxygen). The other part of Gay-Lussac's law is the pressure-temperature law. This law states that the pressure of an amount of gas at a constant volume is proportional to the absolute temperature.

This can be expressed as:

$$\frac{P}{T} = k \quad \text{or} \quad P \propto T$$

AVOGADRO'S LAW In 1811, Italian chemist Amedeo Avogadro hypothesized that two gases with the same pressure, volume, and temperature would also contain the same number of molecules, regardless of any physical or chemical properties. Avogadro's law can be written as:

$$\frac{V}{n} = k$$

V represents the volume, n represents the number of moles (or substance) in the gas, and k is a constant.

From Avogadro's law, it was determined that the ideal gas constant (k) is the same value for any gas, which means:

$$\frac{p_1 \cdot V_1}{T_1 \cdot n_1} = \frac{p_2 \cdot V_2}{T_2 \cdot n_2} = \text{constant}$$

GRAHAM'S LAW Graham's law deals with effusion, the process where molecules escape from a container by a hole and do not collide. Graham's law states that the rate of effusion is inversely proportional to the square root of the molecular masses. Graham's law can be written as:

$$\frac{\text{Rate}_1}{\text{Rate}_2} = \frac{\sqrt{M_2}}{\sqrt{M_1}}$$

Rate_1 and Rate_2 are the rates of effusion for the first and second gases, respectively, and M_1 and M_2 are the molar masses of the first and second gases, respectively.

PLASMA

WHAT IS PLASMA? The three most well-known phases of matter are solid, liquid, and gas. There is a fourth phase, however, known as plasma, and it is the most abundant form of matter in the universe even though it does not have a definite form. Plasma is matter that has a very high pressure and temperature; stars and interstellar dust feature plasma (for example, it is found on the Sun). Plasma is a combination of free electrons (which are stripped from their orbit), neutral atoms, and charged ions. Like gas and liquid, plasma is fluid; however, due to the charged particles, it both responds to electro-magnetic forces and generates electro-magnetic forces.

DEGREE OF IONIZATION
In order for plasma to exist, there must be ionization, where an atom is converted into an ion by removing and adding charged particles. Even a gas that has 1 percent ionized particles will exhibit properties of plasma. The degree of ionization, mostly controlled by temperature, is the ratio of ions to the total number of molecules. To find the degree of ionization, the formula is:

$$\alpha = n_i/(n_i + n_a)$$

where n_i represents the ion density, and n_a is the density of atoms that are neutral.

TEMPERATURES
In order to sustain ionization, extremely high temperatures are needed. (Otherwise, electrons and ions recombine, forming an atom, and the plasma turns into a gas.) Plasmas can be categorized as thermal and nonthermal. Thermal plasma has heavy particles and electrons in thermal equilibrium (meaning at the same temperature). In nonthermal plasma, electrons are much hotter, meaning they are more ionized than the ions and neutrals. The temperature of plasma is measured in kelvins, also known as electron-volts, and is the thermal kinetic energy found in each particle.

DIFFERENCES BETWEEN PLASMA AND GAS
Due to the fact that it has no definite volume or form, plasma is most closely related to gas, which shares this property. It is its own form of matter,

however, and plasma has several differences from gas. While gas has very low electrical conductivity, plasma has extremely high electrical conductivity that can be seen as infinite. While all gas particles behave similarly, in plasma, ions, electrons, neutrons, and protons all act independently. Though for gas, two-particle collisions is the general rule; for plasma, waves made of an organized movement of plasma interact over long areas.

MAGNETIZATION   When a plasma is magnetized, it features a magnetic field that is so strong it can influence the movement of the charged particles. On average, a particle completes a single gyration around the magnetic field before a collision occurs, and the electrons are often magnetized, not the ions. Magnetized plasma is known as anisotropic, meaning the direction parallel to the magnetic field has properties that are different from those that are perpendicular to the magnetic field.

EXAMPLES OF PLASMA   Even though plasma is found in the stars and Sun, there is evidence of plasma on Earth's surface. Lightning, for example, is plasma, with a temperature that can reach ~28,000 Kelvin and densities of electrons that can be up to 10^{24} m^{-3}. Fluorescent lights, sparks, flames, neon signs, plasma displays, and even aurora borealis are all examples of plasma. In neon signs, for example, a glass tube is filled with gas. As the light is turned on, the gas becomes charged by the electricity, creating plasma.

THE SOLAR SYSTEM

WHAT IS THE SOLAR SYSTEM?   The solar system consists of the Sun, Mercury, Venus, Earth, Mars, Jupiter, Saturn, Uranus, and Neptune, the moons orbiting the planets, dwarf planets, and the asteroid belt. The solar system has an elliptical shape and is always in motion. The largest object in the solar system is the Sun, around which all other objects in the system orbit. The solar system is believed to be about four billion years old.

THE PLANETS

There are eight planets in the solar system. Mercury, Venus, Earth, and Mars are known as rocky inner planets. These are smaller and denser planets that contain less gas, and are primarily composed of rock or metals. In fact, Mercury and Mars do not even have atmospheres. The other four planets, Jupiter, Saturn, Uranus, and Neptune, known as outer planets, are larger, with dense atmospheres and small cores.

THE SUN

The Sun is the center of the solar system, the closest star, and the largest object in the solar system. It makes up 99.8 percent of the mass of the solar system. The power of the Sun is produced through nuclear fusion reactions. The energy from the nuclear fusion travels into space in the form of light and heat. The surface of the Sun has a temperature of 5,800 Kelvin.

THE ASTEROID BELT

Asteroids are bits of rock that were left over after the formation of the Sun and the planets. These asteroids are most often found orbiting the Sun between Mars and Jupiter. This area is known as the asteroid belt, and more than 7,000 asteroids have been discovered in it. The total mass of the asteroids found in the asteroid belt is less than the mass of the Moon.

THE MILKY WAY

The Milky Way is the spiral-shaped galaxy that is home to our solar system. Whereas the solar system revolves around one Sun, the Milky Way contains from 100 to 400 billion other stars (with their planets and other objects in orbit). The Milky Way is just one of 100 to 200 billion galaxies that have been observed from Earth.

DWARF PLANETS Until fairly recently, Pluto was referred to as another planet in our solar system; however, it is now referred to as a dwarf planet. Dwarf planets orbit around the Sun, have a mass that gravity has turned round, cannot be satellites to other planets, and have a mass that is larger than an asteroid but not large enough to be considered a planet. Dwarf planets are not categories of planets, but rather different objects entirely. There are three dwarf planets in our solar system: Pluto, Ceres, and Eris.

THE BIG BANG

FROM NOTHING TO SOMETHING The big bang is the most widely accepted theory that explains how the universe began. Before the universe started, there was literally nothing. Then, 13.7 billion years ago, the universe came into existence. This was known as a singularity. Singularities are thought to exist inside black holes and defy the laws of physics that we understand. Black holes have intense pressure from gravity, and finite matter was squished together, forming the singularity.

THE UNIVERSE EXPANDS Once the singularity formed, it began to expand and inflate (the big bang). The big bang was not an expansion of matter in space, but rather the creation and expansion of the space that carried matter. The big bang started at extremely hot temperatures, and as it expanded, it began cooling. The universe is still expanding and cooling even to this day.

EVIDENCE FOR THE BIG BANG There are many pieces of evidence that confirm that the big bang theory is correct regarding the origins of the universe. Scientists are certain that the universe did have a beginning. Hubble's law, discovered in 1929, states that galaxies are moving away at speeds that are in proportion to their distance, which would mean that the universe was once compact and is now expanding. Scientists have also found remnants of heat traveling through the universe, which is believed to be from the initial heat of the big bang.

MISCONCEPTIONS The big bang was not an explosion, as many believe it to be. Rather, it was an expansion (which continues today). Some believe the singularity to be a ball of fire in space, but in all reality, there was no space, time, energy, or matter prior to the big bang. Space actually started in the singularity. Scientists still do not know where the singularity appeared if space did not exist.

OTHER THEORIES The big bang is not the only scientific theory regarding the origins of the universe. Physicist Robert Gentry proposed another theory in 2003, claiming that the foundation of the big bang was a faulty paradigm. Gentry's theory was based on Einstein's static-spacetime paradigm, with the notion that there is a center that neither expands nor contracts. Gentry believes this also explains the evidence that has been found.

DOES GOD HAVE A ROLE? The big bang is a controversial issue because it puts into question the role of God in the creation of the universe. While some religions have welcomed and incorporated the big bang theory into their beliefs, others have refused to believe it. In 1951, Pope Pius XII declared that the big bang theory was in accordance with Catholic beliefs.

GALILEO GALILEI

WHO WAS GALILEO GALILEI? Galileo was an Italian mathematician, physicist, philosopher, and astronomer who played a key role in the Scientific Revolution that began toward the end of the Renaissance and continued through the Enlightenment period of the eighteenth century. Galileo lived from 1564 to 1642. He is considered to be the "father of modern science," and his contributions to the world of science are still extremely relevant to this day.

THE TELESCOPE In 1609, Galileo heard news of an invention in the Netherlands that would make faraway objects appear close—the spyglass. Determined to figure out how the invention worked, Galileo tried making his own, and in only twenty-four hours, without ever having seen the object and going by only the rumors he had heard, he created a three-power telescope. After making some changes, he brought the now ten-power telescope to the Senate of Venice and demonstrated how it worked.

THE MOON During Galileo's time, the widespread belief was that the Moon was actually completely smooth and polished. As Galileo focused his new invention on the Moon, he began noticing a surface that was anything but smooth. The landscape of the Moon was rough, full of cavities and craters, and uneven. People dismissed Galileo's findings, and some even argued that the surface of the Moon was covered with an invisible layer of smooth crystal.

JUPITER By January of 1610, Galileo's telescope was thirty-power. As Galileo fixed his telescope on the stars, he began to focus on Jupiter, noticing three bright stars in a straight line near the planet. When looking the following evening, the three stars had moved to the west of the planet, while still maintaining the straight line. Over time, Galileo came to the conclusion that these were satellites of Jupiter that rotated around the planet. The implications meant that if satellites rotated around another planet, perhaps the Earth was not the center of the universe as many believed.

GALILEO AND THE CHURCH Galileo continued to discover things about the various planets, and his findings started to contradict the beliefs of the Church. Galileo was, in fact, quite religious and believed in the Bible, but he believed they were wrong in this matter and that the Bible should not be taken so literally. This led to charges of heresy from the Church. He was eventually found innocent; however, sixteen years later, he was put under house arrest until his death for a book he had written expressing Copernican theory.

COPERNICANISM AND GALILEO Galileo was a believer and teacher in Copernicanism, the idea first posed by Nicolaus Copernicus that the Earth was not the center of the universe. The ban of Galileo's book that ended in his house arrest was eventually lifted from the Catholic Church in 1822, and in 1992 the Vatican publicly and formally cleared Galileo of doing anything wrong.

THE PERIODIC TABLE

WHAT IS THE PERIODIC TABLE? The periodic table is a table displaying the various elements. There are currently 118 known elements. The elements are placed along the grid in accordance with how they look and how they act. Rows and columns also have particular meaning in the periodic table. If elements are in the same row (each row is considered a period), that means they have something in common. The elements in the center of the table are known as transition elements.

THE HISTORY OF THE PERIODIC TABLE The periodic table of today was created by Dmitri Mendeleev in 1869; however, he was not the first. In 1789, a list of thirty-three chemical elements was published. These were organized by earths, gases, metals, and nonmetals. In 1829, Johann Wolfgang Döbereiner came to the realization that based on chemical properties, elements could be gathered into groups of three, or triads. By 1869, there had been several attempts at perfecting the table, and what made Mendeleev's table so special was that it left gaps for elements not yet discovered. Also, it occasionally ignored the order by atomic weight to better classify elements into chemical families.

GROUPS The vertical columns in the periodic table are called groups. The groups are the most important way to classify elements. In the current format, the groups are numbered 1 to 18 from the left to right. Elements in a group share similar configurations of the atom's outermost electron shells. The groups are given names such as alkali metals, alkaline earth metals, halogens, pnictogens, and chalcogens, to name a few.

PERIODS The horizontal rows in the periodic table are known as periods. All the elements in a period have the same number of electron shells. Currently, the maximum number of electron shells for any type of element is seven. As you move across a period, the atomic number increases. The atomic number is the number of protons found in the atom's nucleus.

BLOCKS A set of adjacent groups is known as a block or a family. There are five blocks: s-block (the first two groups), p-block (the last six groups except for helium), d-block (the transition metals), f-block (part of the lanthanoids and actinoids), and g-block (which is hypothetical; no elements exist in the g-block yet). These blocks reflect the configuration of the electrons.

NAMES OF THE ELEMENTS The naming of the elements is complex. Sometimes it is just the first letter of the element (such as oxygen, O; or hydrogen, H); sometimes it's the beginning of the Latin word (gold is Au, from the Latin *aurum*); while other times it is named for the person who discovered it or for a whole slew of other reasons (polonium is Po, which stands for *Poland*, named after the country that the people who discovered the element were from).

CHEMICAL FORMULAS

WHAT IS A CHEMICAL FORMULA? A chemical formula is a method of expressing how a chemical appears in a simple and easy-to-understand way based on the atoms that make up chemical compounds. When writing out the elements involved in a chemical, if there is more than one atom present in a particular element, then it is indicated by a subscript number after the symbol, showing how many atoms there are. For example, water is H_2O. This means there are two hydrogen atoms and one oxygen atom present in water.

POLYMERS Polymers are macromolecules made up of structural units that repeat. When writing the formula of a polymer, you do not have to write out every one of the repeating units.

Instead, parentheses are used, followed by a subscript to show how many times it repeats. For example, in a hydrocarbon molecule $CH_3(CH_2)_{50}CH_3$, the CH_2 repeats fifty times.

IONS
Ions are atoms that have a positive or negative charge. This is due to the fact that the number of electrons in the atom is not the same as the number of protons. Ions can be represented with a superscript on the right-hand side showing whether it is positive or negative. For example, Na^+. In more complex ions, brackets are used (and parentheses can be used inside of the brackets).

ISOTOPES
Isotopes are versions of the same element with different numbers of neutrons. Isotopes are indicated with a superscript number on the left-hand side of the formula. For example, the isotope Uranium 235 is expressed as ^{235}U. The 235 refers to the number of neutrons and protons combined, or the mass number.

THE EMPIRICAL FORMULA
The empirical formula is the simplest way of expressing the ratio of the elements present in a compound. For example, the molecular formula for glucose is $C_6H_{12}O_6$. However, the empirical formula breaks that down further into its simplest form. So glucose expressed in the empirical formula is CH_2O.

THE HILL SYSTEM
Another system of writing chemical formulas is called the Hill system. With the Hill system, you first indicate the number of carbon atoms, then hydrogen, and then you go down the list of elements alphabetically. For example, uranium oxide in the chemical formula is written as U_3O_8. In the Hill system, it appears as O_8U_3. This system is commonly used for databases.

ISAAC NEWTON

ABOUT ISAAC NEWTON Sir Isaac Newton lived from 1642 to 1727. Newton is known today for developing the law of universal gravitation and the laws of motion. He also invented calculus and discovered the spectrum of colors. He attended Cambridge University in 1661 but had to return home because of a plague epidemic. Six years later, he would return to Cambridge, and in 1668, he invented the reflecting telescope. In 1687, his greatest work, *Philosophiae Naturalis Principia Mathematica* was published, in which he described the role of gravity.

~~~~~~

NEWTON'S LAW OF UNIVERSAL GRAVITATION Newton's law of universal gravitation is perhaps best known by the story of the apple falling from the tree. From noticing the apple fall, Newton concluded that a force, or gravity, must be acting on the apple. Even when the apple tree is the tallest apple tree, this force of gravity still applies. His law of universal gravitation states that every object attracts other objects with a force pointed along the line of centers for the objects. This is in proportion to the product of the masses, and is also inversely proportional to the square of the space between them.

His formula looks like this:

$$F_g = G\frac{m_1 m_2}{r_2}$$

F_g = Gravitational force
m_1 and m_2 = masses
r = distance between the masses
G = Gravitational constant

NEWTON'S FIRST LAW OF MOTION Newton's first law of motion deals with inertia. It states that objects at rest stay at rest, and objects in motion stay in a straight line at a constant speed unless an unbalanced force acts on it. If the sum of all of the forces, or net force, is zero, there will be no acceleration or change in velocity. If the net force does not equal zero, there will be acceleration and a change in velocity.

NEWTON'S SECOND LAW OF MOTION Newton's second law explains how an object's velocity will change when pushed or pulled. Newton states that if one puts force on an object, its acceleration or velocity will change in the direction you force it to. The acceleration is directly proportional to force (if you push twice as hard on something, it goes twice as fast). The acceleration is inversely proportional to the mass. His second law can be summarized as $F = ma$, where F is force, m is mass, and a is acceleration.

NEWTON'S THIRD LAW OF MOTION Newton's third law deals with more than one object. The law states that with every force, there is an opposite and equal force. In other words, for every F, there is a $-F$. If you push something, it will push back. When two objects collide, an opposite and equal force is present.

THE SPECTRUM OF COLORS Sir Isaac Newton is also responsible for discovering that white light is made up of a variety of colors in the color spectrum that are then blended together. With one prism, he was able to separate the light into a spectrum of colors, and then, using another prism, he showed that if you rejoin the colors, it will create white light. He theorized light was made up of particles, but in order to explain refraction, he associated the property of light with waves.

QUANTUM MECHANICS

WHAT IS QUANTUM MECHANICS? Quantum mechanics is the study of particles, such as protons, electrons, photons, and atoms, and their movements at the atomic and subatomic level. According to quantum mechanics, particles at such microscopic levels behave counterintuitively. There are major differences between quantum mechanics and Newton's laws, including the notion that a particle can only have one value for its energy, and only the probability of a particle's location can be determined.

HEISENBERG'S UNCERTAINTY PRINCIPLE One of the fundamental principles of quantum mechanics is Heisenberg's uncertainty principle. German physicist Werner Heisenberg came to the conclusion that every part of observing particles actually affects particles. Even the light that is shone to help physicists see affects how the particles react and change velocity. To understand a particle, it has to be measured, but measuring it affects it. To make up for this, quantum physicists have to create thought experiments that prove or disprove the interpretations of quantum theory.

BLACK BODY RADIATION A black body is the idea of something that absorbs the radiation from all of the wavelengths falling on it. It is the perfect absorber, and it appears black because it does not reflect light at normal temperatures. According to Prévost's theory of exchanges, not only is the black body the best absorber of radiation; it is also the best emitter of radiation. A black body that is hotter will emit radiation with shorter wavelengths, and will appear blue at a higher temperature and red at a lower temperature.

BOHR MODEL The Bohr Model of the atom was modified from the Rutherford model by Niels Bohr in 1915. The model features negatively charged electrons orbiting around a positively charged nucleus. According to the Bohr Model, the orbits of the electrons have a specific size and energy; energy is related to the orbit's size, with the lowest energy in the smaller orbit; and when electrons move from orbit to orbit, radiation is emitted or absorbed. There are several problems with this model, such as not taking Heisenberg's uncertainty principle into account, and it doesn't predict the intensities of the spectral lines.

SCHRÖDINGER'S CAT One of the most famous paradoxes found in quantum theory was created by Erwin Schrödinger. He proposed a theoretical experiment where a cat is placed into a steel box with a vial of a radioactive substance, hydrocyanic acid. If even one atom decays, the vial will break, and the cat will be dead. The observer, however, does not know whether the cat will be dead or alive until opening the box, and in calculations, the cat has to be considered both dead and alive. This is called quantum indeterminacy, and it means there aren't any outcomes until a measurement is observed.

THE PHOTOELECTRIC EFFECT The photoelectric effect was described by Albert Einstein, which led him to win the Nobel Prize in 1921. The photoelectric effect explains that when light shines on a piece of metal, a current will flow through it. The light provides energy to the electrons of the metal's atoms, which makes them move around and create a current. Not all lights will have this effect, however. Einstein concluded that instead of light being thought of as a wave, light was made of photons that acted like particles.

ALBERT EINSTEIN

ABOUT ALBERT EINSTEIN Perhaps one of the most famous scientists of all time, and deservedly so, Albert Einstein lived from 1879 to 1955. Einstein, born in Germany, studied physics and mathematics at Zurich, and he became a Swiss citizen in 1905. In 1909, he became a professor in theoretical physics at the University of Zurich, and a year later, he held the same position at the German University of Prague. In 1913, he was elected to the Prussian Academy of Science in Berlin, and, as he taught at the University of Berlin, he once again became a German citizen. When the Nazi party began to rise in Germany, Einstein left for the United States. He taught at the Institute of Advanced Study in Princeton, New Jersey, until his death.

THEORY OF RELATIVITY Einstein's theory of relativity can be broken up into two parts: the special theory of relativity, first published in 1905; and the general theory of relativity, published in 1915. The special theory of relativity states that regardless of total velocity, the laws of physics remain the same, and the speed of light is always constant. In other words, you cannot know whether you are moving, unless you see another object, but the laws of physics always apply. The general theory of relativity expands upon the ideas from the special theory of relativity, including gravity in the picture. This theory states you cannot know the difference between gravity and inertia, and that gravity, which acts like a force, is not one. Gravity bends space-time.

$E = MC^2$ From Einstein's special theory of relativity came one of the most famous mathematical formulas of all time: $E = mc^2$. What this means is that energy (represented by E), equals mass (represented by m) multiplied by the speed of light (represented by c) squared. The speed of light, 186,000 miles per second, is a gigantic number when squared. So, a small amount of mass will create a lot of energy. This equation essentially says that mass is another form of energy.

TOTAL ECLIPSE Light photons do not have any mass. They do, however, have energy. And according to Einstein's formula of $E = mc^2$, energy behaves like mass. This means that light from stars is also bent by the Sun's gravity. On May 29, 1919, there was a total eclipse. British astronomer Arthur Eddington studied the location of the stars during the eclipse. What he found was that Einstein's theory was in fact true; that when looking at the stars during the eclipse, it appeared as if the stars had changed positions, and that the Sun's gravitational field was in fact affecting the light.

BROWNIAN MOTION In 1905, Einstein's third paper concentrated on the random movement of small particles in liquids and gases. Brownian motion gets its name from Robert Brown, who in 1827 reported on the motion of pollen particles in water. Brown, however, was never able to figure out why the motion happened. Einstein concluded that the motion was due to water molecules hitting the pollen. Though the pollen grains were visible, the water molecules weren't, and so it appeared that these particles were jiggling. Einstein was also able to show the speed the water molecules were moving in and how many molecules hit a single grain of pollen, as well as what properties of atoms could be tested.

EINSTEIN'S BRAIN Albert Einstein died on April 18, 1955, at the age of seventy-six. His body was cremated, but his brain was saved for research. Up until 1999, scientists concluded that Einstein's brain was really no different than any other person's brain. In 1999, however, it was discovered that Einstein's brain lacked a certain wrinkle, called the parietal operculum. To compensate for this missing wrinkle, other sections of his brain, such as the inferior parietal lobe, had to compensate. This part of the brain plays a role in mathematical thinking and visual imagery.

STRING THEORY

THEORETICAL PHYSICS In theoretical physics, math is used to explain aspects of nature. Often, the formulas that are designed cannot be tested with an actual model, which is what separates theoretical physics from empirical physics. A theoretical physics theory should accurately explain and predict certain phenomena with support from known observations. String theory is one of the most well-known theories in theoretical physics, and it is often known as the "theory of everything." String theory tries to explain how gravity fits with quantum physics.

STRINGS AND MEMBRANES When string theory was first developed in the 1970s, it was believed that strings, little filaments of energy, were one-dimensional, and came in two forms: open and closed (think of one rubber band that is broken, and another that is not). These strings, known as Type I strings, could go through five different types of interactions. Physicists believe the closed strings could describe gravity. Later, it was discovered that, in addition to strings, branes were involved. Branes are sheets that the strings attach one or both ends to.

QUANTUM GRAVITY There are two basic laws in modern physics that represent two very different areas of study: general relativity and quantum physics. General relativity studies nature on a grand scale, studying planets, galaxies, and the entire universe.

Quantum physics, on the other hand, focuses on the smallest objects that can be found in nature. String theory is an attempt to unite these two very different theories, and any theory that does so is known as a theory of quantum gravity. It is believed that string theory has the most promise to unite the two.

UNIFICATION OF FORCES There are four fundamental forces found in the universe that string theory attempts to unify: gravity, weak nuclear force, strong nuclear force, and electromagnetic force. Currently, these are four completely separate and different phenomena. String theorists believe that string theory is what unifies these forces. They believe that all four of these forces are described by strings that interacted with one another in the early stages of the universe, when energy levels were extremely high.

SUPERSYMMETRY There are two types of particles in the universe: fermions and bosons. In string theory, it is hypothesized that there is a connection between these two types of particles called supersymmetry, and that for one to exist, the other has to also exist. The idea of supersymmetry was actually discovered separate from string theory, and in the mid-1970s, it was incorporated into the theory, turning it into superstring theory. As scientists have yet to observe the particles, supersymmetry is still a theoretical assumption. Scientists believe supersymmetry to be the case because of how much energy it takes to make the particles; as energy spread due to the big bang, the particles would have collapsed into lower energies.

EXTRA DIMENSIONS Our universe currently has three dimensions of space: up/down, front/back, and left/right. String theory, however, can only make sense if there are more than three dimensions. And scientists have possible explanations for where these extra dimensions are. One explanation posits that there are six dimensions, which are curled up into sizes so small that we will never identify them. Another explanation states that the other dimensions are inaccessible because we are fixed on a three-dimensional brane, and those other dimensions extend off of our brane.

PHOTOSYNTHESIS

WHAT IS PHOTOSYNTHESIS? Photosynthesis is the process that plants and some bacteria perform to convert the energy that comes from sunlight into usable energy. The sunlight is first turned into a sugar, and then through a process called cellular respiration, the sugar is turned into adenosine triphosphate, known as ATP, a form of energy. Plants require water and carbon dioxide, and as a result of photosynthesis, oxygen is released into the atmosphere. Without photosynthesis, life would not exist. The process of photosynthesis can be summarized as:

$$6CO_2 + 6H_2O \rightarrow 6(CH_2O) + 6O_2$$

The products are $6(CH_2O)$, which is energy in the form of sugar and oxygen.

LEAF STRUCTURE The main organs for plants to perform photosynthesis are leaves. Leaves play a critical role in allowing carbon dioxide and water in and oxygen and sugar to escape. As water comes in through the roots of the plant, it is transported to the leaves via cells. A waxy layer, called the cuticle, covers the leaf. This waxy layer prevents carbon dioxide from coming in and oxygen from going out. As a result, leaves have tiny openings called stomata (*stoma* is the singular term), which allow the carbon dioxide to pass and the oxygen to enter.

CHLOROPLAST AND CHLOROPHYLL Plant cells have specialized organelles known as chloroplasts that are not found in animal cells. The chloroplasts make sugar and starch through photosynthesis. They also contain the molecule chlorophyll, which is a pigment that absorbs the energy of light and gives plants their green color. As the sunlight hits the plant, all of the wavelengths are absorbed except for green, which gets reflected back. When the light hits the chloroplast, the chlorophyll uses the Sun's energy to combine water and carbon dioxide, which leads to the creation of sugar and oxygen.

LIGHT REACTIONS There are two stages to photosynthesis: the light-dependent process (also known as light reactions) and the light-independent process (or dark reactions). Light reactions are the processes that occur in the chloroplasts and thylakoids, in which light energy is absorbed by the chlorophyll and converted into chemical energy. During this process, water is split and oxygen is released. Light reactions have two photosystems (photosystem I and photosystem II) that harvest the light. The chlorophyll in photosystem I is the stronger absorber of the light. The two products to come out of light reactions are ATP and $NADPH_2$.

DARK REACTION The light-independent process (or dark reaction) occurs in the stromata of chloroplasts and takes carbon dioxide from the atmosphere and turns it into glucose with the ATP and $NADPH_2$ from the light-dependent process. For this process to occur, light is not necessary, and no matter how much light is available, the process can continue. A 5-carbon sugar is combined with carbon dioxide, creating a 6-carbon sugar. This sugar is then broken into fructose and glucose, which sucrose is composed of.

THE CARBON CYCLE As animals produce carbon dioxide from breathing, plants take in the carbon dioxide and use it to make organic nutrients. The plants are then eaten by an animal (transferring the carbon), and then that animal is eaten by another animal (once again transferring the carbon). When plants and animals die and their bodies start to decay, carbon enters the ground. Some of that carbon will be buried and eventually turn into fossil fuel. As humans use fossil fuels, carbon is released into the atmosphere in the form of carbon dioxide gas. The carbon then travels from the atmosphere into the oceans and other bodies of water.

CELLS

THE BASIC UNIT OF LIFE The cell is the smallest unit of life in an organism's body. Each cell has its own unique feature and function. Some organisms, like humans, animals, and plants, are multicellular, meaning they are made of many, many cells (for humans the number is in the trillions). However, other organisms, such as bacteria, are unicellular and consist of a single cell. Both animals and plants are eukaryotes, meaning their cells have a well-defined nucleus.

PROKARYOTIC AND EUKARYOTIC CELLS There are two basic types of cells: prokaryotic and eukaryotic. *Prokaryotic* means "before a nucleus," and *eukaryotic* means "possessing a true nucleus." Prokaryotic cells have no nucleus, are usually single-celled organisms, and were the first organisms to live on Earth. Bacteria are prokaryotic cells. On the other hand, eukaryotic cells have a nucleus and organelles, and are the types of cells found in humans, plants, and animals.

PLANT CELLS Though structurally similar, there are some major differences between the cells found in plants and those found in animals. Plant cells have very rigid walls made of cellulose and contain chloroplasts. Chloroplasts, which contain chlorophyll, utilize the Sun's light and enable the process of photosynthesis. They are also responsible for the green color found in plants. Plant cells have a large central vacuole and contain, within their cell walls, linking pores that connect to transmit the information.

ANIMAL CELLS Animal cells are much smaller than plant cells and do not have the rigid cell walls that plant cells have. This allows animal cells to take on various shapes. While plants have the ability to make their own food with chloroplasts and sunlight, in animal cells, it is the role of the mitochondria to get energy from food that is consumed.

STRUCTURE OF A CELL The plasma membrane is the outer lining of a eukaryote cell. It protects the cell from the surrounding environment and is composed of lipids and proteins. The nucleus inside of the cell is surrounded by a membrane that separates it from the cytoplasm. Two kinds of genetic material, DNA and RNA, exist inside the cell. The cell's chromosomes are in the nucleus, which is also the location for RNA synthesis and DNA replication.

THE NUCLEUS The nucleus is responsible for regulating all activity in eukaryotic cells. It contains the hereditary information (DNA and RNA) and controls growth and reproduction. The most prominent structure in the nucleus is called the nucleolus. The nucleolus produces ribosomes, which play a critical role in protein synthesis. These proteins are used for a variety of purposes, including, but not limited to, structural support and enzymes to catalyze a reaction.

THE NERVOUS SYSTEM

WHAT IS THE NERVOUS SYSTEM? The nervous system is a complex system that is responsible for sending every electrical impulse and signal throughout your body. These signals are what cause any and all actions, reactions, and thoughts you have, as well as anything you feel. The nervous system is made up of two systems: the central nervous system and the peripheral nervous system.

NEURONS The nervous system works via nerve cells, or neurons. These cells process and transmit information through chemical and electrical signaling. What makes neurons different from other cells is that they have very specialized extensions called axons and dendrites. Dendrites receive information, and the axon carries the message to target cells.

THE CENTRAL NERVOUS SYSTEM The central nervous system consists of two of the most important parts of the nervous system: the brain and the spinal cord. The brain is considered to be the command center of the nervous system, since it controls all of the workings of your body. The central nervous system collaborates with the peripheral nervous system in controlling the behavior of the body.

THE PERIPHERAL NERVOUS SYSTEM The peripheral nervous system consists of the nerves that receive and send the information from the central nervous system. There are two types of nerves: motor nerves, which send signals from the brain to different tissues in the body; and sensory nerves, which receive information in the form of pain, heat, or touch, and then send those impulses to the central nervous system.

THE SOMATIC NERVOUS SYSTEM

THE SOMATIC NERVOUS SYSTEM The somatic nervous system, or voluntary nervous system, is part of the peripheral nervous system. It is responsible for processing sensory information—such as pain, heat, and touch—from an external stimuli, and controlling the voluntary muscular systems. The somatic nervous system allows a person to receive sensory information and react to environmental changes and part of the autonomic nervous system.

THE AUTONOMIC NERVOUS SYSTEM The autonomic nervous system, which is part of the peripheral nervous system, controls involuntary body functions. Two aspects of the autonomic nervous system are the sympathetic nervous system, which is responsible for causing the fight-or-flight reaction; and the parasympathetic nervous system, which regulates more mundane processes in nonemergency situations, causing the body to rest and relax.

THE DIGESTIVE SYSTEM

THE MOUTH When a person eats, the saliva in their mouth has enzymes that start to break down the chemicals in the food. As your teeth chew the food, you begin to break it down into a mushy substance. The tongue then rolls this substance into a ball, and the food is now called bolus, meaning a substance that is broken down to the point that is ready to be swallowed.

THE ESOPHAGUS The tongue pushes the food to the back of the throat, toward the opening of the esophagus. The esophagus is a pipe responsible for moving food from the throat to the stomach. When a person swallows, a little flap called the epiglottis closes the windpipe, ensuring the food goes down the esophagus. Along the walls of the esophagus, muscles squeeze the food until it reaches the stomach.

THE STOMACH The stomach has three roles: to store food, to break down the food into chyme (a semifluid paste), and to empty the chyme into the small intestine. The stomach breaks down the food with the help of gastric juices that line the walls of the organ. The gastric juices start breaking down the food into its essential nutrients, and kill any harmful bacteria that may be in the food.

THE SMALL INTESTINE From the stomach, the food enters the small intestine, an organ that, when stretched out, is 22 feet long in an adult. The small intestine, which breaks down the food further, is where the major amount of absorption of nutrients takes place. The nutrients are then sent to the liver, while what's left of the food is passed on to the large intestine.

THE LARGE INTESTINE The large intestine measures five feet long and is fatter than the small intestine. The small intestine passes waste on to the large intestine. There is no longer any nutritional value to the substance, so the body can't use it and it must be taken out. The substance passes through a part of the large intestine called the colon, which is the last chance for the body to absorb any water or minerals. The result is feces, solid waste that the large intestine then pushes to the rectum.

OTHER ORGANS The liver, gallbladder, and pancreas also play a key role in the digestive system. These organs send digestive juices to the small intestine. The pancreas is responsible for sending juices that digest protein and fat. Bile, a substance created by the liver but stored in the gallbladder, absorbs fat in the bloodstream. The nutrient-rich blood is then sent to the liver, where waste is filtered out.

THE RESPIRATORY SYSTEM

INHALATION The function of the respiratory system is to supply the blood with oxygen, which is then transferred to the rest of the body. Oxygen is received through breathing. The oxygen enters through the nose and mouth. From there, it goes through the larynx and trachea to the chest cavity, where the trachea then splits into small tubes called bronchi. The bronchus then divides once more, creating bronchial tubes, which lead to the lungs.

EXHALATION Inside of the lungs are tiny sacs called alveoli. The inhaled oxygen passes through the alveoli and then diffuses into the arterial blood through the capillaries. As this is happening, the veins send waste-laden blood carrying carbon dioxide into the alveoli, and this carbon dioxide comes out as you exhale. Both inhalation and exhalation are made possible by the diaphragm muscle, which contracts and relaxes below the lungs.

THE LUNGS The surface area of the lung is larger than the surface area of your skin. If you were to line up all of the airways and air sacs inside of the lungs, the distance would cover more than 100 square yards. The lungs are the second line of defense (the first is the nose and throat) against harmful materials that are inhaled. Mucus is produced inside of the lungs, which traps inhaled agents and provides white blood cells for protection.

THE NOSE AND NASAL CAVITY The nose and throat are the first line of defense when it comes to protecting the respiratory system. As air is inhaled through the nose, the dirt is cleaned by the hairs in the nose, and further cleaned by mucus. The nasal cavity is lined with tissue that consists of many blood vessels. These blood vessels provide heat, which warms the air as it is breathed in. The nasal cavity also adds moisture to this air, making it suitable for the lungs.

ASTHMA Asthma is a chronic inflammatory disease of the lungs, in which the airways tighten and narrow. It is the number one reason children chronically miss school, and it affects more than 235 million people in the world. Asthma flares occur when the muscles contract and the lining of the airways starts to swell. This prevents proper airflow, which can result in wheezing, difficulty in breathing, and sometimes death.

CHRONIC OBSTRUCTIVE PULMONARY DISEASE Unlike asthma, which can be treated with medications, chronic obstructive pulmonary disease (COPD) is a narrowing of the airways that will gradually grow worse over time. It is a co-occurrence of emphysema and chronic bronchitis that is usually caused by an irritation of the lungs. The most common cause of COPD is smoking cigarettes. This can lead to wheezing, shortness of breath, a rapid breathing rate, and a chronic cough. Symptoms usually don't appear until significant lung damage has occurred.

THE CIRCULATORY SYSTEM

WHAT IS THE CIRCULATORY SYSTEM? The circulatory system consists of the heart, blood, and blood vessels. It is the body's transportation and cooling system. Your blood moves from the heart via arteries, and to your heart via veins, delivering oxygen and nutrients throughout your body. The blood also picks up any waste products in your system in order for the body to get rid of them.

THE HEART

The heart is a muscle roughly the size of a clenched fist. It is two-sided and has four chambers. Blood enters the heart through the right atrium. The right ventricle pushes the deoxygenated blood to the lungs. The left atrium then receives the oxygenated blood from the lungs and pumps it to the left ventricle of the heart, which is responsible for pushing the blood out of the heart and into the body's circulation.

RED BLOOD CELLS

Blood is constantly flowing through our bodies and carries oxygen, nutrients, water, and waste products to and from our cells. Red blood cells carry oxygen and carbon dioxide. After picking up oxygen from the lungs and delivering it to the cells, the red blood cells transport the carbon dioxide to the lungs, through which it is then exhaled.

WHITE BLOOD CELLS

White blood cells fight germs. During an infection, the body produces more white blood cells that will then try to attack and destroy the infection. When someone is prescribed an antibiotic, it is because the white blood cells need help fighting off the infection.

THE AORTA AND ARTERIAL SYSTEM

The aorta is the largest artery in the body. It originates from the left ventricle and distributes the oxygenated blood. From the aorta, the blood is then sent to the other arteries and arterioles, which are small arteries that deliver oxygen and nutrients to all of the cells in your body. At the end of the arterioles are capillaries, which pass the blood through the venous system.

THE VENOUS SYSTEM The venous system is responsible for bringing the blood back to the heart. From the capillaries, the blood flows through small veins called venules, and from there, the blood then flows to the veins. The superior and inferior venae cavae are the two largest veins in the body, and both end in the right atrium. The superior vena cava enters at the top of the heart while the inferior enters from the bottom.

TISSUES

WHAT IS TISSUE? In the body, specific cells group together to perform a certain specialized function, creating tissue. When many tissues group together to carry out a specific function, it becomes an organ. In animals, there are four types of tissue found in the body: epithelial tissue, connective tissue, muscle tissue, and nervous tissue.

EPITHELIAL TISSUE Epithelial tissue is tissue that covers the entire body, and it forms the covering or lining of internal and external surfaces. It is made up of closely packed cells formed into one or many layers, with close to no intercellular spaces and little intercellular substance. The endothelium is the tissue on the surface of the internal cavities, and its main function is for absorption, excretion, protection, secretion, reproduction, and sensory reception.

CONNECTIVE TISSUE Connective tissue supports and binds to other tissues in the body. It is the framework on which epithelial tissue rests, and it is what nerve and muscle tissues are embedded in. The major cells involved in immunological defense are also found in the connective tissue, and connective tissue is where inflammation, the body's defense against invading microorganisms, occurs.

MUSCLE TISSUE Muscle tissue can contract and conduct electrical impulses and allow the body to move. Muscle is classified as voluntary or involuntary, and smooth or striated. There are three types of muscle tissue: skeletal muscle (which is voluntary, striated, and attached to the bone); cardiac muscle (which is involuntary, striated, and found in the heart); and smooth muscle (which is involuntary, smooth, and found in the digestive system, respiratory system, eyes, and the walls of blood vessels).

NERVOUS TISSUE Nervous tissue is made up of neurons (cells that transmit messages) and neuroglia cells (cells that protect the neurons). Nervous tissue is the main part of the nervous system; it is specialized to conduct impulses and react to various stimuli. Nervous tissue consists of the brain, the spinal cord (making up the central nervous system), and the peripheral nerves (making the peripheral nervous system).

ORGANS Organs are groups of tissues that work together to perform a specific function. In organs, there is usually a main tissue called the parenchyma, which is unique to the specific organ; and sporadic tissues called the stroma, such as connective tissue or blood. Groups of organs that work together to perform a specific function form organ systems.

REPRODUCTION

THE HUMAN REPRODUCTIVE SYSTEM The reproduction system is a system of organs that work together to allow humans to reproduce. In order for reproduction to occur, two different types of reproduction systems must be present: the male reproduction system and the female reproduction system. The differences between these systems allow for the genetic material of both individuals to be passed on to the offspring.

GAMETES There are two types of gametes, or sex cells, involved in human reproduction. The male gamete is called the sperm and the female gamete is called the ovum, or egg. The gametes are produced in organs called gonads. In the male, the sperm is produced in the testes, and in the female, the ovum is produced in the ovaries. Each gamete carries twenty-three chromosomes. The ovum carries only an X chromosome, and the sperm can carry either an X or a Y chromosome. During sexual intercourse, the gametes come together in fertilization. If both have an X chromosome, the zygote will grow to become a female. If the sperm has a Y chromosome, the zygote will become a male.

THE MALE REPRODUCTIVE SYSTEM The role of the male reproductive system is to produce semen, which transports the sperm during sexual intercourse. The external structures of the male reproduction system include the penis, the organ used during sexual intercourse; the scrotum, a sac that holds and moderates the temperature of the testicles; and the testicles, which make testosterone and generate sperm. There are several internal structures involved in the male reproduction system including the epididymis, a tube that transports, stores, and matures the sperm; and the vas deferens, a tube that transports the mature sperm to the urethra, which gets urine and semen out of the body.

THE FEMALE REPRODUCTIVE SYSTEM The female reproductive system is responsible for producing the egg cells and hormones, and transporting the egg cells to the site of fertilization; if conception occurs, the beginning stages of pregnancy take place. If fertilization does not happen, the system is designed to shed the uterine lining, or menstruate. The female reproductive system is located internally in the pelvis and consists of the vagina, the cervix, the uterus (the major organ that accommodates the growing fetus and pushes the fetus out during delivery), the fallopian tubes (the source of fertilization), and the ovaries.

FETAL DEVELOPMENT

FETAL DEVELOPMENT Immediately upon fertilization, the sex of the child is determined. In the first four weeks, neural tubes, the foundation of the nervous system, will develop, and the heart and a primitive circulatory system will form. By the third week, the embryo has developed along with a placenta, and the heart begins to beat. By day forty, the embryo is the size of a raspberry and has five fingers on each hand, and brain waves can be detected. By week twelve, the fetus breathes amniotic fluid, exercises, sleeps, awakens, and can open and close its mouth. By week twenty-one, the fetus now weighs 1 pound. By week thirty-six, the baby will weigh anywhere from 6 to 9 pounds. By week thirty-eight, its heartbeat can be heard from outside of the womb, and the baby is ready to come out.

ASEXUAL REPRODUCTION What was just described was reproduction for humans; however, plants and even certain animals reproduce in a different way—asexually, or without a mate. This is done through mitosis. Mitosis is a process of cell division that involves replicating chromosome material. During asexual reproduction, genetic mixing does not happen, and it is sometimes referred to as cloning because the copies are identical.

GENETICS

GREGOR MENDEL'S PLANTS Austrian monk Gregor Mendel is considered to be the father of genetics. In 1856, Mendel conducted a series of studies on pea plants where he observed seven traits in the plants: the color and shape of the seed, the color of the flower, the color and shape of the pod, the position of the flower, and the height of the plant. Mendel performed tests in hybridization and cross-pollination and found that the first generation of plants only resembled one parent, but in the next generations, dominant and recessive traits appeared.

MENDEL'S LAWS OF INHERITANCE

From his findings, Mendel came up with three laws regarding inheritance. The law of dominance states that if there is a pair of genes, the one that appears in the offspring is most likely the dominant one because that is passed on more often than the recessive gene. Mendel's principle of segregation states that an individual inherits an allele (or a unit of information) about a trait from both parents, and during the formation of the gamete, these alleles segregate from one another. Mendel's law of independent assortment states that the factors for characteristics are distributed independently to the reproductive cells.

INHERITANCE PATTERNS

There are three types of inheritance patterns: single-gene inheritance, multifactorial inheritance, and mitochondrial inheritance. These are all useful in understanding disease. In single-gene inheritance, also known as Mendelian inheritance, a single gene is mutated and then follows the predictable pattern of inheritance. In multifactorial inheritance, it is not due to a single gene but rather several genes and environmental factors. In mitochondrial inheritance, disease is transmitted by the mitochondria, organelles that are inherited only from the mother's egg.

DNA

Deoxyribonucleic acid, or DNA, is a double-helix structure that carries all of the genetic information and is the hereditary material. The double-helix structure is crucial in genetics.

DNA can copy and replicate itself, and each strand in the double helix serves as a pattern for duplication. When cells divide, each new cell gets an exact copy of the old cell's DNA.

GENE EXPRESSION Gene expression is the process of converting the gene's information into messenger RNA (mRNA) through a process called transcription, and then converting the information to a protein in a process called translation. Gene expression is responsible for interpreting the genetic code in the DNA, which gives rise to the organism's traits or phenotype.

GENETIC MUTATIONS Genetic mutations are permanent changes found in the genetic sequence of an organism that alter the nucleic acids, which alter the DNA. Mutations are the main cause of diversity and can lead to evolution, but they can also lead to genetic diseases and cancers. Mutations can either be inherited by parents, or can occur during an organism's lifetime.

MITOSIS

PROPHASE If you recall from the discussion on asexual reproduction, mitosis is cell division. Following interphase, which prepares the cell for division, the next step in the cycle is prophase. In prophase, the chromatin will condense and become chromosomes, which have duplicated and now have sister chromatids. The chromatids are identical to each other and are connected, forming an X. The mitotic spindle, which moves the chromosomes, is formed and set up away from the nucleus. By the end of this step, the nuclear envelope is broken down into vesicles.

METAPHASE In metaphase, chromosomes are aligned along the middle of the nucleus of the cell and are held in place by microtubules of spindle fibers. This is known as the metaphase plate. Chromosomes are oriented so that kinetochores, a protein structure on the chromosomes, are facing the pole, and each tail of the chromosomes are facing each other. The organization allows for the new nuclei to receive a single copy of each chromosome when separation occurs (in the next phase).

ANAPHASE The chromosomes that are paired begin to separate at the kinetochores. The kinetochores then start to move toward the poles. Once this has happened, the polar fibers will elongate, which starts to spread the poles farther apart from one another. The sister chromatids then separate and move toward their related poles.

TELOPHASE Once the chromatids have reached their opposite poles, new membranes begin to form around the sets of chromosomes, forming two nuclei. These two nuclei are, for the time being, in the same cell. RNA synthesis occurs and the nuclear envelope reappears, which then breaks down the chromosomes to the point that they can no longer be viewed with a light microscope.

CYTOKINESIS Technically, cytokinesis is not a part of mitosis; rather, it completes the cell division. After telophase, there are two nuclei in a single cell. All that is left is for the cell to divide in half. Cytokinesis actually begins during anaphase and continues simultaneously through telophase. The cell first begins to furrow, a process where it starts pinching in. The cell pinches until there are two daughter cells, each with its own nucleus. These two cells will then continue the cycle.

MEIOSIS Meiosis is a cell division that occurs to produce germ cells like the sperm and egg, and thus is a necessity for sexual reproduction. In meiosis, a copy of the mother's chromosomes and a copy of the father's chromosomes are taken. Four haploid cells are produced, each with one copy of a chromosome. This process is responsible for creating genetic diversity, because each cell has its own unique combination of chromosomes. A single parent cell will create four daughter cells, and each daughter cell has half the amount of chromosomes as the parent cell.

STEM CELLS

WHAT ARE STEM CELLS? Stem cells are a very special type of cell; during their early life and growth stages, they can actually develop into many different types of cells. Another important feature of stem cells is that in a living body, they can be used as a repair system and divide infinitely, replenishing the other cells. During division of stem cells, the new cells can either turn into different types of cells that have a specific function or they can remain as stem cells. Under certain conditions, stem cells can actually turn into tissue or become organ-specific cells that carry out particular functions.

UNIQUE PROPERTIES OF STEM CELLS Stem cells are not like any other cells found in the body, and they have three properties, no matter the source. Stem cells have the capability to divide and renew themselves over long periods of time, a characteristic that blood cells, muscle cells, and nerve cells do not have. Stem cells are not specialized, meaning they do not have functions like carrying oxygen or pumping blood. Instead, they create specialized types of cells. The process of creating a specialized cell from an unspecialized cell is known as differentiation.

EMBRYONIC STEM CELLS The stem cells taken from embryos are known as embryonic stem cells. These cells are mostly derived from the embryos of eggs fertilized in vitro, which are then donated for further research. These cells are then grown in the laboratory. If grown under proper conditions, embryonic stem cells can remain undifferentiated. If they begin clumping together, they will differentiate spontaneously and begin to form various types of cells. When scientists attempt to generate a specific type of cell, they control the differentiation. Today, scientists have "recipes" that tell them how to make particular cells.

ADULT STEM CELLS Adult stem cells are undifferentiated cells that exist around differentiated cells in a tissue or organ and have the ability to renew and differentiate to create some or all of the specific types of cells in the tissue or organ. In living organisms, stem cells repair and maintain the tissue they exist in. The embryonic stem cell is derived from the embryo, but scientists still do not know where the adult stem cells are derived from. They have been identified in the brain, heart, teeth, skin, skeletal muscle, testes, ovarian epithelium, liver, blood vessels, peripheral blood, and gut.

INDUCED PLURIPOTENT STEM CELLS An induced pluripotent stem cell (iPSC) is an adult cell that is reprogrammed into an embryonic cell-like state with the use of viruses. This is done by forcing the cell to express factors and genes that are necessary for keeping the important properties of embryonic stem cells. Scientists do not know if embryonic stem cells and iPSCs differ in any important ways. Use of iPSCs has been very important in developing drugs and modeling diseases. Scientists hope to use iPSCs with transplantations. Using the viruses to change the adult cells needs further studying, however. Scientists have noticed that introduction of the viruses can cause cancers.

USES OF STEM CELLS Stem cells can be used for a wide variety of things. Human stem cells can be used when testing drugs. For example, stem cells are currently used for screening anti-tumor drugs. Perhaps the most impressive way stem cells can be used, however, is for cell-based therapies. Stem cells offer the possibility of renewing and replacing cells and even generating tissues. This would allow treatment of ailments and diseases such as Alzheimer's, stroke, heart disease, burns, diabetes, rheumatoid arthritis, and osteoarthritis by healing destroyed tissue.

DNA

WHAT IS DNA? Deoxyribonucleic acid, or DNA, is the genetic makeup of each cell in our body, and every characteristic of any living organism and most viruses. Almost every single cell in the body has the same DNA. The DNA is located inside of the nucleus of the cell (called nuclear DNA), though some DNA can also be found in the mitochondria (which is known as mDNA or mitochondrial DNA). Information is stored in the DNA as a code of four chemical bases. The bases are guanine (G), adenine (A), thymine (T), and cytosine (C). There are around 3 billion bases in human DNA. Of those bases, 99 percent are the same in every human.

STRUCTURE DNA is a double-helix molecule that consists of two chains. A single chain is a strand that is made up of a large amount of nucleotides, or chemical compounds, that are linked together. The nucleotides are made up of three things: deoxyribose (a sugar molecule in the center of the nucleotide), a phosphate group (which links to the deoxyribose of the other chain), and one of the bases (A, G, T, or C). When the two chains come together, they form the double-helix shape. Bases are always paired accordingly: A with T and C with G.

PROTEIN SYNTHESIS Inside the DNA are instructions for how to produce protein. Proteins are made up of amino acids, which also determine the function and structure of the protein. The sequence of nucleotide bases in the DNA determine the sequence of amino acids. A triplet (three nucleotide bases) specifies an amino acid. GAC, for example, is the codon (genetic code) for leucine. When the DNA molecule separates into two strands, protein synthesis occurs. Transcription begins, where a part of the strand turns into a template for a new strand, known as messenger RNA. This RNA then attaches to ribosomes, and through translation, amino acids are linked and a protein is formed.

REPLICATION Before a cell divides, the DNA is replicated. This occurs in the nucleus, and involves the polynucleotides separating. These then act as a model for a new complementary chain to be made. When chains separate, nucleotides attract complementary nucleotides, which are joined by hydrogen bonds. This forms the rungs of the new DNA. The phosphate group of a nucleotide is linked to the deoxyribose of the adjacent nucleotide by an enzyme known as DNA polymerase. The process continues, resulting in a new molecule that has a double helix.

DISCOVERY OF DNA In 1868, Swiss physician Friedrich Miescher discovered what he referred to as "nuclein." In reality, these were the nucleic acids. In 1951, the complete DNA molecule was discovered by three scientists, Francis Crick, James Watson, and Maurice Wilkins. By the 1940s, scientists understood that DNA was composed of amino acids and was the basic genetic makeup of life. They did not know, however, what the molecule looked like. Using x-ray diffraction, the scientists were able to conclude that DNA was a double helix. In 1962, the three scientists received the Nobel Prize for their contributions to science.

USES OF DNA DNA is astounding for a number of reasons. Medically speaking, DNA gives insights into the evolutionary past of humankind; it helps people understand diseases, drugs, and birth defects; and DNA can help people understand how to cure genetic mutations and illnesses. DNA is also used to identify people involved in crimes and paternity tests. DNA testing even helped solve the mystery of the missing Romanov children. The last Russian czar (Nicholas II) and his family were executed in 1918. Later, it was found that the skeletons of two children were missing from the mass grave. In 1991, two bodies were found 77 yards away from the grave of Nicholas II, and with DNA, it was proven that these were his two daughters.

RNA

MESSENGER RNA Messenger RNA, also known as mRNA, is the single-stranded molecule that is responsible for encoding a chemical blueprint for the process of protein synthesis. Messenger RNA has a copy of the genetic information found on a strand of DNA. Whereas DNA has the genetic information in the nucleus, messenger RNA transports that information out of the nucleus to the cytoplasm. It is in the cytoplasm that the proteins are put together. As mentioned earlier, messenger RNA goes through transcription and then translation.

RIBOSOMAL RNA Ribosomes create proteins. A part of the ribosome is known as ribosomal RNA, or rRNA. This type of RNA creates polypeptides (which are groups of amino acids that proteins are made of). A ribosome is an extremely small structure found in the cytoplasm. The ribosome has two subunits, and both of the units contain ribosomal RNA and protein. However, from these units, a startling discovery has been made, leading scientists to believe that the origin of life lies in RNA. This is because the larger of the two units of the ribosome features a chemical reaction. This chemical reaction turns genetic information into the beginning of the proteins, and only rRNA is located there.

TRANSFER RNA Transfer RNA, also known as tRNA, is responsible for reading the code and carrying amino acids that will go into the developing protein. Every amino acid has transfer RNA, and there are around twenty different tRNAs. The transfer RNA has an anticodon that reads the codon of the messenger RNA. The reading process occurs by matching base pairs with hydrogen bonds. All transfer RNAs have anywhere from seventy-five to ninety-five nucleotides. Transfer RNAs have also been known to be used in processes other than ribosome-dependent translation.

SMALL INTERFERING RNA Small interfering RNA, also known as siRNA, play an important role during the translation process. The small interfering RNA take part in what is known as RNA interference, or RNAi. The small interfering RNA strand (which is double stranded) has a phosphate group and, at the end, a hydroxyl group. During translation, this hydroxyl group interferes by binding and creating the degradation of the messenger RNA at certain sequences. This prevents the creation of certain proteins based on the sequence of nucleotides and interferes with gene expression, a process that can help in defending against viruses.

PRECURSOR MESSENGER RNA A single strand of messenger RNA, which is considered immature, is known as the precursor messenger RNA (pre-mRNA). Precursor messenger RNA is created by the process of transcription within the nucleus of a cell by a DNA template. Upon being processed, the precursor messenger RNA turns into the mature messenger RNA or, simply, the messenger RNA. After being processed, the new strand of mRNA is exported from the nucleus and translated into the protein, thus starting the cycle.

RNA THERAPEUTICS

Scientists have realized the significance and many applications of RNA. Not only can the molecule be tested with new drugs; it can also provide insight into the formation of diseases. New therapies and treatments are being created based on RNA. RNA acts as a messenger and informs cells (cancer or normal) what proteins to make. Scientists are attempting to have RNA disrupt the message of cancer before it is made. Others are attempting to create an mRNA sequence that will bind to oligonucleotides to target a therapeutic protein.

PART 5

Foreign
Language

LATIN

ANCESTOR OF ROMANCE LANGUAGES Latin is an Indo-European language that was spoken in ancient Rome. It is the ancestor of all modern Romance languages today, including Italian, Spanish, French, Portuguese, and Romanian, just to name a few. Although it is officially a dead language, meaning no one speaks it as a native language, Latin is still used in the Roman Catholic Church.

CLASSICAL LATIN Classical Latin was used by the ancient Romans at the same time as Archaic Latin. Classical Latin was based on the language that was spoken by the more refined, upper classes of Romans, and was found in the literature of the time. Around 75 B.C. to A.D. 14, from the Republic all the way to the reign of Augustus Caesar, Latin literature was at its peak and was written in Classical Latin. This was referred to as the Golden Age.

VULGAR LATIN Vulgar Latin, not Classical Latin, is the closest ancestor to the Romance languages. Vulgar Latin was the Latin spoken by the common people, and was a simpler form of Classical Latin, which was reserved for literature. Vulgar Latin varied across the Roman Empire due to the influence of the languages of local populations. By the time the Roman Empire disintegrated after A.D. 600, the local forms of Vulgar Latin were so distinct, they became the Romance languages.

MEDIEVAL LATIN Medieval Latin was the form of Latin used in the Middle Ages, from A.D. 500 to 1500. While it was primarily used by the Roman Catholic Church, it was also found in literature, law, administration, and science. The major distinction found in the Latin used at this time is that it began to have a wider vocabulary, grammar, and syntax, influenced by the various languages of the time.

RENAISSANCE LATIN Similar to how the Renaissance in Italy placed emphasis on a return to Classicism, the Latin at this time was purged of the changes made in Medieval Latin during the Middle Ages. People wished to return to the language that was used in the Golden Age of Latin literature during the Roman Empire. The humanists' efforts were successful in education, but ultimately, this wish to return to Classical Latin would lead to the extinction of the language.

AN EXTINCT LANGUAGE AND NEW LATIN Because humanists during the Renaissance were writing in an old language, they did not have the proper vocabulary to describe issues of that time period. This gave the language an old, antiquated feel. Over time, less was written in Latin, until ultimately, the language became extinct. From that point on and to this day, the most common form of Latin is known as New Latin. This is Latin used for international scientific vocabulary, systematics, and the classification of species.

SPANISH

THE HISTORY OF THE SPANISH LANGUAGE Spanish is an Indo-European language. The earliest antecedent of Spanish was spoken 5,000 years ago around the Black Sea. Indo-European language speakers migrated throughout the land, leading to fragmentation. With the Romanization of Spain in 218 B.C.,

Latin became the language people used and is the direct ancestor of Spanish and all other Romance languages.

MAKING SPANISH OFFICIAL Early standard Spanish was the direct result of Alfonso X the Learned, king of Castile and Leon. Though Latin was partly abandoned by the previous king, Alfonso X became the first king to establish Castilian, a form of Spanish spoken in northern and central Spain. Castilian was the official language to be used in churches, courts, official documents, and books, instead of Latin.

SPANISH SPREADS When Christopher Columbus, backed by the Spanish Empire, came to the New World in 1492, he opened the door for the Spanish conquest of what is now known as Central America. Four hundred years of colonization of this new land by the Spanish Empire followed, bringing over their culture, religion, and language. The Spanish would come to control Central America, much of North America and South America, and Mexico.

FRAMING A SENTENCE Unlike English, in Spanish the object of your sentence can come before the verb, and the subject is part of the verb. For example, in English, we would say, "I see you." The word "you" being the object, is at the end of the sentence. "I see you" in Spanish translates as "Te veo." The object is "te," and "veo" is actually a combination of "I" and "see."

SPANISH TODAY Today, Spanish is the native language of more than 400 million people, and it is the second-most popular language in the world (behind Chinese). It is the official language of numerous countries including Spain, Colombia, Peru, Cuba, Argentina, Bolivia, Mexico, Honduras, and Costa Rica. By 2018, the number of people in the United States who spoke Spanish as their primary language at home was more than 39 million.

USEFUL SPANISH PHRASES There are several basic things one should know how to say when traveling in a Spanish-speaking country.

Hello!	*¡Hóla!*
Good day.	*Buenos diás.*
Thank you very much.	*Muchas gracias.*
Good night.	*Buenos noches.*
Goodbye.	*Adiós.*
Where is the bathroom?	*¿Dónde está el baño?*
Can you help me?	*¿Me podría ayudar?*
How much does that cost?	*¿Cuánto cuesta?*
Can I get on the Internet?	*¿Puedo conectarme con el Internet?*

FRENCH

THE ORIGINS The roots of the French language date back to 154–125 B.C., when Gaul (the region comprising contemporary France and parts of Belgium, German, and Italy) was conquered by the Romans. When Latin became the spoken language due to Romanization, the Gaulish language was spurned and only used in more rustic areas. Eventually, the north would split from the south, leading to the creation of many distinct dialects. Over time, and due to the political prestige of the area, the dialect spoken in Paris would become the national language.

FRENCH CONSONANTS French consonants are pronounced similarly to the way they are in English. However, there are two major exceptions. Consonants at the end of a word (except *c*, *r*, *f*, and *l*) are not pronounced, and unlike in English, you are not supposed to linger on consonants. They should be short and quick, so that you can move on to the next vowel. The letter *r* is also pronounced from the back of your throat.

FRENCH VOWELS Unlike consonants, French vowels are pronounced differently than they are in English. Vowels do not form diphthongs like in English. Instead of closing the vowel with a "y" or "w" sound, the vowels stay constant, and the tongue remains tense while pronouncing them. The letters *a*, *o*, and *u* are hard vowels, and *e* and *i* are soft vowels. When followed by *m* or *n*, vowels sound nasal, meaning that when pronouncing them, air escapes both the mouth and the nose.

ARTICLES In French, there is always an article in front of the noun, and these change according to gender (masculine, feminine), and number (singular or plural). There are three types of articles: definite (equivalent to *the* in English), indefinite (equivalent to *a/an* in English), and partitive (used when a singular noun can represent smaller parts, such as the word *food*). The articles are:

	Definite	**Indefinite**	**Partitive**
Masculine	le	un	du
Feminine	la	une	de la
Plural	les	des	
Before Vowel	l'	de l'	

FRENCH TODAY French is the native language for approximately 275 million people worldwide, and it is the national language for over twenty-five countries including France, Haiti, Luxembourg, and Monaco, and more than fifteen countries found in Africa. It is also one of the official languages of Canada, Switzerland, and Belgium, as well as one of the six official languages used by the United Nations today.

USEFUL FRENCH PHRASES Here are some helpful phrases to use when traveling in a French-speaking country:

Good morning./Good day.	*Bonjour.*
Good evening.	*Bonsoir.*
Do you speak English?	*Parlez-vous anglais?*
Thank you.	*Merci.*
How are you?	*Comment allez-vous?*
What time is it?	*Quelle heure est-il?*
I need to use the restroom.	*J'ai besoin d'utiliser les toilettes.*
Please repeat.	*Répétez, s'il vous plaît.*

ITALIAN

THE ORIGINS Italian, like the other Romance languages, stemmed from Vulgar Latin, and most closely resembles Latin. Around the fourteenth century, the Tuscan dialect began to dominate as a result of the aggressive commerce centered in

Florence. In 1525, Venetian linguist, lawyer, and, eventually, cardinal, Pietro Bembo set out to make the dialect spoken in fifteenth-century Florence the official language of Italian literature. The first official Italian dictionary was published in 1612.

VOWELS Vowels in Italian are short. They should be pronounced very clearly and not drawn out. The letters *a*, *i*, and *u* are always pronounced in the same way. The letter *a* is pronounced like in the word *cat*, the letter *i* is like the *y* in the word *yellow*, and the *u* is pronounced as in the word *fun*. The pronunciation of the letters *e* and *o*, however, will vary depending on which part of Italy you are in and could have an open or closed sound.

EASY CONSONANTS The modern Italian alphabet features fewer letters than the English alphabet. Missing from the Italian alphabet are the letters *j*, *k*, *w*, *x*, and *y*. The letters *b*, *f*, *m*, *n*, and *v* are pronounced the same way they are in English. One drastic difference when it comes to consonants is that the *h* in Italian is actually silent.

HARDER CONSONANTS These consonants are different than the ones you previously learned about. In Italian, some consonants have two different pronunciations depending on the letter before it. When a *c* is followed by an *a*, *o*, *u*, or a consonant, it is pronounced with a "k" sound, such as in the word *cat*. If it is followed by an *e* or an *i*, it is pronounced with a "ch" sound. If a *g* is followed by an *a*, *o*, *u*, or a consonant, it is pronounced like it is in the word *get*. If it is followed by an *e* or an *i*, it is pronounced with a "j" sound, like in the word *gym*.

ARTICLES Just like the other Romance languages, nouns in Italian must have a gender and number associated with them.

	Singular	**Plural**
Masculine	il	i
Masculine	lo	gli
Feminine	la	le
Masculine/Feminine	l'	gli/le

There are two masculine articles. The first row shows the articles used with a masculine noun that begins with a consonant, unless that word starts with a *z* or begins with an *s* and another consonant. In those cases, you use the masculine articles shown in the second row.

USEFUL ITALIAN PHRASES Here are some helpful phrases to use when traveling in Italy:

Hi.	*Ciao.*
Good morning.	*Buongiorno.*
Good evening.	*Buona sera.*
Where is the bathroom?	*Dove posso trovare il bagno?*
How much is this?	*Quanto costa questo?*
Thank you.	*Grazie.*
Do you speak English?	*Parli inglese?*
Can you help me?	*Può aiutarmi?/Puoi aiutarmi?* (formal/informal)
When does the train leave?	*Quando parte el treno?*

GERMAN

THE ORIGINS German is one of the largest Indo-Germanic languages today. Though it has words based on Latin, it is not a Romance language. The closest relative of German is actually English, but it is also related to Dutch, Norwegian, Danish, and Swedish. The earliest record of the language dates back to 750. The origins of the German language are broken down into three periods: Old German, Middle German, and Modern German.

OLD GERMAN Old German was used from 750 to 1050. Old Low German was known as Old Saxon. This was spoken by people of the northwest coast of Germany and in the Netherlands. During the barbarian invasion, or the migration period, the sound of the German language began to change. This is known as the High German consonant shift, and it's what began to distinguish Old High German from Old Saxon.

MIDDLE GERMAN From Old Saxon came Middle Low German. This was the language spoken around the North Sea and Baltic Sea, and it had a heavy influence on the Nordic languages. From Old High German came Middle High German, which was used from 1050 to 1350. The High and Low refer to that part of the country the people lived in. During this time, a written language developed and Middle High German replaced Latin in official writings.

MODERN GERMAN Modern German began around 1500 and is still being used today. In 1880, the first grammatical rules were established, and in 1901, these were declared the standards for the German language. It is now the official language used in the church, state, education, and the arts.

GERMAN TODAY Today, German is the most widely spoken language in the European Union, and it is one of the three most learned languages. It is the official language of Germany, Austria, Switzerland, Luxembourg, and Liechtenstein, and parts of Belgium, Romania, France, and Italy. German is spoken by more than 100 million people worldwide.

USEFUL GERMAN PHRASES Here are some helpful phrases to know when traveling in a German-speaking country:

Good morning.	*Guten morgen.*
Hi.	*Hallo.*
I'm lost.	*Ich habe mich verlaufen.*
Where is the bathroom?	*Wo ist das Badezimmer?*
How much is this?	*Was kostet das?/Wie teuer ist das?* (formal/informal)
Do you speak English?	*Sprechen Sie Englisch?*
What time is it?	*Wieviel Uhr ist es?/Wie spät ist es?* (formal/informal)

PORTUGUESE

THE ORIGINS Portuguese is the sixth-most spoken language in the world. It is a Romance language that evolved from Latin, which was spoken on the western coast of the Iberian Peninsula. From A.D. 409 to 711, Germanic people inhabited the land, which led to regional variation. From the ninth to eleventh centuries, Portuguese-Galician was first being used in official administrative documents. In the eleventh century, the Christians of the region took over the land, and Portuguese and Galician split.

DIALECTS There are many dialects found in Portuguese, but the two main ones are Brazilian and European. The differences between the two involve different grammatical forms and phonology. The European dialect is more like that spoken by Portugal's former Asian and African colonies. The Brazilian dialect is primarily spoken in Brazil, and is the most common form.

RELATED LANGUAGES Portuguese is a West Iberian Romance language, and is closely related to Spanish, Galician, Fala, Leonese, and Mirandese. Galician and Fala are the closest languages to Portuguese. Galician and Portuguese used to be one language called Galician-Portuguese, and the vocabulary of Galician is still very similar to Portuguese. Fala is a descendant of Galician-Portuguese, and is spoken in several small towns in Spain.

THE PORTUGUESE LANGUAGE ORTHOGRAPHIC AGREEMENT OF 1990 In 1990, an international treaty was made to unify the writing system of Portuguese that would be used by all Portuguese-speaking countries. The treaty made changes in the spelling of both European and Brazilian Portuguese. Some letters were removed, the letters *k, w,* and *y* were added to the Portuguese alphabet, and guidelines were made for the use of the hyphen and capitalization.

PORTUGUESE TODAY Around 279 million people speak Portuguese today, and it is the official language of nine countries. Portuguese is the most widely spoken language of the Southern Hemisphere. Attempts have been made to turn Portuguese into an official language of the United Nations; however, it has faced several challenges, such as the fact that many Portuguese speakers all live on the same continent.

USEFUL PORTUGUESE PHRASES

Here are some helpful phrases to use when traveling in a Portuguese-speaking country:

Hello.	*Olá.*
Goodbye.	*Adeus.*
Good day.	*Bom dia.*
Good evening.	*Boa tarde.*
Yes.	*Sim.*
No.	*Não.*
Thank you.	*Obrigado.*
How much?	*Quanto?*
I don't speak Portuguese.	*Eu não falo Português.*
Hey, ref! Where's the penalty?	*Oí, árbitro! Cadê o penalty?*
Brazil is magnificent!	*O Brasil é lindo maravilhoso!*

POLISH

THE ORIGINS Polish is a West Slavonic language. During the Middle Ages, as the Proto-Slavonic tribes settled in Europe, three groups emerged: West, East, and South. The Polish language began to emerge during the tenth century, when the first

Polish state was established. As Christianity spread through the land, the Polish adopted the Latin alphabet, which allowed people for the first time to write Polish, a language that until then had only been spoken. Over time, additional letters were added.

DIALECTS There are several dialects of Polish. Greater Polish is the dialect of the west; Lesser Polish is spoken in southern and southeastern Poland; Mazovian is spoken in eastern and central parts; Silesian is spoken in the south and southwest; and Highlander is spoken on the border of Poland of the Czech Republic and Slovakia. Highlander is strongly influenced by Romanian, as a result of migrants.

KASHUBIAN Kashubian is one of the more commonly spoken variants of Polish. It is spoken in the north of Poland, west of Gdansk, and in Pomerania. The argument over whether Kashubian is a distinct language on its own or another dialect of Polish has long been disputed. It has been decided that Kashubian is in fact another language; however, the similarities between the languages are striking. Nevertheless, those who speak Polish will not understand Kashubian unless it is written down.

POLISH GRAMMAR Grammar in Polish is heavily influenced by the Old Slavic system of grammar. The endings of nouns, pronouns, and adjectives change according to function, with seven distinctions (nominative, genitive, dative, accusative, instrumental, locative, and vocative). There are also two number classes (singular and plural), and like many Slavic languages, there aren't any definite or indefinite articles.

POLISH TODAY There are 40 million Polish speakers worldwide. Polish is the official language of Poland; however, it is used as a secondary language in some parts of Lithuania, Russia, Belarus,

Kazakhstan, and Ukraine. This is a result of migration, resettlements, and border changes from the Yalta Agreement following World War II. Today, Polish is the third-most widely spoken Slavic language.

USEFUL POLISH PHRASES Here are some helpful phrases to use when traveling in Poland:

Good morning.	*Dzień dobry.*
Good evening.	*Dobry wieczór.*
Hello.	*Cześć.*
Goodbye.	*Do widzenia.* (formal) *Do zobaczenia./ Narazie! Cześć!* (informal)
I don't understand.	*Nie rozumiem.*
I speak English.	*Mówię po angielsku.*
Thank you.	*Dzięki./Dziękuję./Serdecznie dziękuję.*
Where is the toilet?	*Gdzie jest toaleta?*
How much is it?	*Ile to kosztuje?/Po ile to jest?*

RUSSIAN

THE ORIGINS In the sixth century, the Slav people migrated from Old Poland and gradually occupied the Balkans. By the tenth century, Western, Southern, and Eastern Slavonic had emerged as three similar, yet distinct, language groups. Eastern Slavonic is a direct ancestor of what would become Belarusian,

Ukrainian, and Russian. The languages shared many grammatical rules, and were able to share one written language (and only a written language), known as Old Church Slavonic.

CYRILLIC   In the ninth century, Constantine and Methodius, two missionaries, were ordered to write down the language of Old Church Slavonic and preach to the people of Moravia about Christianity. Constantine, who on his deathbed changed his name to Cyril, created a Slavonic alphabet that is now known as Cyrillic. The Cyrillic alphabet was closely based on the Greek alphabet, with additional letters added for sounds not found in the Greek system.

PETER THE GREAT REFORMS THE LANGUAGE   In the early eighteenth century, Peter the Great came to power in Russia. With his political reforms came a reform of the alphabet that modified and simplified it and removed some of the Greek letters. Some vocabulary from Western Europe was introduced, and the language reflected post-Renaissance Europe instead of the Byzantine Empire's way of pronouncing words.

A NEED TO CHANGE THE LANGUAGE   By the middle of the eighteenth century, there was a need for the written Russian language to reflect the actual spoken language. Three distinct styles were distinguished: high style, also known as Church Slavonic, spoken for religion and poetics; middle style, used for science and prose; and low style, used for low comedies and personal correspondence. The middle style would come to form the Russian language that exists today. It was a combination of East Slavonic and Church Slavonic.

THE SOVIET UNION'S SPELLING REFORM OF 1918   Shortly   after the Russian Revolution, and as a direct result of political ideology, the Russian language was simplified once again. This time, four letters were removed, and one silent letter used at the end of words was also removed. New political terminology was introduced, and the politeness characteristic toward the upper classes was also removed. These steps were characteristic of what the new authoritarian regime set out to accomplish.

USEFUL RUSSIAN PHRASES Here are some helpful phrases to use when traveling in Russia. Note that these are not written with the Russian alphabet, but rather are pronunciations that have been written in English.

Good day.	*Dobry den.*
Hi/Hello.	*Privet.*
Do you speak English?	*Govorite li vy po angliyski?*
I need to use the restroom.	*Mne nuzhno otoyti v tualet.*
What time is it?	*Kotoryy chas?*
Goodbye.	*Do svidaniya.*
Yes.	*Da.*
No.	*Net.*

GREEK

MYCENAEAN GREEK Mycenaean Greek is the oldest form of the Greek language. It was spoken from the sixteenth to eleventh centuries B.C. in Mycenae and Crete. The Linear B script tablets, which showed a system of writing based on a syllabic alphabet, is the only record of Mycenaean Greek. The language consisted of eighty-eight signs representing syllables and made no distinction between long and short vowels or double consonants.

CLASSICAL GREEK

CLASSICAL GREEK Classical Greek, or Ancient Greek, was widely spoken throughout the Roman Empire. It is the language found in the works of Homer and all of the famous Athenian philosophers. There were three distinctive forms and dialects of the language based on the different tribes and their locations: Dorian (the coast of Peloponnesus), Aeolian (the Aegean islands), and Ionian (the west coast of Asia Minor).

HELLENISTIC GREEK

HELLENISTIC GREEK Hellenistic Greek, or Koine Greek, is traced back to the Hellenistic colonization created by the conquests of Alexander the Great. It was the first common Greek dialect, and it was developed from a mixture of the Attic dialect (a subdialect of Ionic spoken in Athens) and other Greek dialects. It became the lingua franca across the Mediterranean, meaning the common language among people who spoke various languages. This was also the language used in the translation of the Christian New Testament.

MEDIEVAL GREEK

MEDIEVAL GREEK Medieval Greek, also known as Byzantine Greek, was spoken during the Byzantine Empire from 600 to the Ottoman conquest of Constantinople in 1453. It was the only language used in government, and it is still the language used in the Greek Orthodox Church. Medieval Greek is considered to be the link between Ancient Greek and Modern Greek. Over time, neighboring languages and the languages of conquerors came to influence and shape the language.

MODERN GREEK

MODERN GREEK Modern Greek refers to the language spoken from the fall of the Byzantine Empire in 1453 until now. There were two forms of the language spoken: Demotic and Katharévusa. Katharévusa was used for literature, scientific, administrative, and juridical purposes, and it was an imitation of the Classical Greek language. In 1976, Demotic was announced as the official language of Greece, and this is now known as Standard Modern Greek.

USEFUL GREEK PHRASES
Here are some helpful phrases to use when traveling in Greece:

Hello (singular).	*Yia sou.*
Hello (plural).	*Yia sas.*
Thank you.	*Efharisto.*
Excuse me.	*Signomi.*
Please.	*Parakalo.*
Where is the toilet, please?	*Pou ine i twaleta, parakalo?*
Where is the beach?	*Pou ine i paralia?*
Sorry, I don't speak Greek.	*Signomi, ala then milao elinika.*
How much is it?	*Poso kani?*

BULGARIAN

ABOUT BULGARIAN Bulgarian is a South Slavic language spoken by 7 million people today. It is the official language of the Republic of Bulgaria, though there are also Bulgarian-speaking minorities in neighboring countries such as Greece, Turkey, Macedonia, and the Ukraine. Bulgarian is believed to be the first Slavic language that was written, and the language evolved in three periods: Old Bulgarian, Middle Bulgarian, and Modern Bulgarian.

OLD BULGARIAN

Old Bulgarian was also known as Old Church Slavonic (which you might recall from the lesson on Russian). It was spoken from the ninth century to the eleventh century, and it was the first written Slavic language that was used universally throughout the land. Old Bulgarian shared many qualities that other Slavic languages had; however, certain sounds were found only in Bulgarian.

MIDDLE BULGARIAN

From the twelfth century to the fifteenth century, the language changed dramatically. Middle Bulgarian was the official language used in the administration of the Second Bulgarian Empire. Many vowels lost their nasal quality, and consonants were harder in the West, while in the East, there was still a difference between hard and soft consonants. Also during this time, a new class of verbs developed.

MODERN BULGARIAN

Modern Bulgarian started in the sixteenth century and borrowed many words from Greek and Turkish. The present-day written language, which was based on the vernacular language, was standardized in the nineteenth century and included Russian, German, and French words. There are no definite rules when it comes to stress in language, so the accent of each word must be learned. Unlike other Slavic languages, Bulgarian has definite articles and has dropped almost all case forms for nouns, using prepositions and positions like English.

DIALECTS

Even though the written language is used across the entire country, there are several variations in the spoken language. The differences in pronunciation of consonants that was found in Middle Bulgarian between the East and West still hold true today. Another one of the main differences can be found in the pronunciation of vowels, and there are even words only used in certain areas.

USEFUL BULGARIAN PHRASES Here are some helpful phrases to use when traveling in Bulgaria:

Hello/Hi.	*Zdravey./Zdrasti.*
Good morning.	*Dobro utro.*
Good evening.	*Dobar vecher.*
Yes.	*Da.*
No.	*Ne.*
Thank you.	*Blagodarya.*
I do not understand.	*Ne razbiram.*
Where is the bathroom?	*Kade e baniata?*
How much is this?	*Kolko struva tova?*
Can you help me?	*Moje li da mi pomognete?*
Do you speak English?	*Govorite li angliiski?*
My Bulgarian is bad.	*Balgarskiiat mi e losh.*
Goodbye.	*Chao.*

ALBANIAN

THE ORIGINS Albanian does not belong to any other family of the Indo-European languages. The vocabulary of Albanian is distinct, though the language does borrow from Germanic, Balto-Slavic, and Greek. Albanian is believed to have originated from Illyrian, a language spoken in the Western Balkans until the sixth century; however, others believe it is a descendant of Dacian or

Thracian, languages spoken in the Balkans until the fifth century. Albanians call their language Shqip.

INFLUENCES The earliest language that Albanian borrowed from was Doric Greek. From the second to the fifth centuries, Albanian also began absorbing Greek and Latin. Latin had the largest influence on the language. From the seventh to the ninth centuries, the language absorbed Southern Slavic and Proto-Romanian, a result of tribes settling in the Balkans.

DIALECTS There are two dialects found in Albanian, Tosk and Gheg, and the two have diverged for at least a millennium. Gheg is spoken to the north of the Shkumbin River, and Tosk is spoken south of the river. The Tosk dialect is considered the official language of the country. A transitional language is spoken in central Albania.

THE ALBANIAN ALPHABET Over the course of history, the Albanian alphabet has been written in several different ways, including using the Greek alphabet, the Turkish alphabet, and Cyrillic. In the 1900s, the Albanian government made a form of the Latin alphabet the standard alphabet. The Albanian alphabet appears as:

A B C Ç D Dh E Ë F G G Gj H I J K L L Ll M N Nj
O P Q R Rr S Sh T Th U V X Xh Y Z Zh

GRAMMAR Nouns in Albanian have a case, a gender, and indefinite and definite forms. Definite and indefinite articles (such as the word *the*) are not stand-alone words but are attached to the words as suffixes. Adjectives come after the nouns and match the gender and number of the nouns. The conjugation of verbs shows tense and person.

USEFUL ALBANIAN PHRASES Here are some helpful phrases to use when traveling in Albania:

Hello.	*Tungjatjeta.*
Goodbye.	*Mirupafshim.*
Thank you.	*Faleminderit.*
Yes.	*Po.*
No.	*Jo.*
I don't speak Albanian.	*Nuk flas Shqip.*
I don't understand.	*Nuk kuptoj.*
Do you speak English?	*Flisni Angisht?*
Excuse me.	*Më falni.*
Good morning.	*Mirëmëngjes.*
Good afternoon.	*Mirëdita.*
Good evening.	*Mirëmbrëma.*
Good night.	*Natën e mire.*
What is your name?	*Si ju quheni?*

DUTCH

THE ORIGINS Dutch is a part of the West Germanic dialect, and, more specifically, it is a West Low Franconian language. Dutch can be traced back to A.D. 500, when Old Frankish was split by the High German consonant shift. The Dutch language is broken down into periods: Old Dutch, which lasted from 500 to 1150; Middle Dutch, which lasted from 1150 to 1500; and Modern Dutch, which began in 1500 and is still spoken today.

DIALECTS Dialects in Dutch are extremely diverse, and there is said to be about twenty-eight distinct dialects. Flemish is the term used for the type of Dutch spoken in Belgium; in Flanders there are four types of Flemish: West Flemish, East Flemish, Brabantian, and Limburgish. Flemish is considered a softer dialect, and it favors older words. Netherlandish Dutch, in contrast, is considered to be harsh and even hostile sounding. In the east of the country, Dutch Low Saxon is spoken, and in Holland, Hollandic is spoken.

CHANGES TO THE LANGUAGE Pronunciation has changed over the past century in Dutch. Voiceless pronunciation with some letters—meaning saying hard sounds instead of using one's voice—has started to become the standard for the language. This change mirrors a movement to make the spelling of Dutch words as phonological as possible. Another change that has not been declared an official change to the standard language, but rather has begun appearing in the younger generation, is known as Polder Dutch.

POLDER DUTCH Polder Dutch is a variation of Dutch spoken by the younger generation. In Polder Dutch (a term coined by Jan Stroop), diphthongs are pronounced with a wider mouth, and are pronounced lower. Polder Dutch seems to have begun around the 1970s, and originally it was middle-aged women and the upper-middle class who were pronouncing these diphthongs in this way. It has since spread.

DUTCH TODAY Dutch is currently the native language of Belgium, the Netherlands, and the Republic of Suriname. Dutch is said to be somewhere in between German and English; however, it most closely resembles German. It is spoken by 23 million people worldwide and was standardized in the seventeenth century. The Dutch of today has started to sound more like the dialect found in Holland.

USEFUL DUTCH PHRASES Here are some helpful phrases to use when traveling in a Dutch-speaking country:

Hello.	*Hallo.*
Good morning.	*Goedemorgen.*
Good afternoon.	*Goedemiddag.*
Good evening.	*Goedenavond.*
Have a nice day.	*Nog een prettige dag.*
I don't understand.	*Ik begrijp het niet.*
Excuse me.	*Neem me niet kwalijk.*
How much is this?	*Hoeveel kost dit?*
Thank you.	*Dank U.*
Where's the toilet?	*Waar is de WC?*
Goodbye.	*Tot ziens.*

SWEDISH

THE ORIGINS Swedish is a North-Germanic language, influenced by Middle Low German. It originally stemmed from Old Norse, which in the ninth century split into Old West Norse and Old

East Norse. Old East Norse consisted of Sweden and Denmark, and in the twelfth century, the language between those two lands began to change, turning into Old Swedish and Old Danish.

OLD SWEDISH

Old Swedish was the language spoken in 1225, and it lasted until the late fourteenth century. It was much more complex than what is spoken today, and the influence from Middle Low German was very clear. The Christian Church played an important role in society, and documents were written in Latin script. Words from Latin, Greek, and Dutch were all incorporated into Old Swedish.

MODERN SWEDISH

With the printing press and the Reformation, the Swedish language began to undergo changes. Gustav I Vasa, the king of Sweden, ordered that the Bible be translated into Swedish. This version, which blended Old Swedish with the colloquial Swedish of the time, remained the most common Bible in Sweden until 1917. During this time, changes were made to certain sounds in the language, such as the softening of certain consonants and assimilation of consonant clusters.

CONTEMPORARY SWEDISH

Nusvenska, literally meaning "Now-Swedish," is the Swedish language spoken today. It began toward the end of the nineteenth century, and much of the written language appeared closer to the spoken language, moving away from formal restrictions. By the time of the spelling reform of 1906, the language was standardized, and in the 1960s, a major change was made, known as du-reformen (the "you-reform"), replacing standard titles and surnames with "du."

DIALECTS

There are six main dialects in the Swedish language: North Swedish, South Swedish, Finland Swedish, Svealand Swedish, Götaland Swedish, and Gotland Swedish. These dialects are separate from the standard language and developed independently from as far back as Old Norse. They are very localized, and speakers of these dialects also speak the standard language.

USEFUL SWEDISH PHRASES
Here are some helpful phrases to use when traveling in Sweden:

Hello.	*Hej.*
Good morning.	*God morgon.*
Good afternoon.	*God eftermiddag.*
Good evening.	*God kväll.*
Good night.	*God natt.*
I don't understand.	*Jag förstår inte.*
How much is this?	*Hur mycket kostar det?*
Where's the toilet?	*Var är toaletten?*
Cheers!	*Skål!*
Excuse me.	*Ursäkta.*
Thank you.	*Tack.*
Goodbye.	*Hej då.*

FINNISH

THE ORIGINS Finnish is a Uralic language. It came from the Proto-Finnic language Sámi. The Proto-Finnic language was not actually spoken in Finland but around what is now St.

Petersburg. As the language began to spread north, one of the daughter languages turned into Finnish. Around the first century, the Finnic languages separated, which still has great influence on the Finnish dialects.

FINNISH DURING THE MIDDLE AGES Before the Middle Ages, Finnish was only an oral language. During the Middle Ages, Finland was annexed to Catholic Sweden. The administrative language was Swedish, the language used in religion was Latin, and business was transacted in Middle Low German, leaving little room for Finnish to be spoken. However, the first evidence of Finnish writing is found from this time period, dating to around 1450.

THE WRITING SYSTEM In the sixteenth century, Finnish bishop Mikael Agricola created the first comprehensive Finnish writing system as well as the system to translate the Bible. The orthography was based on Latin, Swedish, and German. Agricola's system was revised to make a more phonemic system at a later time, and certain phonemes were lost.

MODERNIZATION OF FINNISH In the nineteenth century, there was a great need to improve the Finnish language. Since Agricola's writing system first appeared, written Finnish was almost solely used for things pertaining to religion. As support for a national language grew, efforts were made to modernize and improve the language. By the end of the nineteenth century, Finnish, with Swedish, became the official language of journalism, literature, science, and administration.

DIALECTS There are two types of dialects found in the Finnish language: Western and Eastern. The two dialects are fairly similar, but do have slight differences in diphthongs, rhythms, and vowels. The most obvious distinguishing factor between the two dialects is how the letter *d* is pronounced. Otherwise, much of the same grammar, vocabulary, and phonology are the same.

USEFUL FINNISH PHRASES Here are some helpful Finnish phrases to use when traveling in Finland:

Hello.	*Terve.*
Good morning.	*Hyvää huomenta.*
Good afternoon.	*Hyvää päivää.*
Good evening.	*Hyvää iltaa.*
Yes.	*Kyllä.*
No.	*Ei.*
Thank you.	*Kiitos.*
Do you speak English?	*Puhutteko englantia?*
I don't speak Finnish.	*Minä en puhu suomea.*
I don't understand.	*Minä en ymmärrä.*
Where's the toilet?	*Missä on WC?*
Goodbye.	*Näkemiin.*

ICELANDIC

THE ORIGINS Icelandic is a Northern Germanic language and is actually a dialect of Norwegian. During the ninth century, settlers from Norway came to Iceland, speaking Old Norse. Due to the geographic location of Iceland, the language began to diverge from Norwegian over time. The language also had influence from other Scandinavian settlers, and as a result, the common traits to all of the different languages were reinforced, with the differences disappearing gradually.

MIDDLE ICELANDIC From 1350 to 1550, the differences between Norwegian and Icelandic grew significantly. There was a dichotomy in Icelandic: Part of the Icelandic language remained pure and the other went through a significant transformation. Among the changes made was a diphthongization of long vowels, short vowels became less tense, previously absent consonant phonemes appeared, and unvoiced consonants were now aspirated. These changes were never written but were phonetic.

MODERN ICELANDIC Modern Icelandic formed around 1550 with the introduction of the printing press, the Lutheran Reformation, and the translation of the Bible. Several changes have been made to both the vowel system and the consonant system. The modern alphabet was established in the nineteenth century and based on that of the twelfth century, with some changes made to fit Germanic conventions. In the twentieth century, *é* was adopted, replacing *je,* and the letter *z* was abolished.

INFLUENCES ON ICELANDIC Though at one point Danish was the official language of Iceland, little of the language has stuck. In the nineteenth century, the language was purified to get rid of any Danish influence, and only a few Danish words are still used today. Though Latin influences can be seen from its Germanic roots, Icelandic has not been heavily influenced by any other languages with the exception of English, which the younger generation has adapted to the Icelandic morphological and phonetic system.

PHONOLOGY Due to the fact that Icelandic is spoken by a small number of speakers in one concentrated area, there are relatively few dialects of the language. The language features diphthongs, monophthongs (pure vowels with a fixed articulation), and consonants that can be both voiced and unvoiced. In Icelandic, there is a contrast of aspiration (burst of air) between plosives (a consonant sound that stops airflow).

USEFUL ICELANDIC PHRASES Here are some helpful phrases to use when traveling in Iceland:

Hello.	*Halló.*
Good morning.	*Godan dag.*
Good afternoon.	*Godan daginn.*
Good night.	*Goda nott.*
Thank you.	*Takk.*
I don't understand.	*Eg skil ekki.*
Do you speak English?	*Talardu ensku?*
How much is it?	*Hvad kostar?*
Goodbye.	*Bless.*

CROATIAN

THE ORIGINS Croatian is a South Slavic language. The language developed from Old Church Slavonic, which, in the ninth century, became the official language of the land. Based on the local dialect of Old Church Slavonic, Croatian developed and used three alphabets: Cyrillic, Glagolitic, and Latin. Over time, the language was strongly influenced by Slovenian and Serbian.

ATTEMPT AT STANDARDIZING CROATIAN

In the seventeenth century, there was an attempt to unify Croatia, which at the time had been ruled by two dynasties. Ikavian-Kajkavian was chosen to be the unifying dialect because it was an intermediate between all of the other dialects. However, when the dynasties were overtaken by the Holy Roman Emperor, the standard language was abandoned and replaced by Neo-Shtokavian.

THE ILLYRIAN MOVEMENT AND FORWARD

In the nineteenth century, there was an attempt to create a common South Slavic literary language. This was known as the Illyrian movement. The Shtokavian dialect was chosen as the standard language to be used among Croats and Serbs, and the Serbo-Croatian language was standardized. In 1954, the Novi Sad Agreement established Serbo-Croatian as one language with two variants, and this remained until the collapse of the Socialist Federal Republic of Yugoslavia in 1991, which led to several disputes.

PHONOLOGY

Croatian has a total of thirty letters in its alphabet (which stems from the Latin alphabet), with twenty-five of those letters being consonants and only five being vowels. Vowels can be long or short, and when they are stressed, they carry a rising or falling tone. Understanding consonants is a bit more difficult, and they are affricate (begin as a stop and end with a sound of incomplete closure) and palatal (where the tongue is raised to the hard palate).

CROATIAN TODAY

Croatian is spoken by 6 million people today, and is the national language of Croatia. The language is also spoken in Herzegovina, Bosnia, Slovakia, Italy, Austria, and Hungary. Though Croatian, Bosnian, and Serbian are extremely similar, speakers emphasize differences between the languages as a result of a deep and complicated cultural, political, and religious history.

USEFUL CROATIAN PHRASES Here are some helpful phrases to use when traveling in Croatia:

Hello.	*Zdravo.*
Pleased to meet you.	*Drago mi je.*
Good morning.	*Dobro jutro.*
Good day.	*Dobar dan.*
Good night.	*Laku noć.*
Yes.	*Da.*
No.	*Ne.*
Please.	*Molim.*
Thank you.	*Hvala.*
Excuse me.	*Oprostite.*
I don't understand.	*Je ne razumijem.*
How much is it?	*Koliko kosjta?*
Where's the toilet?	*Gdje je zahod?*
Goodbye.	*Zbogom.*

CZECH

THE ORIGINS Czech is a West Slavonic language that was known as Bohemian until the nineteenth century. The earliest written documents in Czech date back to the eleventh century, and they were written in the Latin alphabet. Due to geographical location and a turbulent political history, the Czech language is greatly influenced by German, and has grammatical and phonetic features of both German and Slavonic.

THE FIFTEENTH CENTURY In the fifteenth century, Jan Hus, a religious reformer, standardized the spelling of the language. In his reform, he attributed one letter to every sound. By adding certain accents (in the form of dots or lines) to certain letters, Hus was able to create a standard of spelling based on the Latin alphabet. This system is still in use to this day.

THE "PEASANT TONGUE" Up until the fourteenth century, the Czech language was suppressed. It was considered to be a language spoken by peasants, not worthy of literature or any kind of standardization. For the first time, following the work of Jan Hus, Czech appeared in literature. In the nineteenth century, a movement to standardize the dialect to an older form of Czech took place. In Moravia and Silesia, this dialect is still spoken.

CZECH AND SLOVAK The Czech language and the Slovak language are very similar. The two countries were once a single country, Czechoslovakia. However, when the Communist regime fell, they broke apart, becoming the Czech Republic and Slovakia. Though there are slight differences, speakers of Czech can understand and read Slovak, and vice versa.

DIALECTS Two major dialects can be found in the Czech language relating to geographic location. The most commonly used dialect is called Common Czech, which is used around Bohemia. The other dialect pertains to Moravia and Silesia, which is based on standard Czech. Moravia and Silesia have more localized dialects than Common Czech. In Silesia, for example, there exists a community that speaks a combination of Czech and Polish.

USEFUL CZECH PHRASES Here are some helpful phrases to use when traveling in the Czech Republic:

Hello.	*Dobrý den.*
Good morning.	*Dobré ráno.*
Good evening.	*Dobrý večer.*
What's your name?	*Jak se jmenujete?*
I don't speak Czech.	*Nemluvím česky.*
I don't understand.	*Nerozumím.*
Thank you.	*Děkuji.*
Where is the bathroom?	*Kde jsou toalety?*
How much is this?	*Kolik to stojí?*
Goodbye.	*Na shledanou.*

HUNGARIAN

THE ORIGINS The Hungarian language, called Magyar, is a Uralic language. Uralic languages are not related to Indo-European languages and emerged in the Urals of Russia. The history of the language can be broken down into five periods: Proto-Hungarian, when the Hungarian language first came to be; Old Hungarian (during the Middle Ages); Middle Hungarian (the language turned into a form similar to today's); New Hungarian (when the language underwent some reforms); and Modern Hungarian (the language as it is spoken today).

TURKIC INFLUENCES From 400 to 896, the Hungarians lived as nomads. When they settled on the coast of the Black Sea, they came into contact with the Turkic people. The Huns had come to the area after the fall of Attila and settled there, ruling over the Hungarians. Between the sixth and the eighth centuries, the Huns fell into decline and were replaced by the Turks. Hungarians were introduced to the Turkic writing system, which the Old Hungarian writing system was based on. The word *Magyar* comes from the Turkic *onugor*, and the phonetic language was extremely influenced by the Turkic language.

THE FOUR-TIERED LEVEL OF POLITENESS In Hungarian, there are four different ways to express levels of politeness. Uses of the different levels include when showing respect to the person being addressed; when distancing oneself from the person being addressed; a system similar to the previous two but with additional words (this would be used when talking to the family friends of parents, for example); and a form of being polite that doesn't fit into the other three categories.

WRITING SYSTEM When Stephen I of Hungary came to power in the year 1000, the Old Hungarian system of writing was gradually replaced by the Latin alphabet. The Hungarian system of today still uses the Latin alphabet, although it has expanded, modifying characters with accents (such as *á, é, í, ú, ö*, and *ü*) to represent sounds not present.

DIALECTS There are eight major dialects in Hungarian: Alföld, Danube-Tisza, West Danube, King's Pass Hungarian, Northwest Hungarian, Northeast Hungarian, Székely, and West Hungarian. These are all mutually intelligible. The most significant dialect is Csángó. Due to its isolation (it is located in the Romanian area of Bacău), it has the most differences of any of the dialects.

USEFUL HUNGARIAN PHRASES Here are some helpful phrases to use when traveling in Hungary:

Good morning.	*Jó reggelt kívánok.*
Good afternoon.	*Jó napot kívánok.* (also used as "hello")
Good evening.	*Jó estét kívánok.*
Good night.	*Jó éjszakát.*
Thank you.	*Köszönöm.*
I don't understand.	*Nem értem.*
I can't speak Hungarian.	*Nem beszélek magyarul.*
Excuse me.	*Elnézést.*
Where's the toilet?	*Hol van a mosdó?*
Goodbye.	*Szia.*

KOREAN

THE ORIGINS The Korean language is a Ural-Altaic language. Ural-Altaic languages originated in northern Asia and include the Turkic, Mongol, Finnish, Hungarian, and Manchu languages. Despite grammatical similarities, a relationship between Korean and Japanese has not been discovered yet. From 108 B.C. to A.D. 313, the Chinese occupied northern Korea, and by the fifth century, Classical Chinese was the written language and much of the Chinese language was borrowed.

THE KOREAN WRITING SYSTEM The Korean alphabet, Hangul, was created in 1444. The consonants got their shape based on the shape the mouth made when the sound was pronounced. The writing direction (vertically and right to left) and method of writing the symbols in blocks was taken from the Chinese. After Hangul was created, most Koreans could write in both Hangul and Classical Chinese, and during the nineteenth and twentieth centuries, a mix of the two systems (Hanja) became popular until 1945, when use of Chinese characters diminished.

VOCABULARY The vocabulary of the Korean language is a blend of pure Korean words and Sino-Korean words, which were taken from written Chinese or Korean words in Chinese characters. This is similar to how Indo-European languages infused Greek and Latin into their languages. Today, many of the loanwords are from the English language. The vocabulary of North Korea favors the native Korean vocabulary over the Sino-Korean vocabulary.

DIALECTS There are many dialects found in Korean. In South Korea, the standard language is based on the dialect of Seoul.

In North Korea, the standard language is based on the dialect of Pyongyang. The dialects found in both North Korea and South Korea are mutually intelligible. The dialect that is most noticeably different is that of Jeju Island, which features many archaic words that have since been lost in the Korean language of today.

NORTH KOREAN AND SOUTH KOREAN DIFFERENCES Though North Korea and South Korea speak the same language, the lasting separation from one another has created subtle differences in the languages. While they both use the same letters, called jamo, some of the letters have different names. Also, the North uses a stroke in one jamo that is different from the South; compound vowel and tense consonant jamos are not treated separately in South Korea but are in North Korea; and some jamos have different names.

USEFUL KOREAN PHRASES Here are helpful phrases to use when traveling in Korea. Note that these are written out phonetically.

Hello.	*Annyeonghaseyo.*
How are you?	*Eotteohke jinaeseyo?*
Pleased to meet you.	*Mannaseo bangapseumnida.*
Good morning/afternoon/evening.	*Annyeong hashimnikka.*
I don't understand.	*Moreugesseumnida.*
How much is this?	*Ige eolmayeyo?*
Thank you.	*Kamsahamnida.*
Where's the toilet?	*Hwajangsiri eodiyeyo.*
Excuse me.	*Shillehagessumnida.*
Goodbye.	*Annyeonghi gyeseyo.*

JAPANESE

THE ORIGINS Japanese is a Japonic language, and is related to Altaic and Ryukyuan languages. The Japanese language has gone through four distinct phases: Old Japanese (which ended around the eighth century A.D., a period that saw the beginning of significant influence from Chinese); Early Middle Japanese (from 794 to 1185); Late Middle Japanese (from 1185 to 1600, where European languages began influencing Japanese); and Modern Japanese (from 1600 to today).

THE WRITING SYSTEM The Japanese writing system of today is a blend of the Chinese writing system, two kana syllabaries (alphabets based on symbols developed during the ninth century to simplify writing), and Roman numerals and letters. From the third to the fifth century, Japanese used Classical Chinese as the official writing system. As the language evolved, several distinct differences separated the Japanese form of writing from the Chinese. One notable difference is that Chinese is a monosyllabic language (all words are one syllable), and Japanese is polysyllabic.

SOUNDS OF THE LANGUAGE The Japanese language does not have any diphthongs. Instead, it is composed of monophthongs, meaning the vowels in the language are pure. There are five vowels in Japanese—*a, i, u, o,* and *e* —and each has a long and short form. Most of the syllables in Japanese end with a vowel sound. Japanese has a pitched accent, meaning pitch falls following the syllable that is accented.

POLITENESS There is a very complex system in the Japanese language when dealing with the issue of politeness, and at least four different levels of how to address a person. How to address someone is based on a variety of factors such as age, job, and experience, and there is even a different form of politeness when asking someone for a favor. There are differences between the polite language, teineigo; the respectful language, sonkeigo; and the humble language, kenjōgo; as well as differences between honorific and humble forms.

DIALECTS Due to the mountainous terrain and a history of internal and external isolation, there are many dialects of Japanese. These differ in vocabulary, pitch accent, morphology of certain types of words, and sometimes pronunciation. The dialects fall into two main categories: Eastern and Western. Eastern dialects emphasize the sounds of consonants, and the Western dialects emphasize vowels.

USEFUL JAPANESE PHRASES Here are some helpful phrases to use when traveling in Japan. Note, these are spelled out phonetically.

Hello./Good morning.	*Konnichiwa.*
How are you?	*O genki desu ka?*
Pleased to meet you.	*Hajimemashite.*
Good morning.	*Ohayō gozaimasu.*
Good evening.	*Konbanwa.*
Excuse me.	*Sumimasen.*
How much is this?	*Ikura desu ka?*
Thank you.	*Dōmo.*
Where's the toilet?	*Benjo wa doko desu ka?*
Goodbye.	*Sayōnara.*

MANDARIN

THE ORIGINS There are many variations in the Chinese language. Mandarin is spoken in southwestern and northern China and is a Sino-Tibetan language. It began as the language of the courts starting in the Ming Dynasty, with the dialect of Beijing being very influential. By the seventeenth century, schools were set up to teach the Beijing style, and this dialect was established as the national language in 1909. The Beijing style continued to be the national language when the Republic of China came to power and there was a greater need for a common language.

OLD MANDARIN From 960 to 1127 B.C., Emperor Taizu of the Northern Song Dynasty conquered the lands that we now know as China. When the Northern Song Dynasty came to an end, what is referred to as Old Mandarin, a new common speech, developed. Literature and art flourished during this time and were written in this vernacular form. Much of the grammatical elements, rules, and syntax are retained in the Mandarin spoken today.

THE LANGUAGE BECOMES STANDARDIZED Even when the Qing Dynasty fell and the Republic of China came to power, Mandarin remained the official language. When the People's Republic of China came to power in 1949, the effort to make Mandarin the national language continued, and the Beijing dialect became the official language, now known as Standard Chinese. Mandarin is the official language used in the media and in education. Though Taiwan and some of mainland China (such as Hong Kong) still speak Cantonese, Mandarin is spoken fluently as well. Officially, there are two types of Mandarin: one that the PRC (People's Republic of China) government refers to, and one that the ROC (Republic of China, or Taiwan) government refers to.

DIFFERENCES IN PHONOLOGY Mandarin is known as a stress-timed language. What this means is that syllables, as in English, can last for different lengths of time, but there is still a constant amount of time between the stressed syllables. Mandarin differs from other Chinese languages such as Cantonese and Min Nan for this very reason. Cantonese and Min Nan are known as syllable-timed languages, where each syllable takes the same amount of time.

DIALECTS Mandarin is one of the most widely spoken languages in the world, and due to China's size and population, there are many Mandarin dialects spoken. The dialects include the Northeastern dialect, the Southwestern dialect, the Beijing dialect (which Standard Chinese is based on), the Zhongyuan dialect, and the JiLu dialect. Almost all of the cities in China have their own variation on Mandarin.

USEFUL MANDARIN PHRASES Here are some helpful phrases to use when traveling to China. Note that these are written in Pinyin, which is a phonetic spelling that uses the Latin alphabet (with the inclusion of *zh, ch, sh,* and no *v*).

Hello.	*Nǐ hǎo.*
Good morning.	*Zǎoān.*
Good afternoon.	*Wǔān.*
Good evening.	*Wǎnān.*
I don't understand.	*Wǒ tīngbùdǒng.*
Excuse me.	*Duìbùqǐ.*
Where's the toilet?	*Cèsuǒ zài nǎli?*
How much is this?	*Zhège duōshǎo qián?*
Goodbye.	*Zàijiàn.*

SIGN LANGUAGE

THE ORIGINS The origins of sign language can be traced back to ancient Greece, where Socrates believed it only made sense for the deaf to communicate with their hands and other body parts. In 1520, Pedro Ponce de Léon created a system based on gestures to educate the deaf, mostly working with a family in Spain. From 1715 to 1780, Léon's system spread across Europe, incorporating handshakes to represent sounds. In the late eighteenth century, the National Institution for Deaf-Mutes was established in France, with the intention of instructing the deaf. In 1817, Thomas Gallaudet, an American who studied with Laurent Clerc in France, brought the sign language to America with Clerc, establishing the Connecticut Asylum for the Education and Instruction of Deaf and Dumb Persons. Laurent Clerc is responsible for much of the work that would lead to American Sign Language (ASL).

ABOUT DEAFNESS When there is a complete loss of the ability to hear out of either one or both ears, it is known as deafness. Deafness can be caused by a number of factors. It can be inherited, or caused by diseases (such as meningitis), complications at birth, the presence of ototoxic drugs, and exposure to extreme noise. Deafness can appear at birth (known as congenital deafness), or come on either gradually or suddenly. There are two main types of deafness: conductive (when transmission of sound waves is interfered with) and sensorineural (when nerve impulses cannot reach the brain). In the fourth century B.C. it was believed that deaf people were also unable to speak and were thus unteachable, and this stigma lasted with the deaf community for centuries.

RELATIONSHIP WITH ORAL LANGUAGES Sign languages do not depend on oral languages, and they have their own grammatical structures. Sign language does have something known as finger-spelling, where letters of the alphabet are represented with hand signs; however, this is only one part of sign language. In general, sign languages are completely separate from oral languages and have different paths of development. Even though British and American hearing people speak the same language and can understand each other, the American Sign Language and the British Sign Language are completely different, so deaf people using sign language from the US and the UK cannot understand one another.

DIFFERENT TYPES OF SIGN LANGUAGE There are many different forms of sign language. Although these languages emerged separately and unrelated to the spoken languages of countries and are different grammatically, they do feature manually coded languages; that is, they have incorporated the languages of their countries. Several sign languages are mutually intelligible as well. For example, Danish Sign Language, Icelandic Sign Language, and Norwegian Sign Language (which are descendants of Danish Sign Language) are, for the most part, understandable by those who speak Swedish Sign Language. An International Sign Language (IS) has been created as well and is used at international events.

WRITTEN FORM The written form of sign language also differs from the oral forms of languages. This is known as SignWriting. SignWriting was created in 1974 by Valerie Sutton, and is actually based on the graphic notation used for writing ballet steps. The system uses visual symbols to express the handshapes, facial expressions, and movements found in sign language. In other words, the alphabet shows how the hands look. SignWriting is currently the written form for twenty-seven Sign Languages.

SIGN LANGUAGE WITH PRIMATES Language is not only a form of communication, but a uniquely human experience. Studying whether primates have the ability to develop language could lead to some great discoveries about the earliest humans. Washoe, a chimpanzee who lived from 1965 to 2007, was the first nonhuman to ever learn sign language and communicate with humans. Since the 1960s, chimpanzees and gorillas have been learning to use sign language for communication. Koko, a gorilla who lived from to 1971 to 2018, was introduced to sign language in the 1970s. In 2004, Koko was featured in news reports when she signed to her caretakers that she had a toothache and needed to go to a dentist.

INDEX